Gender in Popular Education

Gender in Popular Education
Methods for empowerment

EDITED BY
SHIRLEY WALTERS AND LINZI MANICOM

CACE Publications

Zed Books

LONDON AND NEW JERSEY

Gender in Popular Education: Methods for empowerement was first published by Zed Books Ltd, 7 Cynthia Street, London N1 9JF, UK, and 165 First Avenue, Atlantic Highlands, New Jersey 07716, USA, in 1996.

Published in Southern Africa by CACE Publications, CACE, University of Western Cape, Private Bag X17, Bellville, 7530, South Africa, in 1996.

Cover designed by Andrew Corbett.
Cover picture by Dominique Roger/UNESCO.
Set in Monotype Ehrhardt by Ewan Smith.
Printed and bound in the United Kingdom by Biddles Ltd, Guildford and King's Lynn.

A catalogue record for this book is available from the British Library.

Library of Congress Cataloging-in-Publication Data

Gender in popular education : methods for empowerment / edited by Shirley Walters and Linzi Manicom.
       p.   cm.
     Includes bibliographical references and index.
     ISBN 1–85649–349–0. — ISBN 1–85649–350–4 (pbk.)
     1. Feminism and education—Cross-cultural studies.
2. Popular education—Cross-cultural studies.   3. Women—Education—Social aspects—Cross-cultural studies.   1. Walters, Shirley.   II. Manicom, Linzi, 1952—
LC197.G44   1966
370.19'345—dc20   96-16263
                                               CIP

ISBN 1 85649 349 0 cased
ISBN 1 85649 350 4 limp

Contents

Acknowledgements

Given the lives we have chosen to lead as feminist educators and activists, this book has inevitably been born in the midst of the juggling of professional, personal and political commitments. Many people contributed to making its production possible.

In our homes, Johan Walters and Keri O'Meara have been the two closest to the heat and have made sacrifices to enable us to work when we could have been with them. At work, there have been several contributors to the process. First, all the women who have written for the book have shown great stamina and commitment over an extended period of time. They are part of a community of feminist popular educators with whom we have worked, discussed, shared ideas, and who inspired the idea of this collection.

Secondly, colleagues at the University of the Western Cape, particularly Lehn Benjamin, Eunice Christians and David Kapp, have helped with administrative back-up, and they, and others, have been a part of the creative development of popular education work at the Centre for Adult and Continuing Education. Shauna Westcott has provided excellent editorial assistance. Lynda Yanz, former co-ordinator of the Women's Programme of the International Council for Adult Education, Helene Moussa, Budd Hall and Partnership Africa Canada supported the project in its vulnerable early days. At Zed Books, Robert Molteno and latterly Louise Murray gave us the encouragement we needed.

The book is testimony to our friendship and to our determination to realize the vision of making visible the innovative, challenging, creative work being undertaken by feminist popular educators, sometimes under the most trying conditions. We have enjoyed working together and have learned a great deal from one another and from other members of feminist popular education communities.

For feminist popular educators around the world

Introduction

SHIRLEY WALTERS AND LINZI MANICOM

Rationale

The story of this book – how it came to be, its context and content – broadly echoes themes and concerns of feminist popular education as it has been developing transnationally over the past decade or so. It bears the imprint of international feminist and women's politics, confirming the commonality of many issues for women around the globe, just as it reminds us of the differences in what it means to be 'woman' in various classes and cultures. The book has been constrained by the parameters, pressures and interruptions of activists' lives, taking three years of moments stolen here and there to complete. It reveals the learning and creativity of women educators and grassroots women's organizing in contexts ranging from city pavements to political parties, hostels to health programmes, classrooms to community centres, and more.

It is a book rooted in the longer history of the Women's Programme of the International Council for Adult Education (ICAE), an international network of feminist popular educators, which was co-ordinated in Toronto by Lynda Yanz between 1982 and 1990. We met through the Women's Programme in 1988 and quickly became friends. We are both South Africans. Shirley, an activist and educator within the popular democratic movement, was director of the Centre for Adult and Continuing Education at the University of the Western Cape. Linzi, a political exile now living in Canada, was then working part-time with the Women's Programme and doing feminist academic work.

The objectives of the Women's Programme paralleled those of other international feminist networks that were being established during the 1980s: to build solidarity between women around the world struggling with similar issues; to support those challenging masculine dominance and the exclusion of women in their fields; and to facilitate the exchange and sharing of ideas and resources. What made the ICAE Women's Programme a little different was its particular concern with the educational aspects of women's organizing, although, of course, it was also well recognized that the boundaries between emancipatory education, feminist organizing and the political mobilization of women are not easily drawn.

Coming out of this network was an exciting range of innovative educational work being developed with women and around gender issues in social movements, development projects, non-governmental organizations (NGOs) and community-based organizations in different regions.

It is this loosely defined body of work that we are gathering here under the umbrella term of 'feminist popular education'. The wide reach we are according the term is open to challenge for, as some of the chapters will reveal, 'popular education' is not a term that is used across the board in different places, in different periods. Non-formal educational practices which aim to challenge injustice and oppression are variously called 'community education', 'radical adult education', 'education for change', 'people's education', 'liberatory' or 'emancipatory education', 'transformative education' and 'education for empowerment'. The names pick up on different political lexicons and trends.

In recent years, however, the term 'popular education' has gained an international currency and ascendancy among organizers and educators who have been influenced and inspired by the writings of Brazilian educationalist Paulo Freire and the educational work carried out in Latin American communities over the past three decades. For our purposes here, we can say that the educational work addressed in the chapters that follow represents 'feminist popular education' in that it is oriented towards transforming gendered power relations and shares the basic methodological principle of valorizing, and building analytically and practically upon, the experiential knowledge of learners themselves.

There was very little documentation (in English, anyway) of feminist popular education outside the inevitably dry and diluted reports to funding agencies, bland summaries of conference proceedings and the occasional informally circulated academic paper. The one form in which popular education process did make its way into print and circulate among educators was that of a handbook or 'how to' manual, setting out examples of workshop design and exercises. Although such handbooks are very useful and certainly have been well used by nascent women's groups, what these texts do not capture is precisely what we consider the most valuable aspect of popular education practice: its inventive, perceptive and provocative process, the intuition and critical reflection that lie between the lines, behind the words. Why are some methods chosen rather than others? What is revealed in the process? What is learned by the learners and the educator?

Popular education involves an inherently self-reflective, reflexive and non-dogmatic approach. It works to make space for the collective, participatory production of knowledge and insight, and builds on what emerges from the experiences of those actively participating. The richness of the approach lies, therefore, in the thought and implicit analysis that has gone into the design of the specific educational events or programmes, and in the spontaneous, sometimes serendipitous, process as it unfolds at a particular moment, yielding even more challenges and possibilities. Where gender is the focus, the educator (whether working with women-only or mixed-sex groups) is engaged in the process of deconstructing and constructing gender. Understanding how this happens is essential to feminist practice.

It was to capture and make accessible to a wider audience this developing tradition of feminist educational work that we proposed this book. We hoped it would provide a stimulus, an opportunity and an encouragement to feminist educators, pushing them to write up some of that texture as it has been lived and deeply pondered by them. We therefore charged the contributors to the book with drawing on their own specific experiences as feminist popular educators and with trying to make sense of which educational methodologies work and why. (Translating these experiences into text was, of course, easier said than done. Edited collections are notoriously difficult to co-ordinate and with this one we had to contend with the vagaries of international communications and the multiple commitments of all our lives.)

There were two further motivations for the book. In recent years, the development of feminist analysis within all academic disciplines has produced a broad range of relevant theory and opened up important new ways of thinking about popular education. We are referring here, particularly, to the influence of Foucault and post-structuralism and the field of feminist pedagogy. Equally, the practices being developed in grassroots women's education had relevance for the feminist approaches being explored within radical educational approaches. The lack of impact of feminist popular education on the discipline of adult education was of particular concern to us. As Gore (1993) notes, different theoretical discourses and literatures within even the narrower sphere of radical education have not been mutually engaged. Some of the chapters in the book explore the implications of new theoretical approaches for understanding popular education and vice versa. The relevance of feminist popular education to mainstream adult education, critical pedagogy and women's studies will become clearer with wider exposure to and engagement with it.

Secondly, we also see popular education as having something to offer political theory concerned with social mobilization. Feminist popular education is embedded within social activism and democratic organizations of civil society working for material and substantive transformation of women's lives and conditions. A persistent question that preoccupies popular educators is the relationship of local popular educational initiatives to broader political movements (popular, democratic and feminist), and to transformations in forms of governance. Questions of state and civil society, their complex integration and their current shifting formations globally, as well as critical examinations of 'the market', are thus central preoccupations for feminist popular education. These themes are not particularly developed in this collection but they are certainly present as a strong subtext.

The collection

The book consists of eleven chapters from six countries. A wide call for contributions went out but ultimately it was active solicitation through direct or directed contact that produced draft chapters. Some of the chapters are written by women long associated with the Women's Programme. Others are from women we haven't yet met who responded to our requests for submissions publicized through regional women's adult education networks. Some articles we'd hoped for in order to give a sense of a substantive area of work or work in a particular region didn't come through.

The final selection is less than ideal in terms of regional representation, but does give a sense of the spread of feminist popular education and the different political cultures in which it is located. The inclusion of accounts of popular education among women from oppressed communities in the North makes the point that it is not an exclusively Third World form (see the chapters by Bingman, Pritchard Hughes and Nadeau).

That there are three chapters from South Africa is, of course, indicative of our greater number of contacts there, but is also rationalized as helping to redress the effects of the apartheid-induced curtain of isolation and bringing to a broader readership examples of the kind of educational work that has been developing there. We strove for articles from other parts of Africa, hoping to have examples of the lively methodology that is so closely linked with economic development for women, but without success. However, both Canadian contributions (Nadeau and Stuart) demonstrate transnational flows of influence and exchange in this kind of work.

The most glaring and paradoxical gap in terms of regionality is the absence of a contribution from Latin and Central America, which historically have had perhaps the strongest tradition of feminist popular education grounded in social movements. Although we had good contacts and the prospect of chapters from Latin America, these didn't materialize as texts. While the influence of the Latin American popular education tradition is evident in the chapter by Nadeau, and while it is also clear that there has been a large degree of 'internationalization' of feminist popular education, the book is located firmly within the Anglo-American linguistic community (and related influences of Anglo-American feminist literature) as these traverse the world.

Another glaring issue of representation is the fact that all the South African contributors, including ourselves as editors, are white women. This is a blatant legacy of the educational privileges that the apartheid system bestowed on whites in South Africa and the consequent networks that developed. We should say quickly that we don't subscribe to the rather mechanical and formulaic regulation of representation that can often become a dangerously depoliticized response: that is, the model that requires, regardless, inclusion of at least one 'representative' from a list of 'identities of oppression'. We are more concerned, as are the contributors to this collection, with deepening our understanding of how to tackle racism, homophobia, cultural supremacy, poverty and sexism, and adjusting our educational practice accordingly.

Few popular educators are drawn directly from the constituencies with which they work, and it does not necessarily follow that those who presumably are most affected by particular oppressions either confine themselves to educational work around those oppressions, or are effective educators. It is probably fair to say, however, that educators who do have experience in the issues around which they work, or share some common history with their learners, bring a deeper, empathic understanding to the educational processes that they devise.

All the authors take up questions of race,[1] class, cultural and ethnic-based differences and hierarchies of power, taking into account their own inevitably higher education, their social identities and greater social power, and reflecting on how these shape their capacities as emancipatory educators.

All the authors are both activists and educators, and some are also academics. Activists' lives are, by nature of the work, over-subscribed. The time and space needed for standing back from a process, reflecting upon and analysing it, engaging with bodies of literature and then undertaking the slow, extractive process of writing, is not easy to come by, particularly when it is not released time or time that is paid for. It is not surprising or coincidental that almost all of our contributors are now based, at least part-time, at tertiary educational or research institutions, affording them a little space in which to write and do work which is related to their jobs. Nevertheless, their contributions still involved stolen moments, stops and starts, and many hours that they could ill afford, suggesting that they share with us a sense of urgency about getting this work into circulation and stimulating debate among those who are themselves similarly engaged.

Surveying the chapters that we finally have in hand for this collection, assessing them in terms of representation of different kinds and contexts of feminist popular education work, we recognize the lacunae and imbalances. We certainly see the need constantly to evaluate the politics of representation in the production of collections like this one, and to work harder to encourage and ensure a wider range of voices in print. Despite these reservations, however, we remain pleased by the variety of accounts of feminist popular education experience gathered here, and committed to getting the material out where it can be engaged with, discussed and developed.

Feminist popular education

Feminist popular education developed in the early 1980s as a critique of the male-biased popular education that was dominant in social movements in different parts of the world. Parallel feminist challenges to forms of educational practice and theory were developing in different sites of social action, as we will go on to outline. These also influenced the work of our contributors and account for their variety of approaches.

The chapters are varied in their perspectives. Some focus on a particular educational event or process, others record work with specific constituencies or on particular issues, and others again involve evaluations, over a period of time, of a range of different methodologies. They are all linked, however, by their major concern, which relates to the design and facilitation of educational and organizational events that maximize participation in defining and carrying out action aimed at changing situations or relationships experienced as oppressive. Although there is a certain replication in the kinds of educational strategies, principles and issues that are discussed, we don't see them as adding up to a checklist of universal features or steps that can be applied in any context.

The differences in the approaches adopted and in ways of understanding the educational process are revealing of the extent to which popular education practice is embedded in its social context, as well as within distinctive gendered cultures and political and theoretical discourses. Recognition of this embeddedness cautions against the appropriation and translation of models of popular education directly from one context to another. If educational methodologies are to be effective, they must be critically rethought and reframed within their target contexts, taking into account the broad range of factors that enable and constrain the empowerment of women. We see the contributions in this book as offering insights, critical analyses, concrete examples and general principles of transformative education which we hope will stimulate ideas for approaching local educational work in different ways.

Is it possible or useful, then, to define 'feminist popular education' more tightly at this point? Some of the contributors to this book explicitly set out a working definition, while others offer a more implicit definition by elaborating their objectives. We see feminist popular education as having a core orientation and offer the following characterization: it is a participatory, democratic, non-hierarchical pedagogy which encourages creative thinking that breaks through embedded formats of learning. It valorizes local knowledge, working collectively towards producing knowledge, the principle of starting from where people are situated, and working to develop a broader understanding of structures and how these can be transformed. It strives to foster both personal and social empowerment. Feminist popular education obviously focuses particularly on the conditions and positions of women and the renegotiation of gender relations; but, given that gender is a social category, referring to the historically and culturally defined constructs of masculinity and femininity, feminist popular education must simultaneously engage with the ways in which the social categories of race, ethnicity, culture, age, social class, sexuality and physical ability are implicated in constructions of gender.

Taking another view, there are two central dimensions to popular education in general. Fink (1992) refers to them as the pedagogic and the political, while Gore (1993) talks about the instructional aspect and the aspect of social vision. However, these two aspects or dimensions are absolutely intertwined and it is this that makes popular education distinctive. The pedagogical choices implement the political objectives. The pedagogical cannot be separated from the political, unless popular education is to be reduced to a series of formats, games and techniques. For, in fact, very similar techniques are employed in corporate boardrooms, and so is an almost identical vocabulary, for example, 'empowerment', 'working with diversity', 'training for equity'.

The degree of emphasis given to either the political or the pedagogical dimensions of popular education in the chapters that follow can be seen in relation to the immediate setting and political location of the work. As represented in the chapters by Medel-Anonuevo and Patel, popular education is an integral part of social and political movements and part of the social and political fabric. Here, the pedagogical component is subsumed under the organizing strategy. Where popular education is occurring in a formal classroom or workshop setting, as in the accounts of Pritchard Hughes, Stuart and Von Kotze, the pedagogical or instructional aspects are more direct and obvious.

A prime source of the contestation over the meaning of popular education is, of course, the political dimension, or the implicit social vision. Who is the 'subject' of popular education and what is the goal?

In the 1970s and early 1980s, popular education tended to be linked and closely associated with a clearly defined social movement, national liberation struggle or women's movement and a sense of the end-point of 'liberation'. In recent years, particularly since the demise of formal socialism and the emergence of feminist and post-colonial critiques of the unitary narratives of such movements, there is much more fragmentation of social opposition. The building of civil society, of non-governmental organizations and of relations with states, is now much more the context of feminist popular education, although this obviously varies from country to country.

Broadly speaking, the politics of feminist popular education can be defined as the struggle against gender oppression. But, since gender has been understood increasingly as constructed in relation to race, class and so on, feminist popular education has been working to integrate all aspects of power inequalities structured along social identities. None of the authors in this volume articulates her vision of feminist politics in very explicit terms but, while there are clear differences in their understandings of the constructs of 'woman' and 'gender', it is evident that they share a view of feminist popular education as positioned to support the struggles of women in oppressed communities, rather than 'women' in general. It is this that distinguishes feminist popular education from, for example, gender training or feminist pedagogy which tend to be conducted for an undifferentiated category of 'women'.

Context

During the last thirty years, women's political engagement has been influenced by fundamental changes in international economic relations, reduced national capacities to solve problems, remarkable transformations in political regimes and a rise in religious fundamentalism, as well as the growth in the international component of the women's movement. This book, particularly the chapters by Chan and Nadeau, shows that the effects of global economic crisis and restructuring policies can be seen as starting-points for feminist popular education.

Some of the most notable international changes have been policies promoting macro-economic stabilization and internal structural adjustment introduced by the World Bank and the International Monetary Fund to respond to economic instability, particularly in the countries of the South, but also in the emerging democracies of Central Europe and the more industrialized countries of the North. New economic conditions emerging over the last two decades have exacerbated the economic problems of most women in all these situations.

Decreased expenditure on education, health and food subsidies means that increased costs are borne by women, who must work longer hours, take more time to shop around for less expensive food, spend more resources on basic health-care, and face lower wages and fewer job opportunities as the wages in female-dominated industries decline. As Nadeau's graphic description makes clear, it is women's labour and women's bodies that absorb much of the impact of reduced public spending. It is the gendered aspects of these global economic processes that often provide the focus for feminist popular education and organization.

Changes in the nature of nationalism and the rise of many forms of religious fundamentalism have also affected women's status over the last three decades. In the era of rebuilding and decolonizing after World War II, achieving and strengthening the political power of the nation-state were the dominant focuses of nationalism. For most of the world's women, this state-focused political nationalism was accompanied by formal (though not actual) legal equality. Recently, however, state-focused political nationalism has been increasingly challenged by the rise of ethnic, communal and regional forces that seek to alter the nature of national control of politics. The reconfiguration of regional political and economic formations, such as the North American Free Trade Agreement and the South-East Asian Trading Bloc, is reshaping women's struggles, as Nadeau and Chan describe. The politicization of ethnic and racialized identities which tend to designate specific and limiting roles for women, as 'bearers of culture' or 'mothers of the nation', for example, are also posing complex challenges for educators concerned with extending the possibilities and choices for women.

The rise in religious fundamentalism poses similar challenges but, although it is noted as a focus of growing concern by Medel-Anonuevo, this phenomenon is not otherwise dealt with directly in this book. However, several chapters, notably those by Myles and Tarrago, and Von Kotze, underline the need for sensitivity to cultural constructions of gender and highlight the difficulty of working with the sometimes contradictory tension between respecting cultural difference and advancing feminist goals. This area is a focus of current developments in popular education practice.

The growth of international feminism and global feminist networks, as well as of national women's movements, has encouraged an increasing flow and exchange of ideas and practices. Women's movements and women's activism have grown stronger, more varied and more accepted as indigenous expressions of women's interests over the last twenty years. Early in this wave of women's organizing, nationalists in countries of the South and Marxists world-wide often discredited women's movements as imperialist or bourgeois. They voiced concerns about the local applicability of feminist ideas originating in Western Europe and North America. But women in the South came to articulate directly their own awareness of male domination and forms of resistance to it. These developments are reflected in the chapters describing work in India, the Philippines and South Africa.

Influences on feminist popular education

A central influence on much of the writing contained in this book, whether directly or derivatively, is the Latin American work based on the ideas of Paulo Freire, which were first generated in the 1960s. Critical pedagogy, strongest in North America, also traces its roots to Freirean ideas, but has been developed more in relation to critiques of schooling and cultural politics. Itself gender-blind in its earlier formulations, the critical pedagogy school has been subject to a series of recent challenges by feminist theorists whose work has influenced some of the authors in this collection, for example, Chan, Von Kotze and Walters.

Closely related to this literature, but more powerfully influenced by feminist theory, is feminist pedagogy, which has been developed within women's studies programmes in colleges and universities around the world. This contributory strand is evident particularly in the chapters by Pritchard Hughes and Walters. Another body of educational theory and practice which is clearly influential is adult education more broadly, which focuses on learning and on design and facilitation.

An important site of work relevant to feminist popular education is that of women and development, particularly the approach known as the empowerment model (Sen and Grown, 1987). The focus in recent years on training and education in development work with women is somewhat of a response to earlier practices, which neither addressed the educational components of development projects adequately, nor involved women in their design and implementation, a reason for the failure of so many. Training components are now necessarily part of any gender-sensitive development. The years of economic crisis and structural adjustment policies have seen more recent work in 'women and development' focusing on poverty alleviation strategies such as micro-enterprises, income-generating and credit schemes, all of which necessarily have central training and capacity-building components oriented towards sustainable development.

We mentioned above the relevance to popular education of the profound theoretical developments in feminism over the past two decades. One strand of this influence traces through feminist rethinking in fields concerned with the personal and social empowerment of women (for example, psychology, social work, health and theology), and is apparent in several chapters, for example, those by Myles and Tarrago, Friedman and Crawford Cousins, and Nadeau. This points to the broader, well-discussed question of the uneasy relationship between feminist theory, or the academy, and feminist practice, or the women's movement(s).

We are not going to rehearse the various contours of the debate but it is one that is posed directly in the field of popular education because of the political commitment and activism inherent in this approach. The distance and tension between feminist theory and practice have been exacerbated in some ways as some forms of feminist scholarship have grown and become more institutionalized, developing increasingly esoteric and exclusive languages. Nevertheless, we would argue that theory is integral to popular education in a number of ways. The process of bringing to light aspects of experience, reflecting upon and making sense of them, finding concepts and drawing connections, pulling out and exposing the assumptions – this is theorizing, and this is precisely what happens in a popular education process and what, we hope, is reflected in this book.

Emergent themes

In this final section, we identify several themes and tensions that emerge in the chapters that follow, seeing these as raising and representing some of the critical questions within the field of contemporary feminist popular education. The themes relate closely to each other and overlap in places, suggesting that different terms might be used to talk about quite similar issues and pointing to their embeddedness within different feminist discourses and political problematics. Many of the themes resonate with complex, contested issues in feminist and educational theory. Here we can only point to the varying emphases and tensions of different approaches within feminist popular education practice as discussed in these chapters. The intention is to stimulate further debate and clarification and the hope is that others will take up the threads and tease them out further.

Starting from where women are Probably the most agreed-upon 'principle' of both popular and feminist education is that of starting from the lives and preoccupations of women themselves. This tenet is, at one level, a clear and straightforward one. In practice, however, there are various interpretations of 'where women are'. Some draw on the geographic location of women's activities: the domestic setting, the workplace, the neighbourhood; others draw on more metaphorical locations: the place of feelings and emotion, the 'private' sphere with which women tend to be associated, and women's subjectivity as it is culturally shaped. The chapters in the book illustrate this range well.

Attention to the feelings and emotions of learners is perceived as critical in feminist popular education. It was these aspects that were overlooked or under-emphasized within earlier gender-blind models of popular education. The practice of consciousness-raising, associated with the rise of contemporary feminism in the North, closely parallels popular education in this regard, creating conditions in which women can open up about their feelings of oppression before working together to analyse the dimensions and relations of that oppression. Chan's work with Malaysian 'factory women' provides a rich example of educational practices designed to elicit the expression of suppressed feelings and emotions.

Nadeau, reflecting an important contemporary theme in feminist analysis, comes at emotion from a different angle. Exploring the ways in which the oppression of women is imprinted on the body, she makes a strong case for popular education to incorporate body-work, in order to release tensions and rehearse alternative ways of being 'in the body'. In fact, many popular education exercises, such as 'sculpturing' and various 'energizers', rely on a notion of physical doing, of embodied action, both to shake off tensions that might be blocking creativity and to stimulate experience in ways that might generate insights. The work in the Philippines that Medel-Anonuevo describes included a focus on a more specific aspect of women's embodiment, one where very specifically gendered oppressions are centred, namely sexuality. Domestic violence and sexual oppression are often starting-points of work with women because they are aspects of women's lives that are often dangerously hidden and, at the same time, provide a basis for understanding the relations of patriarchy.

Spirituality is another aspect of 'where women are' as they seek to make sense of the world. This is touched on only briefly by Nadeau and, to a lesser extent, by Friedman and Crawford Cousins, but it is a theme that is increasingly significant within popular education practice as culturally distinct groups, such as indigenous peoples, women recovering 'womanist' traditions and ethnic collectives, draw on cultural and spiritual symbols in healing and transformative education.

Walters refers to the notion of *cotidiano* central to the Latin American tradition of popular education for women. *Cotidiano*, the everyday, refers to the daily activities of women that revolve around family, domestic work and community. The basic point is that if popular education is to be effective for women, it must start with concrete reference to these realms of life, rather than with some abstracted notion of capitalist patriarchy, for example.

A number of the contributors to this book pose, as the central challenge for popular education, the question of how to move from the starting-points of women's immediate concerns to a broader analysis and to political action aimed at transforming oppressive relations. Medel-Anonuevo sees the challenge as 'how to relate the micro lives of the women to the larger national picture'. For Nadeau the issue is relating the poverty and sense of despair experienced by the women she works with to the effects of free trade policies and global economic restructuring.

Many accounts of feminist popular education have drawn on the linked concepts of women's practical needs and their strategic interests in thinking about how to make connections between women's immediate lives and broader social relations. While useful in pointing to the different focuses of organizing work with women, this construct has been questioned increasingly in recent years. It has been argued, for instance, that the dichotomy implied in distinguishing between two kinds of women's interests does not take adequate account of the fact that they are interlinked. Changes in the ways that women organize to address their everyday needs invariably produce changes in gender relations, as Patel's chapter shows clearly.

Another critique of the practical/strategic couplet is that it implies a hierarchy of women's issues, that strategic interests show more evidence of a 'feminist consciousness' and therefore are more politically advanced. In the context of general questioning of who defines feminism, and what its issues are and should be, and the argument that much of what has been advanced as strategic interests pertains more to the lives and concerns of middle-class, Western women, the distinction between practical and strategic concerns becomes problematic. The different starting-points or salient concerns of women that are discussed in the chapters of this book reinforce the doubts raised against this popular way of defining women's issues and struggles. Sexuality, sexual pleasure and exploration are shown to be strategic in the lives of poor women; emotional release is critical for women of all classes.

Although the authors of this book vary in the issues they focus upon and the extent to which they draw connections between local and global developments (a difference which, of course, reflects the context and objectives of the projects involved), what they have in common is the valorization and politicization of the lives and concerns of women. As their chapters show, it is not an instrumental question of paying attention to women's concerns as a jump-off point for tackling 'the real' political issues. It is rather one of showing the *cotidiano* as intrinsically political, and as integrated with broader social relations and hierarchies of oppression. However, there is a tension here for popular educators between validating and celebrating the daily concerns of women as significant, on the one hand, and challenging the gender relations and constructions of 'the domestic sphere', of 'women's work' and of emotional responses that confine women to ways of being in the world that are limiting, disempowering and rob women of choice and agency, on the other.

Experience and expertise   Closely related to the preceding theme, but coming at it from a slightly different perspective, is the issue of experience as the central form or basis for women's knowledge. Women's experience is seen as the point of departure for feminist popular education.

The concept of 'experience', however, is a highly contested one within contemporary feminist theory. Some of the issues that have been raised in debate are relevant to feminist popular education. First, it is argued, privileging 'women's experience' as a basis for knowledge tends towards an essentialist construction of 'women'. For that experience tends to be lodged in some foundational definition of women, such as reproductive capacity, or mothering, or the gendered division of labour. What about women who are differently located, who experience different things differently? How are the different claims to truth of different women's experiences mediated? Appealing to 'women's experience', that is, tying experience to a particular identity, carries the danger of reproducing the ideological system that defines 'women' and their worlds in particular and limiting ways.

There are further issues. When women's experience is given epistemological status as the standpoint from which an overall analysis can be built, there is the problem of accounting for the limitations in perspective that are assumed to be the consequence of an oppressed and excluded status. One of the rationales for promoting women's experience as a source of knowledge is to counter the masculine and class dominance of rational, abstract modes of analysis. But all experience and knowledge, it is argued, is mediated by language or discourses which shape what is possible to know and speak about. Experience is not a pristine category.

These complex questions translate into strategic issues for feminist popular educators. One such fine line is that between validating experience as it is articulated by women learners, and engendering a stance among the learners of critical reflection on that experience, on how it comes to be associated with gender or with other social attributes. As can be seen from the authors' accounts, appeal to the notion of women's experience is attractive, even where educators might have reservations about an implied fixed and ahistorical identity of women, because it tends to produce a quick sense of recognition and solidarity between learners and facilitators.

The challenge is to find ways of drawing on women's experiences to illustrate that the category 'women' is not homogeneous, that it is socially constructed and that there are many ways of being women. Indeed, it is another form of the challenge of moving from women's everyday experiences to an analysis of the structures of gender oppression that govern women's lives, and this process is discussed explicitly in a number of chapters. There is a subtle range in these chapters between those implicitly seeing women's experience as a standpoint, a source of 'truth', and those understanding experience as a starting-point for the production of knowledge or the building of an analysis.

The accounts in the book also differ in regard to the degree to which the introduction of expertise is emphasized and how it is timed. Again reflecting the differing objectives and parameters of their respective programmes, some of the educators work extensively with the resource of women's experience, while others argue for the strategic introduction of relevant skills and expertise. The work in India with women pavement dwellers that Patel describes, for example, was concerned to ensure that women picked up skills for negotiating with government officials and for deciding upon appropriate housing. In a time-limited popular education process, as so many of them are, finding the balance between eliciting the wealth of understanding and perception that is present in women's collective experience, and imparting useful knowledge and analysis, presents a real challenge. When the concern is understanding and analysing social relationships, much of that expertise takes the form of new discourses, new words in which to make sense of experiences, as well as new forms of action.

However, notwithstanding differences in the weight given to experience and expertise, all contributors share a perception of experiential knowledge as particularly effective educationally. Popular education definitely privileges experiential knowledge over knowledge that is imparted by the experts. As is evident in the chapters that follow, much of popular education activity is organized around two processes: drawing on pre-existing experiences of the learners, and creating experiences in the workshop setting, setting up situations which allow learners to identify with, feel and experience ways of seeing that side-step the usual, often limiting, mediation of attitudes, rational logic and language. The chapters by Stuart, Nadeau, and Friedman and Crawford Cousins provide good examples of this kind of learning.

Silence and voice   A dominant metaphor within both feminism and popular education is that of silence and voice. Freire wrote of 'the culture of silence'; popular education, particularly that which involves literacy training, often speaks in terms of 'breaking the silence' and 'giving voice'. These words come up frequently in the chapters of this book.

Although this metaphor is often used in a simple way, with the replacement of silence by voice seen as the unquestioned goal, the authors here uncover a much more nuanced picture. Silence, as Friedman and Crawford Cousins maintain, can be a strategy of resistance or one for holding on to power. Silence can also mean a strategic suppression, as in the case of the women with whom Chan worked. If the only voice on offer is 'his master's voice', keeping silent can make sense. Clearly, the question has to be looked at in context, particularly taking into account the dimension of public and private and the different discourses available to women. It is often the case that women have vibrant voices within a non-official, more private, community space, whereas they are silent/silenced in more public situations. Women may also be silent in the dominant forms of communication, such as official or more formal language.

The lesson of the perspectives on silence/voice offered here is that feminist popular education has to be sensitive to the context of silences and the power relations that they reflect. Equally, it must search for those media of 'voice' with which women learners are most comfortable and which offer ways to express often submerged feelings and perceptions.

Empowerment   The term empowerment is a prevalent one in feminist and popular education discourses. In recent years, however, its extensive use and appropriation by a very broad range of political positions has drained it of any clear referent and, in many contexts, of its more politically transformative meaning.

The implicit meanings of empowerment in the various chapters of this book range from an individual to a collective focus, and from self-validation and the building of self-esteem to working actively and concretely to change social conditions. Popular education that is located historically and politically within defined and organized social movements, as in the Philippines, South Africa and among the urban pavement dwellers of India, tends implicitly to support a notion of empowerment that involves the achievement of social and political objectives. Patel defines empowerment in these terms.

Where this is not the case, empowerment tends to refer to gaining more decision-making capacity, to deepening an understanding of the relations configuring one's life and to controlling conditions affecting one's life; advances which may or may not be shared with a group. The over-all political context in which popular educators work, and the strength of women's movements in particular, contribute significantly to the extent to which small, local instances of empowering education contribute to broader, political and social changes.

Perhaps the most important result of the current focus on the notion of empowerment, and one which feminist popular education has contributed to developing, is the attention given to the subjective aspects of political change or, in other words, to the construction of political subjectivity. As discussed in the following chapters, the process of reflecting on experience and collectively building alternative interpretations of the relations shaping one's life, produces shifts in subjectivity as well as building confidence and capacity. This aspect of subjective transformation has led some to question the relationship or overlap between feminist popular education, which works self-consciously to elicit feelings and emotions, and psychotherapy. Nadeau argues that the collective focus of popular education distinguishes it from individualized therapy, although clearly similar learning processes and reinterpretations are taking place.

Difference Like empowerment, the term 'difference' has become a catch-all category, embracing a range of meanings. In the chapters of this book it is generally used to refer to the different identities of women in terms of race, class, ethnicity, age, sexual orientation and so on. Inasmuch as these differences between women involve differences in power, privilege, life conditions and experience, as well as potential conflict and antagonism, they present a set of issues for the feminist popular educator that must be addressed in the design and conduct of the education process.

One of the central dynamics in feminist popular education derives from the difference in the class positions of the educators, who tend to be highly educated middle-class women, and the learners, who are mainly working-class, poor women and men. The other central dynamic flows from the power differences between participants, which are broadly structured by socially significant markers of identity, such as race. The account, by Friedman and Crawford Cousins, of working self-consciously with this dynamic provides a vivid illustration of the complexity involved. Various popular education practices work to equalize power within the education process, deploying fairly mechanical devices to redress power imbalances, or drawing attention to the social weighting of different attributes to diminish their authority.

Another meaning of 'difference', which is rather more implicit in some of the chapters, refers not to different gendered identities but rather to the different and changing constructions of the category 'women'. Underlying this meaning of difference is the understanding of gender as not referring merely to sexual difference, but also to the cultural, social and often racialized constructions of masculinity and feminity. Unpacking these different constructions of gender through popular education offers learners an understanding of the possibility of being women in less fixed, less oppressive ways. This understanding also makes better sense of the experience of many women who do not always see themselves primarily as women, but in particular contexts and struggles identify more as racialized or class subjects, for instance.

As all the chapters demonstrate, and particularly those by Stuart, Von Kotze, Myles and Tarrago, and Friedman and Crawford Cousins, working with difference is extremely challenging but critical to effective process. It demands sensitive, self-reflective responses and understandings of the various dimensions of difference. Because of the self-knowledge and tensions that power inequalities can provoke, educational work that fully engages with difference has the potential to be very generative and catalysing of learning and transformation.

Facilitation and control   One of the characteristics that differentiates the examples of popular education in this book is the degree of direction given to learners. This is sometimes expressed as the continuum between a free or open-ended process and goal orientation.

It was suggested earlier that the political objective was a primary dimension of popular education. But what that objective is can range from a radical democratic one, in the sense of attributing full control of the education process to participants and supporting whatever analysis and objectives emerge from it, to working educationally with women in order to impart a political analysis and realize a plan for action. One could argue that feminist popular education is by definition concerned with raising gender awareness and improving the life conditions of women. However, there is a considerable range within this broad orientation.

Myles and Tarrago, for instance, describe a very open-ended process of cross-cultural consultation, designed specifically to provide as much space as possible for the emergence of non-dominant cultural understandings. By contrast, the community work of women in the Appalachian mountains described by Bingman is a relatively spontaneous process with the implicit goal of finding ways to build the confidence and capacities of local women. A number of the workshop-based experiences had specific objectives with a fairly flexible process: for example, the creative writing programme described by Von Kotze, the women's studies class analysed by Pritchard Hughes and the training of development workers in Stuart's account. The learning process described by Patel, on the other hand, was directed by clear goals set by the women with whom she worked.

Another aspect of the tension between eliciting and directing popular education is that of dealing with participants who are antagonistic to the pedagogical process and to its feminist or anti-oppression orientation. Those contributors who describe educational experiences with mixed-sex groups elucidate the complex dynamics that emerge between women and men in relation to examining gender. Within all-women groups, hostility often erupts around race and class identity, or sexual orientation. Friedman and Crawford Cousins usefully designate the role of 'the disturber' and argue that the dynamic produced around this role, while disruptive and detracting in some ways from the process, is one that can be embraced to reveal some of the underlying tensions of power hierarchies.

There is also, of course, the question of how to deal with those who do no disturbing. Given that participation is a principle of popular education, facilitators are faced with choices about the extent to which they want to enforce participation. How much does one intervene to establish a putative 'equality' in participation in the education context? Or should those with more socially conferred power be given less opportunity to dominate proceedings? Should hierarchies and roles be allowed to emerge within a learning group? Different strategies for dealing with these questions are found in the chapters which follow. Finding the balance between allowing a spontaneous and creative process to emerge and directing the process to complete an agenda is an ongoing tension in popular education work.

Finally, feminist popular educators require particular skills, knowledge and understanding and these must often be acquired 'on the job'. The development of training programmes for feminist popular educators has not yet been undertaken on a wide scale, a gap particularly visible in tertiary institutions. The chapter by Walters describes a possible curriculum outline which demonstrates the complexity and multi-layered nature of the tasks feminist popular educators undertake and for which they need training and support.

Gender awareness and feminist politics A sub-theme of the general tension between facilitation and control in popular education is whether to allow gender awareness to emerge in an undirected process, or to work with a more explicit feminist analysis and the objective of promoting critical reflection and transformation of oppressive gender relations. 'Gender training', which has become a significant field of popular education in recent years, has the clear orientation of raising sensitivity to the ways in which gender structures social and economic developments. However, even within this explicit orientation there is a range of interpretations of gender and its implications.

The tension of being a facilitator with 'two agendas' is referred to in the chapter by Von Kotze, where she grapples with the conflicting demands of her feminist commitment and her role (negotiated with participants) as facilitator of a creative writing course for a mixed-sex group of factory workers. Pritchard Hughes argues that 'free process' is important to feminist education, while Patel is very goal-orientated, stressing that improvement to the lives of the women living on pavements in the cities of India requires that they be unified and organized together with the men.

In working with conceptions of women and gender there is always a fine line between reinforcing particular constructs and meanings, and questioning not only the relations that produce women's oppression but also the prevailing conceptions of femininity. (None of the chapters reflects much on masculinity and how it might relate to social change.)

Space, time and place for learning Many of the chapters in this collection refer to the importance of a particular space for popular education with women. Given the responsibilities of most women for family care and household management, a place away from 'the everyday' and from home is often a catalyst in an empowering education process. Bingman recounts how the experience of doing community work together, away from home, and sharing their stories prompted shifts in the confidence of women and in their understandings of themselves. Similarly, Patel describes how a sense of a shared space from which to venture into the public realm of state bureaucracy imparted an enormous sense of confidence to the pavement dwellers of Bombay.

Building trust is an important condition for a learning space, as Chan's work emphasizes particularly. In situations where women are as massively silenced and undermined as she describes, the reproduction of a sense of 'home', of sanctuary, can be crucial to popular education work.

The time, or temporality, of the learning process is also significant. Myles and Tarrago draw attention to this dimension in their cross-cultural communication project with Aboriginal women. Time away from everyday rhythms creates space for reflection and for coming to understand social relations from a broader perspective. The temporal parameters of an education project allow for very different depths of work. Much popular education takes place within a workshop format of very limited duration, and various methodologies for maximizing the political and psychic space and time for learning are illustrated in this collection. Ways have to be found of immediately engaging participants with a sense of community and commitment to shared goals. Physical relaxation and energizing exercises help to build the necessary focus.

However, the limitations of workshop education experiences are well known. Participants can experience transformations in their under-standings, feel empowered and even carry away very concrete skills, but on returning to their home or work situations, get weighed down by unchanged relations of oppression. Where popular education workshops are linked to an ongoing process or social movement, their effect can be cumulative and supported.

Feminist popular education, as these themes show, is riddled with fine lines to be drawn and knife-edges to be negotiated. In designing pro-grammes and processes, and in executing them, educators are called upon to make complex and quick judgements in order to optimize the learning moment and make it as transformative as possible. Our hope is that the chapters of this book, in raising questions, reflecting on the different perspectives and possibilities and sharing strategies, will offer other feminist popular educators more clarity about the choices to be made and more understanding of the range of factors that are involved.

Notes

1. A number of the terms used are contentious. We have not tried to standardize their use across chapters but have left authors to speak from their own contexts. For the sake of clarity, we have avoided using inverted commas around certain terms. In some contexts it is convention to refer to 'race' in this way to signal that the term is understood as not natural but a socially constructed

category. While we share this understanding, we have not used the convention. We also use with some reservations the terms North, South, West and Third World because of the way they often homogenize those regions and implicate all the inhabitants in the politics of imperialism, obscuring class, racial or ethnic differentiation. We understand these terms as designating constructs referring to degrees of relative poverty or affluence, rather than to geographical regions.

Bibliography

Fink, M. (1992) 'Women and Popular Education in Latin America', in Strom-quist, N. (ed.), *Women and Education in Latin America: Knowledge, Power and Change*, Lynne Rienner, Boulder, CO.

Gore, J. (1993) *The Struggle for Pedagogies: Critical and Feminist Discourses as Regimes of Truth*, Routledge, New York.

Luke, C. and Gore, J. (1992) *Feminisms and Critical Pedagogy*, Routledge, New York.

Sen, G. and Grown, C. (1987) *Development Crises and Alternative Visions: Third World Women's Perspectives*, Monthly Review Press, New York.

Training gender-sensitive adult educators in South Africa

SHIRLEY WALTERS

The first educational workshops in South Africa for the training of gender-sensitive adult educators were held in 1990. These workshops provided the basis for three important initiatives: publication of a highly successful handbook (Mackenzie, 1992); an ongoing training project at the Centre for Adult and Continuing Education (Cace) which has sought to deepen gender and anti-racism educational work among adult educators; and the start of a network of gender-sensitive adult educators from different regions of the country. The workshops also established a concrete base from which to explore the question of curricula for the training of gender-sensitive and feminist adult educators.[1]

This chapter elaborates the elements of a core curriculum for the training of gender-sensitive and feminist adult educators, through discussion of key themes in the workshops and in the literature on feminist pedagogy. It begins by discussing briefly the goals of adult education in relation to the empowerment of women in general, and in South Africa in particular. It argues that adult educators who wish to challenge oppressive gender relations need to become self-conscious actors who reflect on their own privilege and oppression and act, alongside others, to change both themselves and society.

The quest for empowerment[2]

Women in most societies lack institutional and decision-making power. They are seen as inferior to men because of their sex. Gender ideologies promote and reinforce patriarchy, which can be defined as 'the social organization of the family, the community, and the state, in such a way that male power is reinforced and perpetuated' (Stromquist, 1991: 7).

The first pillar of patriarchy is the sexual division of labour that assigns men and women to different occupations and thus to different levels of prestige and reward. The second is male control of women's sexuality which both seriously constrains women's space and physical mobility and shapes conceptions of what 'women' should be. These two pillars of patriarchy function in a mutually supportive manner, one seeming to justify the other. The combination appears totally natural and renders the questioning of either a formidable task, since economic benefits and deeply internalized norms are at stake. While the particular ways in which the division of labour and control of female sexuality manifest themselves are significantly influenced by social class, technological levels of development and religious and cultural norms, the two pillars nevertheless constitute the basis for women's subordination in most societies.

Adult education that is to 'empower' women must challenge these two pillars of patriarchal ideology and practice. It must contribute to meaningful change in the condition and position of women.[3] Fortunately, more and more South African women are realizing that if any real change in the position of women is to occur, women themselves need to attain real power as part of a process of economic, political and cultural transformation. In other words, women must gain access to and participate in decision-making structures at all levels in society. As Manzini (1992) argues, the mobilization of women and men to struggle for social justice for women as part of the political process of attaining social justice for all South Africans, is essential for changing the position and condition of women. This was the realization that, for the first time in the history of South Africa, united women from extremely diverse political and cultural backgrounds in the project of drawing up a Women's Charter for insertion into the national constitution-making process. The charter was handed over to President Nelson Mandela on 9 August 1994, National Women's Day.

Adult education concerned with the empowerment of women cannot stand apart from these developments. It needs to be an integral part of the political processes in which women's political, economic and social demands are asserted at national, regional and local levels. However, it is not enough to focus at the level of the constitution and state structures. Critical adult education work also needs to be addressed to the level of the family and community. In the face of this daunting task of helping to confront women's subordination on multiple levels, the training of adult educators takes on a singular importance.

The Cace workshops[4]

The first attempt by Cace to develop and run educational workshops to train feminist adult educators consisted of a series of two workshops held in October and December 1990. Run over five days and three days respectively, the workshops aimed 'to develop educational tools for gender analysis within community and worker organizations' for use by South African adult educators. The workshops were part of an ongoing action research process in Cace which aimed to develop relevant theory and practice with and for adult educators.

The workshops were attended by thirty-nine women from various parts of the country who were working as educators in a variety of sectors: within non-formal education organizations, political organizations, church-linked organizations, sports bodies, cultural organizations, trade unions, youth organizations, women's organizations, universities and health projects. The participants ranged in age from twenty-four to sixty years old. Most (72 per cent) were black. Their education levels ranged from ten years of schooling to post-graduate degrees. The majority were from urban areas; a few worked in rural areas.

The first workshop began with attempts to build a level of trust between the participants in order to make the workshop a relatively safe space in which we felt able to talk, reflect, analyse and play. It moved very soon into a focus on personal experiences through a story-telling exercise, which used household objects to trigger memories of being subordinated as women. For example, one woman who picked up a coat-hanger recalled: 'It was when I was sixteen years old. A boy said, "You think too much of yourself." He clubbed me. He ripped my clothes. And then he left.'

Another woman picked up a teacup and said: 'My mother had come to tea. She looked so disappointed in me. How could I sit there and accept a cup of tea from my husband?'

This exercise ignited very deep feelings and graphically demonstrated the subjective and objective realities of subordination for all the women, across colour, age, social class and religious and cultural traditions. It provided the basis for analysing commonalities of experience and for starting to identify and question the underlying reasons for the oppression of women in these various ways.

On the second day, the focus was on differences among the women. As the facilitators said:

> We assume that we cannot challenge gender subordination without acknowledging our difference of colour, sexual preference, class, cultural practices and the complexity of the interrelationships between these social categories. The most useful way of exploring gender is by recognizing these interconnections and learning how to identify them. Difference is seen as positive and there can be unity in diversity. (Author's workshop notes.)

In order to investigate differences and to problematize understanding of the intersection of colour, class and gender, an experiential exercise involving 'human sculpture' was developed after participants had listed their questions about the intersections of the various social categories. Each person had an opportunity to re-create a 'moment of subordination' and to analyse that experience.

The situations 'sculpted' in this way included women taking their wedding vows in different cultural settings; a young, pregnant, unmarried Muslim woman being counselled by an older Muslim woman who was a medical doctor; sexual harassment and assault on public transport; and being silenced in meetings. The exercise evoked a rich tapestry of experiences in which the complexities of subordination were identified and explored. We then began to construct a theoretical framework for an analysis of gender subordination, drawing on both these experiences and input from the facilitators.

The workshop shifted from a focus on personal experience to an analysis of gender relations within organizations. We began by exploring gender issues in relation to a fictitious case study of a small non-governmental organization (NGO) working in literacy and situated in Khayelitsha on the outskirts of Cape Town. Drawing on this exercise and our earlier analysis of personal experiences of subordination, we developed a symbolic 'gender tree' to provide theoretical tools for analysis of gender relations. The roots of the tree represented the systems of power which shape gender relations, the trunk the values and beliefs that sustain these relations, while the branches and leaves symbolized the visible outcomes of these structures in women's daily lives. These three aspects were then applied to case studies of organizations.

The next phase of the workshop was an analysis of the socio-economic and political contexts within which gender relations exist, and identification of spaces for effective challenges to subordination. Participants used paper, flowers, sticks and anything else they could find to create collages and sculptures to represent the social forces at play in these contexts. This formed the basis for planning by participants of strategic interventions within their own contexts by means of individual and group action. The interventions developed included formative thinking around the founding of a workers' college for Cape Town, actions by the African National Congress (ANC) Women's League designed to impact on the male-dominated ANC, and actions aimed at changing gender relations within certain NGOs, universities and families.

The last major exercise before the close of the first workshop involved practising specific assertive behaviours. In particular, participants practised what they would do and say on their return to work when confronted with dismissive and derisive comments from certain colleagues about being 'bra-burning feminists' and the like.

At the end of the first five-day workshop, the women undertook to implement in their families and organizations the strategic interventions they had developed and to return two months later to participate in the second three-day workshop.

The second workshop focused specifically on developing gender-sensitive educational skills and practices among participants. It presented opportunities for design and facilitation of mini-workshops which promoted gender awareness. Prior to the skills training, however, participants examined the social construction of knowledge by analysing the history and meaning of feminism, particularly 'African feminism' (Savane, 1990).

Participants offered a wide range of meanings given to the term 'feminist' by different women and men. Examples included:

— Some say a feminist is a woman with loose morals because she is often single and doesn't need a man
— She is not 'well cooked', not a whole woman
— She is someone who works for a culture of caring
— She has success in a man's world because she is being like a man
— She is someone who has concern for human rights.

Participants then analysed why these divergent understandings had developed. The last stage of the workshop involved 'visioning' activities in which the women created an alternative vision of a society where oppressive gender relations had been overcome.

In summary, there was constant shifting in the workshops between personal, organizational and socio-political experiences and analyses. There was constant movement between intellectual activity, emotional expression, including the space to have fun, and strategizing about changing the situations within which participants lived and worked. There were processes of consciousness-raising, theoretical analysis and practical skills training. Participants were engaging at one moment as women, as black or white women, as rural or urban women, as older or younger women, and as educators – educators with or without much experience and educators working in very different contexts. The design and the facilitation of the workshops strove to accommodate precisely such movement across these dimensions, ending with plans to continue to build solidarity among gender-sensitive and feminist adult educators in South Africa.

Key themes

With hindsight it is clear that the approaches used in the workshops resonated strongly with those described in the literature on feminist pedagogy, including feminist popular education. The particular themes that are debated within the literature and which have relevance for this discussion are: consciousness-raising and the use of experience as a basis for both social analysis and validating how women see their lives; the acknowledgement of difference, including a particular focus on racism, as a vital consideration in the design and facilitation of educational workshops; social activism; and the position of the educator. This section explores these themes, beginning with some background to the literature on feminist pedagogy.

Feminist pedagogy Feminist pedagogy is part of and an elaboration of critical pedagogy. Critical pedagogy in general is concerned with transforming the position of the oppressed. Feminist pedagogy deepens and extends this with a particular focus on improving the position of women. It developed as a critique of critical pedagogy which in the past largely ignored gender as a key social category (Ellsworth, 1989; Weiler, 1991).

The theoretical discussions in English of feminist pedagogy seem to have emanated mainly from the growth of women's studies courses at colleges and universities in North America and Western Europe. This has limited much of the discussion to pedagogy within formal educational institutions with students enrolled in formal degree programmes. It has also constrained feminist pedagogy within the need to deal with the contradictions and difficulties of work in formal institutions (Bannerji et al., 1991). However, in Latin America, the Philippines, the Caribbean and elsewhere, there is apparently vibrant dialogue around feminist popular education.[5] An additional source of debate is the work of 'gender trainers' in the area of gender and development (Population Council, 1991).

Defining what feminist pedagogy is, in practice, is not easy. Weiler (1991) states that it is easier to describe the various methods used than to give a coherent definition. Briskin (1990) argues that feminist pedagogy speaks to the gendered character of the classroom and to the curriculum. It is about teaching from a feminist perspective. She argues that it is more than 'good teaching' and is concerned with contributing to changing the subordinate position of women. Others (Weiler, 1991; hooks, 1988; *Women's Studies Quarterly*, 1987) agree that the key intention of feminist pedagogy is to provide learners with the skills to continue political work as feminists. Feminist pedagogy across the range of political perspectives – radical, socialist, Marxist, liberal and post-modernist – echoes the struggles of its origins and retains a vision of social activism. It usually reflects this critical, oppositional and activist stance.

Consciousness-raising A fundamental aspect of consciousness-raising is reliance on experience and feeling. During the 1960s and 1970s, as women's movements grew around the world, this focus on women's experiences came from a profound distrust of accepted authority and truth. The need to challenge patriarchal structures, which had defined common sense, meant that women had nowhere to turn except to themselves. Another aspect of consciousness-raising was the sharing of experience in a 'leaderless' group (Walters, 1989: 36), a process similar to testifying in the black church in the United States and dependent on openness and trust between those participating. The assumption underlying this sharing of stories was the existence of commonality among women.

In Latin America, the consciousness-raising process has usually begun with the *cotidiano* or 'daily lived experience'. Doerge (1992: 9) elaborates the importance of starting here, with the most immediate experience and most known, including all aspects of life, at home, at work, in the community, in organizations: 'By focusing on social relations in the *cotidiano*, all contradictions in society can be made evident.'

Consciousness-raising has also been closely linked to political action. It has been seen as both a method for arriving at truth and an impetus to organization and action. What was original in consciousness-raising was its emphasis on experience and feeling as guides to theoretical understanding, an approach that reflected the reality that women's subjectivities and the conditions of their lives were socially defined. However, at some stages and in certain contexts, consciousness-raising groups tended towards a loss of political perspective and too narrow a focus on the individual, to the detriment of political activism.

Weiler (1991) has pointed out the contradiction in an approach that treats experience and emotion as sources of knowledge, on the one hand, while acknowledging, on the other, that both experience and emotion are socially constructed. The resolution she offers is Lorde's argument that human beings are not completely shaped by dominant discourses, that we retain the capacity for self-critique and may challenge our own ways of feeling and knowing. When tied to a recognition of positionality, therefore, validation of feeling can be used to develop powerful sources of politically focused feminist education (and action).

Many feminist adult or popular educators in Latin America would agree with Lorde in all likelihood. They work actively to integrate the emotions, the intellect, the body and the spirit in order to deepen consciousness, reconstruct the self-esteem of individual women and build solidarity among them. Body consciousness, spiritual connectedness and acknowledgement of the importance of emotions are all seen as integral to the conscientization process, according to Doerge (1992). In the United States, Fisher (1987) has pointed out the importance of emotional expression in building a sense of community among learners, which in many instances provides the basis for feminist pedagogy. Melamed (1991) writes about the importance of reclaiming playfulness as a contribution to serious learning by women. Clearly, there are many feminist educators who argue for the importance of emotion in the pedagogical process.

The Cace workshops confirmed the validity of this approach. Participants' experiences and the feelings associated with them, explored through stories evoked by household objects and 'human sculpture', were important reference points throughout the workshops. They provided the basis for the introduction of theoretical frameworks, for the identification of commonalities and differences among the women, and for building solidarity and a sense of a learning community. As interpreted by participants, these experiences also provided the base from which strategic plans were developed.

Significantly, the sharing of experiences in an atmosphere of mutual trust placed 'difference' firmly on the workshop agenda. At the same time it demonstrated in a profound way the existence of a degree of common experience across such divides as colour, culture, age and political ideology.

The question of difference   Black women (Collins, 1990; hooks, 1988; Carty, 1991; Aziz, 1992), post-modernist feminist theorists (Lather, 1991; Luke and Gore, 1992) and critical Third World feminists (Sen and Grown, 1987; Mbilinyi, 1992) converge in their critique of the concept of a universal women's experience. This notion of a unitary and universal category of women has been critiqued for its racist assumptions. Recently, in addition, feminist theorists influenced by post-modernism have pointed to the need to consider the social construction of subjectivity and the 'unstable' nature of the self. They argue that it is when individual selves are viewed as being constructed and negotiated, that we can begin to consider what those forces are in which individuals shape themselves and by which they are shaped. The category 'women' itself is challenged, as it is seen more and more as part of a system of ideology. Critical Third World feminists point, also, to the imperialist assumptions behind the notion of universal women's experiences. Black women, lesbians and women from the Third World ground such critiques on analyses of their experiences, which reveal that it is not only sexism that must be considered and dealt with by feminist theory and practice, but also racism, homophobia, class oppression and imperialism.

Investigation of the experiences of women leads to a view of the world that both acknowledges difference and points to the need for an integrated analysis and practice based on the fact that the major systems of oppression are interlocking. Acknowledging the reality of tensions and differences between women does not mean abandoning the goal of social justice and empowerment for all women, but it does mean recognizing that claims are contingent and situated and, at the same time, turning a critical eye on how our own histories and selves are constructed.

As hooks (1988: 25) argues: 'We need to work collectively to confront difference, to expand our awareness of sex, race and class as interlocking systems of domination, of the way we reinforce and perpetuate these structures.' It is by these means that 'we will learn the true meaning of solidarity', through a new commitment to a 'rigorous process of education for critical consciousness'. hooks's view is shared by others involved in feminist pedagogy. We still look to consciousness raising as a key element in the educational process, but we do so with a more developed theory of pedagogy and an acute consciousness of the importance of difference.

A complementary methodological approach to the question of difference calls for coalition building. Diffference is recognized and validated but so is the need for mobilization around common goals. As Mbilinyi (1992: 27) argues, 'coalition and the crossing of (class/gender/race-ethnic) borders is necessary to successfully face the growing power of the far right, nationally and globally'. Nevertheless, coalition politics do not remove the need for marginalized people to get together to 'formulate thought and theory that includes them and their experiences' (Serote, 1992: 24).

In planning the Cace workshops, which were run prior to the first democratic election in South Africa in a context of continuing statutory racism and minimal political space for challenging sexism, the organizers felt that they could make few assumptions about the common experiences of women in the country. Before the 1990 workshops there had been very few occasions when women from diverse backgrounds could explore their positions in any depth. The assumption was therefore that there would be many different experiences and the design of the workshop encouraged the expression of these differences.

Various methods were used to create space for differences to be heard. For example, during one session in the second workshop, participants were divided into small working groups on the basis of racial classification, that is, into white, coloured and black groups. This was done with the consent of participants and as a way of acknowledging the need to explore differences and commonalities in experience related to race. Other differences, relating to factors such as age, political outlook and educational level, surfaced at different times and in different ways during the workshops. However, exploring difference in any depth clearly takes time and time in the workshops under discussion was very limited.

The position of the educator The recognition that people are shaped by their experiences of class, colour, gender, imperialism and so on has powerful implications for pedagogy, in that it emphasizes the need to make conscious the subject positions not only of learners but of educators as well. Feminist theorists in particular argue that it is essential to recognize that we cannot live as human subjects without in some sense taking on a history. The recognition of our histories necessarily implies articulating our subjectivities and our interests as we try to interpret and critique the social world. It requires educators to acknowledge their power and privilege, although this will vary according to circumstance. For example, those who have the power and authority to grade learners in formal programmes will clearly be in a different position from educators in non-formal settings where grading is not an issue.

As Weiler (1991) remarks, feminist writings point to the need to articulate and claim a particular historical and social identity and to build coalitions on the basis of a recognition of the partial knowledges of our constructed identities. Educators and learners need to recognize and actively acknowledge differences while building solidarity in the quest for the empowerment of all women. Thus, feminist educators are involved in a particular form of Freirian dialogue with learners, recognizing differences and commonalities of experience and knowledge at different points. Doerge (1992: 14) puts it like this: 'My role, as for any feminist popular educator working across difference, is to listen to women of other positions in the world, reflect upon our own privilege and oppression, and act, with these women, so as to transform myself and society.'

In educational programmes, an important way of taking into account the differences among the learners and the educators/facilitators is to ensure that the group of facilitators is representative of social differences. While this strategy carries the danger of essentializing social categories, it can be argued that it still has validity in the South African context.

Social activism   In addressing women's oppression, feminist pedagogy operates from the assumption that the status quo must change. While political activism is assumed in both Freire's work and the literature on feminist pedagogy, there is little discussion on what this might entail or what theories of social transformation underlie particular forms of social action. This neglect is being tackled by certain popular educators in Latin America and Canada (for example, Arnold et al., 1991), and to some extent by gender trainers whose primary concern seems to be with achieving gender equity within organizations, projects and programmes.[6]

The meaning of social activism for feminist pedagogy clearly will be shaped by the specific context within which it is operating. In many situations, particularly within formal educational institutions, learners participate as individuals. Social activism in these circumstances is limited in most cases to the development of critical consciousness among the individuals and in their individual interpretations of what they have experienced. In informal educational settings, particularly when participants come from political, cultural, worker or other social organizations, the curriculum can include space for detailed planning and strategizing for collective social action. In certain situations the line between education and social activism will be quite blurred.

The Cace workshops included sessions which involved planning for personal, organizational and broader social change. Strategies for personal change included the practising of assertive behaviours at work and in the family. On the organizational level, strategies were developed on the basis of an analysis of what was needed to challenge women's subordination in each case. On a broader level, networking and the building of solidarity among participants were discussed as conscious strategies for building the capacities of gender-sensitive and feminist adult educators in the field.

An emerging curriculum?

Critical reflection on both the Cace workshops and feminist pedagogy in general brings to light a number of issues for consideration in the construction of a curriculum for training gender-sensitive and feminist adult educators. The list may well be incomplete, as it is based largely on experience in training women. It is unclear as yet what may be required for the training of men and this lack of experience and theorization is a major limitation of this chapter. The importance of training men to challenge unequal gender relations cannot be over-emphasized but I am unaware of literature that explores this issue in any detail.

Another difficulty in making general proposals relating to a curriculum is that they must stand in a vacuum, seemingly in contradiction to the common knowledge that material conditions are key. For example, the length of the course, the formal or non-formal institutional context, the profile of the participants and so on will determine what is possible. Nevertheless, I would argue that the issues discussed below will need to be considered regardless of context, although the specific situation will obviously shape how the issues are interpreted and addressed.

Consciousness-raising As has been argued above, educators need a high level of self-consciousness if they are to deal constructively with the content and the practice of gender oppression. They must be able to locate and identify themselves within their own subjectivities, acknowledge the interconnections between various social categories, and deploy critical self-knowledge to 'paint themselves into the picture' when dealing with learners' legitimate questions as to where they stand in relation to the latter and their issues (Arnold et al., 1991: 32).

Thus, educators need to go through processes of consciousness-raising which enable them to confront their own experiences and understanding of gender relations, race relations and other relations that are oppressive.

Facilitation skills In order to be able to assist learners to identify and work through their own experiences and understandings, educators have to develop facilitation skills. Fundamental to the development of such skills is the educator's own prior experience of grappling with her (or his) issues in a self-conscious way. In the training of adult educators, there is thus a tension between two processes: the process of dealing with one's own issues, and the process of learning to help others do the same thing.

It is important to recognize the difference between these two necessary processes and to be conscious of when one or the other is operating. There can be slippage between the two which can cause confusion.

Beyond this, facilitators have to be able to think on their feet, to deal with emotional responses of various kinds, to integrate experience with theoretical analysis, to shift between intellectual engagement, personal feelings and the need to strategize. They need, finally, to be able to help women develop the skills to assert themselves confidently and to challenge oppressive behaviour.

Feminist theories Educators need to be introduced to critical pedagogy and to feminist pedagogy in particular. They need to be able to locate themselves within and engage the various educational debates.

In addition, if they are to help learners to make sense of their experiences and to deepen their understandings of gender oppression, educators need theoretical frameworks which can help them to unpack the 'common sense' of gender ideologies. A theoretical understanding is crucial to the planning of strategic interventions, whether in programmes, organizations or families, if actions are to be developed which confront the fundamental issues which give men power over women. It is not enough to tackle the condition of women; their position must be dealt with also.

Thus, educators need an understanding of 'the two pillars of patriarchy': the sexual division of labour and male control of women's sexuality. In the context of the new international division of labour, which highlights the interconnections between women workers globally, an international perspective and analysis are at least useful and possibly essential (Hart, 1992). Educators also need to be able to deal with issues relating to sexuality on both a theoretical and practical level.

While there are several competing feminist theories, a working knowledge of the different positions is important, as is an acquaintance with the theories underlying Women in Development (WID) and Gender and Development (GAD), particularly in relation to planning social actions. WID emphasizes changing the conditions of women without necessarily changing the relations between men and women. GAD assumes that women are neither 'the issue' nor 'the problem' in development and focuses on how relations between women and men are defined and structured, with a view to transformation that enables equality.

Social transformation The need for action aimed at changing the position of women is integral to educational programmes which challenge gender subordination. 'Action' refers both to theoretical analytical work and practical implementation. Theories of organizational and social change which are based on an understanding of the interconnections between gender, race, class and imperial relations are crucial. Mbilinyi (1992) argues, and I would be inclined to agree, that 'critical third world feminism' provides an important theoretical frame.

A variety of strategies for social transformation have been developed by feminists in programmes, projects, organizations and social movements around the world. Knowledge of these various practices is important if successful actions are to be designed and implemented. There is a need to deepen collective analysis of feminist organizing strategies within specific contexts, in order to enhance understanding of the processes of social transformation and prospects for success.

Difference and solidarity There is a need to acknowledge both differences and commonalities among learners and educators. Differences such as social class, religio-cultural background, colour and age complicate the building of solidarity, even among women who share an understanding of gender oppression. It is useful for the educator to be able to work with all forms of oppression simultaneously, facilitating the exploration of differences. In South Africa, educators need particularly to be able to confront racism.

Being able to facilitate the building of solidarity is an important aspect of the educator's role, since the experience of challenging gender subordination is emotionally charged and risky. Individuals and groups need support to be able to sustain their commitment to change. For most women, in addition to any organizational change it may reveal as necessary, challenging gender relations means attempting to change very personal relationships. This is often traumatic and there is a clear need to build support networks, so that women can sustain each other in the process of necessary but painful change.

Participation in design Decision-making in relation to the aims, content and process of a programme is extremely important. There must be space for differences to be acknowledged, a milieu in which participants feel comfortable enough to participate, and a process for setting up the programme that inspires confidence in those involved. In the absence of such a respectful approach, dialogue across differences is not possible, as Ellsworth (1989) notes. In addition, various techniques for maximizing participation should be considered to enable the voices of all to be heard.

Conclusion

This chapter has argued that adult educators who wish to challenge oppressive gender relations must become self-conscious actors who reflect on their own privilege and oppression and act, alongside others, to change both themselves and society.

In order to be able to do this, they need training which takes into account the individual, organizational, societal and educational dimensions of challenging the position and condition of women. Gender-sensitive and feminist adult educators require educational skills, theoretical understandings and commitment to social activism if they are to make a difference. A start has been made in South Africa in the development of training programmes for feminist adult educators. The broad outline of a potential curriculum is emerging. However, much remains to be done, in terms of both evaluation of progress to date and ongoing development for the future.

Notes

I wish to acknowledge the very useful comments made by colleagues at Cace and Linzi Manicom in response to a first draft of this chapter and subsequently by Lehn Benjamin. This chapter was first published under the title 'Training Gender-sensitive and Feminist Adult Educators in South Africa: An Emerging Curriculum' in *Perspectives in Education*, Vol. 15, no. 1, Summer 1993/94, and I thank the editors for permission to publish it in this volume.

1. I refer to gender-sensitive and feminist educators in this chapter in acknowledgement of the many South African women who feel uncomfortable with the label 'feminist' because they associate it with North America and Western Europe. My use of the term, however, follows Marie-Angelique Savane (1990). She argues that for African women feminism is a hope, as it offers the conceptual and methodological tools necessary for understanding their position and role in the economy, for questioning the laws and taboos that legitimate oppressive traditional practices, and for organizing their liberation. Feminism, in this sense, is a political commitment to ending the oppression of women as part of the struggle to end all oppression. Sexist oppression cannot be separated from other oppressions any more than a woman can separate her sex from, for example, her colour and her class. They are all integrated and make up who she is.

2. I purposely use 'quest for empowerment' as Nelly Stromquist (1991) does, since the empowerment of women will mean fundamental transformation of social structures and this is unlikely to be brought about in the forseeable future.

3. I use the terms 'condition' and 'position' of women as developed by Young (1988). 'Condition' means the material state in which women find themselves: their poverty, lack of education and training, excessive work burdens, restricted access to modern technology and so on. 'Position' refers to women's social and economic standing relative to men. The condition of women is the subject of much of the development literature on women, and most of the development projects aimed at women focus on improving their condition through the provision of ameliorative resources, rather than by radically changing the structures which underlie the condition. Thus, the emphasis on women's condition has inhibited a focus on the structural factors which perpetuate women's position. Clearly, both the condition and position of women need to be of concern to adult educators who aim to 'empower' women.

4. One of the outcomes of the workshops was the production and publication of a handbook (Mackenzie, 1991). The account of the workshops in this chapter is a personal one and I accept that there could be various, differing accounts.

5. Doerge (1992) and Fink (1992), among others, have begun to make the debates in Latin America accessible to English-speakers.

6. Gender training seems to be concerned with the implementation of institutional strategies for achieving gender equity. There are a number of dif-

ferent approaches. Some are based on notions of rationality: for example, you need facts and figures to demonstrate that targeting women is a way of making development processes more effective. Others recognize the need to deal with people's attitudes and values in order to change the environment in which they work.

Bibliography

Arnold, R. et al. (1991) *Educating for a Change*, Between the Lines and Doris Marshall Institute for Education and Action, Toronto.

Aziz, R. (1992) 'Feminism and the Challenge of Racism: Deviance or Difference', in Crowley, H. and Himmelweit, S. (eds), *Knowing Women: Feminism and Knowledge*, Polity Press, Cambridge.

Bannerji, H. et al. (1991) *Unsettling Relations: The University as a Site of Feminist Struggle*, Women's Press, Toronto.

Briskin, L. (1990) *Feminist Pedagogy: Teaching and Learning Liberation*, Canadian Research Institute for the Advancement of Women, Toronto.

Carty, L. (1991) 'Black Women in Academia: A Statement from the Periphery', in Bannerji, H. et al., op. cit.

Collins, P. (1990) *Black Feminist Thought: Knowledge, Consciousness and the Politics of Empowerment*, Unwin Hyman, New York and London.

Doerge, S. (1992) 'Feminist Popular Education: Transforming the World from Where Women Stand', working paper, University of Toronto.

Ellsworth, E. (1989) 'Why Doesn't This Feel Empowering? Working Through the Repressive Myths of Critical Pedagogy', *Harvard Educational Review*, Vol. 59, no. 3, August.

Fink, M. (1992) 'Women and Popular Education in Latin America', in Stromquist, N. (ed.) *Women and Education in Latin America: Knowledge, Power and Change*, Lynne Rienner, Boulder, CO.

Fisher, B. (1987) 'The Heart has its Reasons: Feelings, Thinking and Community Building in Feminist Education', *Women's Studies Quarterly*, Vol. XV, nos 3/4, Fall/Winter.

Ford-Smith, H. (1989) *Ring Ding in a Tight Corner*, International Council for Adult Education, Toronto.

Giroux, H. (1992) *Border Crossings: Cultural Workers and the Politics of Education*, Routledge, New York.

Hart, M. (1992) *Working and Educating for Life: Feminist and International Perspectives on Adult Education*, Routledge, New York.

hooks, b. (1988) *Talking Back: Thinking Feminist, Thinking Black*, Between the Lines, Toronto.

Lather, P. (1991) *Getting Smart: Feminist Research and Pedagogy with/in the Postmodern*, Routledge, New York.

Luke, C. and Gore, J. (1992) *Feminisms and Critical Pedagogy*, Routledge, New York.

Mackenzie, L. (1992) *On Our Feet: Taking Steps to Challenge Women's Oppression.*

A Handbook on Gender and Popular Education Workshops, Cace, University of the Western Cape, Bellville.

Manzini, M. (1992) 'Women and Power: Implications for Development', paper presented at the World University Services (SA) 'Conference on Utilising Development and Political Process to Entrench the Rights of Women', Johannesburg, August.

Mbilinyi, M. (1992) 'An Overview of Issues in the Political Economy of Adult Education in the 1990s', keynote address to the African Association for Literacy and Adult Education 'Workshop on the Political Economy of Adult Education', Kenya, July.

Melamed, L. (1991) 'Living and Learning: The Choice to be Playful', *Women's Education des Femmes*, Vol. 8, nos 3/4, Winter.

Population Council (1991) *Gender Training and Development Planning: Learning from Experience*, report of conference held in Bergen, Norway, May.

Savane, M.A. (1990) 'Women in Development in Africa: Challenges for the 1990s', paper presented at the African Association for Literacy and Adult Education general assembly, November.

Sen, G. and Grown, C. (1987) *Development Crises and Alternative Visions: Third World Women's Perspectives*, Monthly Review Press, New York.

Serote, P. (1992) 'Issues of Race and Power Expressed During Gender Conferences in South Africa', *Agenda*, no. 14.

Stromquist, N. (1991) 'Women's Literacy and the Quest for Empowerment', keynote address to a seminar organized by the Vrouwenberaad Ontwikkelingssamenwerking, The Netherlands, November.

Walters, S. (1989) *Education for Democratic Participation*, University of the Western Cape, Bellville.

Weiler, K. (1991) 'Freire and a Feminist Pedagogy of Difference', *Harvard Educational Review*, Vol. 61, no. 4, November.

Women's Studies Quarterly (1987) Special Edition on Feminist Pedagogy, Vol. XV, nos 3/4, Fall/Winter.

Young, K. (1988) *Women and Economic Development: Local, Regional and National Planning Strategies*, Berg/Unesco, Oxford.

2

Embodying feminist popular education under global restructuring

DENISE NADEAU

I look around the circle of women at a church workshop on 'Women and Free Trade'. This is a small town in rural British Columbia. About twenty are here, all of us white, most of us mothers or grandmothers, some middle-class, some working-class. I see drooping shoulders, anxious frowns and many bodies slumped in their chairs. These women look tired and I sense they feel overwhelmed by the North American Free Trade Agreement (Nafta) and the entire economic picture of cut-backs, privatization, lack of affordable housing and day-care, and increasingly part-time, low-paying work for women. The workshop is coming to a close and I'm not sure what to do.

I want to leave them with some sense of hope. I decide to take a risk. I have learned a slogan in Mexico which women use in marches: 'Women struggling transform the world.' I ask the group to get up and practise saying the slogan, then practise yelling it, then lift their fists. At first hesitant, the women stand up. Yelling is something they are not familiar with but they are willing to try it. Suddenly the energy in the room is transformed, the older women joining in with as much vehemence as the younger. Fists raised, chanting, together we have taken a stand with our bodies. The sense of powerlessness is broken.

I share this story as a way of naming what has been the central challenge of my work as a popular educator in the last few years. I work in British Columbia, Canada, with a variety of popular movement groups in both rural and urban areas. Since 1987 I have been educating and organizing around economic issues: free trade, the feminization of poverty, the future of women's work and women's labour rights.

At a certain point I found my work was stuck. The women in my workshops were not 'moving to action' in any real sense. The analysis of global restructuring and free trade we were uncovering didn't seem to connect directly with our lives or give us a sense of hope. Usually the opposite happened. The women felt powerless in the face of forces that seemed too large and too far away for us to have any impact on them.

However, using our bodies and voices at the end of the workshop in British Columbia gave us the beginnings of a feeling that we had some power. Despite the fact that the workshop participants were Christian and presumably had a sense of hope from their spirituality, they had not felt empowered to act. But standing up, yelling and lifting their fists had allowed them to vent their feelings and get in touch with the energy that sustained them.

This experience was about embodying the spirit, bringing to voice and gesture our vision of transformation and our solidarity with other women. I also realized this moment carried a significant lesson for my own work: it was time seriously to explore how to integrate the body more systematically into popular education.

Since that moment in 1991 I have been cautiously and gradually shifting how I do this work. In this chapter I will share some of the methods I have been using, especially in the area of educating and organizing women around global economic restructuring. While I assume that working with the body is working with the spirit, I have chosen to focus here on the constraints and possibilities of incorporating body-work in feminist popular education. I do so because very little has been written on the role and function of the body in popular education.

I am also using the term 'body' in a very specific way. While it has many meanings, in this chapter I am referring to the physical body as a site to which popular education must attend. As I argue below, it is women's physical body that is the primary site of struggle under the global restructuring of capital.

My evolution as an educator has been connected to a realization of the need to integrate my 'private' and 'public' lives. My interest in body-work is rooted in a life-long love of dance. In the early 1980s I realized that my modern dance classes were helping me to deal with a very difficult personal crisis. The idea that dance might have a deeper function than performance and exercise was new and exciting to me. I then began to explore sacred and liturgical dance when I was attending a Christian theological school. Using dance to explore and express sacred texts and rituals reinforced my intuition that movement could both heal and reveal. In the early 1990s I took a course in movement and healing, a programme which helped me move through my internalized oppression.

These personal experiences of transformation are the sub-text of my story as a feminist popular educator. The question of integration, of linking mind, body, spirit and emotions, is a challenge I face as an educator and a human being. Yet I am not alone in this. Feminist popular educators in Canada, Mexico and Central America are asking similar questions and also experimenting with new approaches to working with the body. Because many women's organizations are now linking internationally to fight the consequences of global economic restructuring, we have been able to share and discuss these developments in our educational practice. This chapter tells the story of some of these approaches and the lessons I have learned and applied in my own work.

The absent body

I have called myself a feminist since the early 1970s. In retrospect I would describe what I did in the 1980s as 'popular education with women' rather than feminist popular education. Because I named myself a feminist, because the content was often women's issues, and because popular education is a democratic, inclusive and participatory method that does not contradict feminist aims, I did not see a distinction for many years. However, as I began to educate and organize around economic issues with women, I found there were limitations in both my theory and my practice.

I realized I was using a method that on the surface looked integrated, looked as if it involved the whole person in learning, but in fact was not and did not. In no significant way was the popular education I was practising linking body and mind, spirit and emotion. In fact, by emphasizing social analysis it seemed to reinforce the abstractness of topics like free trade while also increasing women's sense that 'there is nothing we can do about it'.

I define popular education as a method of group education and organizing that starts with the problems in people's daily lives. It then moves through a process of critical analysis of common experience to having the group look for and learn the resources and skills they will need to solve their problems collectively.

Within this basic definition there are different approaches that vary with culture, context and history. For example, there are significant variations in how popular education is practised in the Philippines, South Africa, Brazil and Canada. I myself had adopted a form of popular education that developed in Central America in the late 1970s and early 1980s in the context of the Nicaraguan revolution. The theoreticians of this movement were men and their analysis of oppression and their vision of alternatives were defined primarily in terms of (male) participation in class struggle and national liberation movements. Because this approach focused on the economic exploitation of the working class, with a strong emphasis on social analysis which was missing from my middle-class, North American feminism, I embraced this form of popular education uncritically.

In the last few years I've discovered that Latin American feminist popular educators started to critique this traditional framework in the mid-1980s (Doerge, 1994; Pineda, 1986). Not only did they challenge language such as 'the people' and 'the New Man', which excluded women by assuming a male generic, they also broadened the definition of key social actors in response to the development of popular movements in Latin America. The social movements that emerged in the 1980s were based in the neighbourhood and led by women. Feminist popular educators quickly recognized that women, youth, the urban poor and indigenous people were playing central roles in building popular resistance and in creating alternatives located not in political parties but in the social movements.

These social movements addressed such issues as violence against women, sexuality, health, self-esteem and machismo as much as issues traditionally understood as 'political': housing, clean water, electricity, transport. In fact, by the late 1980s, feminist popular educators in many countries were exploring sexuality, reproductive rights and domestic violence with urban poor and rural and peasant women. As the impact of structural adjustment programmes imposed in the 1980s began to be felt, Latin American feminists also realized that traditional popular education had failed to address the reality of women's domestic and community lives: the invisible 'private' sphere and the specific problems and possibilities of women as workers both inside and outside the home (Fernandez et al., 1991).

It was on the basis of this perception, that traditional popular education had failed to address the many sites where women confront economic oppression, that feminist economists and theorists from the South developed a gender analysis of global restructuring, now often referred to as Gender and Development (GAD) theory. GAD analysis has shown how the intersection of multiple oppressions – race, class and gender as well as colonial history – has shaped women's economic subordination. It also uncovers how the exploitation of women's un-waged domestic and community work is built into the dynamics of global restructuring. Traditional popular education, which emphasized a structural analysis of the economic, political and ideological mechanisms of male workers' exploitation, had not developed tools or a framework for examining the complex realities of women's daily lives.

Underlying this omission is a basic assumption about social change. Popular education has usually stressed the development of critical analysis as the key to transformation. In other words, the belief is that once the oppressed realize the nature and structure of oppression, they will act to change it. However, I have found that people do not necessarily take action once they understand their situation. I have seen women arrive at a critical understanding of the dynamics of their oppression but at the same time begin to feel overwhelmed and powerless. The initial euphoria of making critical links was not translated into action. I gained more insights into this pedagogical dilemma when I read the writings of those American and Australian feminists whose work has been labeled 'feminist post-critical pedagogy'.

These writers have developed a critique of radical pedagogies like popular education for their grounding in a 'rationalist masculinist ideology'. In other words, they have been developed from the standpoint of male experience and make universalist assumptions that are based on norms most applicable to European, white, middle-class, Christian, able-bodied, heterosexual men (Ellsworth, 1992). Underlying these pedagogies is a belief in the rules of reason as the key to realizing the truths necessary for liberation, and a 'gendered division between male public and female private, culture and nature, reason and emotion, mind and body' (Luke, 1992: 34).

For me, the key to overcoming this 'gendered division' has been the body. Traditional popular education uses the body to some extent but limits its function. While techniques such as sculpture and socio-drama involve the body in collective representations, they primarily serve as a distancing mechanism to help the group develop a collective analysis of a problem that before seemed individual. The body is used as a prop. Rarely are feelings debriefed and rarely is the body itself seen as a source of knowledge.

In working at integrating the domains of body and mind, in adding emotional, spiritual and physical knowing to the transformation process, feminist popular education is making the link in its practice between the private and the public. It attempts to access the deeper levels of the human psyche where it is often determined whether people will act or not. Women are involved daily in maintenance and care of the body: in nurturing their families, transmitting culture, providing health-care, preparing food and generally sustaining body and soul in family and community. Much of women's work whether reproductive work, productive work, or community work, revolves around the body and its needs. The political economy of women's bodies revolves around women's work as consumers, sex partners, sex trade workers, free trade zone workers, home workers, domestic workers, and as reproducers of workers in their roles as mothers, teachers, nurses, day-care workers and so on. This labour is so critical that church and state try to manage women's bodies – their reproductive capacities and freedoms and their sexualities. Men as individuals and groups try to discipline women through rape, beatings, disappearances and murder, that is, through the body. In many ways the body is the key site of struggle for women.

Starting from women's experience

I am hurrying along a crowded Mexico City street, dodging street vendors, carts and cars, trying to keep up with my *companera* from Mujer a Mujer [Woman to Woman]. We are on our way to a workshop on free trade which Mujer a Mujer is running with the regional women's committee of the Urban Popular Movement. She is discussing analysis and strategy as we walk: 'For women in Mexico free trade is already a reality. Their lives have changed. Trying to stop this deal [Nafta] is denying women's reality. We need to look at different ways of organizing that address this reality and that acknowledge what women are going through and how women can struggle in this new framework.'

Soon we are entering the regional women's committee building, moving past a community kitchen space and upstairs to a cool dark room where about forty women are gathered on low benches. On the walls are several collective drawings done by the women, whose titles in Spanish translate as 'our health', 'our use of time', 'our community and neighbourhood', 'our plans for our children'. This is the workshop on Nafta and it has started from where women are hurting the most.

This visit to Mujer a Mujer early in 1992 was a turning-point in my analysis and understanding of how we needed to organize women in the context of free trade. In all my organizing in Canada against Nafta, I had missed women's daily reality. Since 1987 I had played the role of bringing the 'women's perspective' into coalition work organizing against free trade deals, deregulation, privatization, workplace reorganization and social programme cuts. Free trade was largely understood in terms of its impact on paid employment – usually male jobs in resource and manufacturing industries – and on sovereignty, democracy, the environment and social programmes. In the campaign literature or discussions about free trade, women would then be added on to the list, as if we weren't integrally involved in all the other areas.

This framework affected how I did my education work. A group of women would share what they knew about free trade and we would then look at what it meant for women in terms of job loss, lower wages and poverty. Yet large parts of women's lives and daily reality – their unpaid work in the home, their family relationships, their responsibilities in the community – were being excluded from this discussion of free trade.

I learned in Mexico that women had been experiencing the impact of economic restructuring with the imposition of structural adjustment programmes since the early 1980s. Like many women throughout the world, Mexican women now have a triple or quadruple day, carrying two or three part-time jobs or working in the informal economy as well as in the home and in the community. Restructuring forced them to increase their workloads to compensate for government cut-backs in food subsidies, health-care, education and social services. Mexican women know from direct experience that global restructuring is built on the continued and increasing poverty and exploitation of women.

How to manage this triple (or quadruple) role is a critical issue for women experiencing economic restructuring everywhere. Most low-income women and many middle-class women must balance reproductive work (childbearing and rearing, household maintenance), productive work (income generation) and community management work (involvement in community activities to fight for resources for community and families). This applies to women in Canada as well as in the South, though women in the North tend to have appliances and other consumer commodities as aids in domestic work as well as a higher standard of living.

Restructuring often means that women must work longer and harder at paid work, often for less pay and fewer benefits, and longer and harder at home because of cut-backs in areas such as health, education and social services. The pressure and stress on women increase as their 'unseen' labour is exploited. As they try to manage multiple roles, women's health is placed in jeopardy. Research with women in a low-income neighbourhood in a city in Ecuador concluded that this pressure divided women into three groups: those who were 'coping', those who were 'hanging on' and those who were 'burnt out' (Moser, 1993).

It is at this level of daily life, where women are experiencing economic restructuring differently to men, that we must start.

Popular education's task is to help women understand their daily situation within a structural or macro-economic analysis and to encourage them to explore what they can do to transform this daily reality. The perspective of the triple role (women balancing reproductive work, productive work and community management work) makes it possible to go directly to the core of women's daily lives: not only the pressures they feel but also their dreams and fears for their children, their concern for the safety and quality of living conditions in their neighbourhoods, their difficulties in relation to finding affordable housing and feeding their families. These are areas close to women's hearts and, I would argue, close to women's bodies. If we start economic literacy work from these points, women can begin to see how economic policies relate to their lives. These are the areas they have energy and passion for changing.

When I returned to Canada I experimented with the exercise whose fruits I had seen in Mexico City. At a workshop with women belonging to a women's centre in a small town, I asked participants to break up into small groups and discuss 'our plans for our children', 'our use of time', 'our health', 'our neighbourhood and community organizations'. The women reported back with much excitement, using collective drawings or skits, and in the ensuing discussion began to see the connections between the changes they were experiencing and 'far away' economic policies. In workshops for organized workers I substituted 'workplace organization' for the fourth category to get at such issues as the intensification of work in 'total quality management' or, more accurately, 'management by stress' schemes.

I decided to try more body approaches to these same issues when I realized that the bodily stress that most women experienced in daily life was a key to uncovering their situation. I have a 'soft' approach: guided meditation. This involves group members first doing quiet breathing, either sitting or lying down, and then using a visualization to lead them to their intuitive knowledge.

An exercise I have used is one adapted from an African workshop about women and structural adjustment. Participants are asked to visualize a normal day in their lives ten years back. The women are then guided to move forward to the present and again to visualize a normal day. After they come out of the meditation they share in small groups how things have changed and why (All Africa Conference of Churches, 1992). The effectiveness of this approach is linked to the fact that memory is activated in the semi-trance state induced by the breathing, relaxation and quiet.

One movement exercise I use is adapted from a popular theatre game called 'twenty-four hours'. In this exercise participants use mime and voice to demonstrate physically what they do over a twenty-four-hour period. The animator 'starts the clock' and slowly goes through each hour, asking the participants to act out with their bodies what they might be doing at that hour. After the exercise, participants reflect on their experience, what they felt and also what they observed of others in the room.

'Twenty-four hours' reveals the extent, complexity and intensification of women's work: how busy women are, how they have no time for themselves, and how they are often pushed to breaking-point. It also reveals similarities and differences across class and race lines (taking the bus or walking versus having a car). When used with men and women, it shows the glaring differences between the lives of the sexes (men playing darts and drinking beer between 4 and 6 p.m., while women are frantically picking up children, shopping and cooking dinner). When used with a group of paid workers such as hospital workers, it leads to an analysis of workplace restructuring and how it is tied into economic restructuring. It also can be used to identify areas members of the group want to act on to help each other.

Another body exercise I have used is called 'the triple role'. Each participant takes out of a container a folded-up piece of paper on which is written a triple role. For example: 'You are cooking dinner while your two-year-old is pulling on your leg, crying, and the phone rings with someone requesting that you go over the workshop design for tomorrow.' Or: 'You are working in the cafeteria when a phone call comes from your daughter's school to inform you that she is sick, while your union shop steward has just slipped you a note saying there is a meeting about your grievance this afternoon.' At the count of three, participants mime what is on their sheet and without speaking find others who are acting out the same triple role. They group together, have a few minutes to prepare and then present their scenario to the group. After all the scenes have been presented and identified, the participants discuss how the skits reflect their reality and what it means. Not only can this exercise lead to a gender analysis of work and restructuring, but it also has led to one group of women identifying ways to help each other to alleviate the stress of the triple role.

The 'collective body scan' is another short exercise I have developed. I read a list of physical symptoms or illnesses common to those who experience high stress in the workplace. Participants, who are standing, can slowly lower themselves to the floor as they recognize symptoms they have, or they can choose to mime what each symptom feels like and how it affects their bodies. This exercise is very effective in immediately grounding the stress in participants' bodies, thus bringing the whole person to the ensuing discussion. It also extends the experience of distress beyond the personal: participants realize that it is not their individual inability to cope that is the cause of their pain but rather that something larger is happening.

More and more feminist popular educators are choosing to start from the physical symptoms of dis-ease or stress to get first at occupational health and safety issues and then at global restructuring. An organization called Women and Work based in Vancouver, Canada, holds occupational stress workshops to help women develop an analysis of how repetitive strain injuries are linked to the restructuring of work. Another group that has developed an educational programme around health, the triple role and economic restructuring is the Grupo de Educación Popular con Mujeres (GEM) in Mexico City. Their programme is called 'The Working Woman and Health' and they use the slogan 'Our health is not for sale'.

Starting from the body and an analysis of the body's centrality in women's daily experience of economics, women can discover the gendered dimensions of global economic restructuring. But this is only the first step in a much larger process. It is very hard for women to move to action if they are 'just coping' or 'barely hanging on'. With the intensification of work dictated by restructuring, most women are usually too tired, too stressed, too busy or too despairing to take on anything more. The challenge for feminist popular educators is to explore what we can bring to the educational process that can release, transform and heal these feelings. This involves paying attention to the body in a different way.

Claiming our bodies

Taller Educación Corporal (Body Education Workshop) ... I immediately catch the title as I look at the notice-board in this Mexican hotel where the 'First Tri-national Conference of Women Workers Against Free Trade and Economic Integration' is taking place. I hurry down the white-tiled hallway to a sparse lobby space where chairs have been pushed back. About twenty Mexican women are standing in a circle. A short, auburn-haired woman dressed in loose clothing stands in the centre. She is about to begin a workshop on bioenergetics which she uses in her work with women in the free trade zone along the Mexican border with the United States of America.

I quickly join the circle and am soon swinging my arms, releasing tension in my fingers and kicking out anger and frustration. As I look around I see faces alert and alight with energy, some laughing with pleasure, others focused and concentrated on these new movements. This is not a group of middle-class professionals; beside me is an indigenous woman from Oaxaca, across from me women from the urban poor movement, and to my left union workers in telecommunications and banks from Mexico City.

I soon feel energy and vitality throughout my body and I am excited when our leader later shares the fact that this approach has become central to how her group is organizing women in free trade zones. I realize that I had to come all the way to Mexico to find the piece that was missing in my own work in Canada.

It had never occurred to me to use bioenergetics in group work with women, and certainly not with women in the free trade zone. Bioenergetics is a form of body-work that focuses on releasing emotional pain and other feelings that are often trapped in the body. It has been developed and used extensively for individual therapy in middle-class circles in Britain, Europe and North America.

The initial impetus for bioenergetics was the work of Wilhelm Reich, an Austrian psychoanalyst who moved beyond traditional psychoanalysis after realizing that social conditions were creating and maintaining his clients' problems. He began to focus on the body and on ways to release blocks and enhance energy. Bioenergetics is a form of body-work developed from his theory that held or repressed feelings have power, and that when a feeling is freed it becomes possible to liberate not only the energy of the feeling itself but the energy that has been used to repress it.

The woman who led the body-work workshop in Mexico was from the women's programme of an organization called Service, Development and Peace (Sedepac), which has been organizing with women in the free trade zones on the border between Mexico and the US. It is very difficult to organize through trade unions in these zones because the women can easily be labelled, fired or otherwise victimized if they are discovered 'agitating'. The women are also extremely tired from long hours of factory and family work. Sedepac therefore started to work outside the factory with Christian communities and women's community groups. Its starting-points were women's health issues and the role and cultural identity of southern women who come to border towns as migrants.

Bioenergetics was first introduced to help the women release their pain, anger and stress and become more familiar with their bodies. Now integrated into regular sessions, bioenergetics serves to build up women's strength and release energy for the struggle to improve economic and social conditions in the *maquilladoras* or free trade zones. Given that free trade zone factories are known to hire young women because they are seen as more 'docile' than men or older women, the use of bioenergetics could become one of the more subversive tactics of the new modes of organizing.

When I returned to Mexico City in 1993 I discovered that the women's committee of the Urban Poor Movement was also using bioenergetics to 'recover the political power of the body' and as an integral part of its training of community health workers. I now use bioenergetics to help women move beyond the feelings of despair and hopelessness that often emerge when discussing global economic forces. I also use simple techniques such as punching and kicking the air to release anger. The discharge of these feelings helps participants to move on and also frees creative energy for action.

Bioenergetics, guided meditation and exercises such as 'twenty-four hours' are based on the assumption that the individual body is a source of knowledge, insight and wisdom. Using such body-work and imaging techniques is to work intentionally with the body's wisdom in order to link deep emotions to rational analysis. The result is often 'embodied insight', a deep and often prior knowledge that cannot be accessed by reason alone.

When education methods focus solely on the mind, the body-self that has been silenced or locked away in denial is not permitted to emerge. That silencing or denial is often at the root of the deep sense of powerlessness which makes women feel unable to act. If popular education fails to uncover these deeper levels of subordination, women can continue to reproduce oppressive behaviour even while using the language of liberation. But where the popular educator can draw on the body as a resource, challenging internalized oppression becomes an achievable goal.

Claiming our history

In North America many people have internalized a sense of futility, a belief that nothing can change. This condition has been called 'surplus powerlessness' (Lerner, 1991). Surplus powerlessness is created by the structure of work and family life in a sexist, racist, classist society. One of the consequences of the stated North American belief in meritocracy is that many people blame themselves for the failures in their lives. This self-blaming is reinforced by the dominant cultural forms which present events in such an ahistorical way that people have no sense of being able to enter history in order to change it; in fact, many people have no sense of history at all.

One of the objectives of feminist popular education is to recover women's histories of resistance and struggle. Recovering our histories of resistance functions at several levels in challenging powerlessness. First it uncovers the 'dangerous memories' of victories, voice, strength, and the power of saying 'no'. Recovering historical memory helps to build identity, affirming who we are, where we've come from and what we might become. Because this remembering is done collectively, a sense of collective dignity and identity is developed which is critical to the capacity of any group to believe that it can act in and on its present historical reality. In fostering the development of an oppositional voice, historical memory work is very subversive.

As a way of helping women to discover their own histories of resistance, Mujer a Mujer ran training workshops for *promotoras internacionales*, organizers with an international perspective on women and global restructuring, where women were asked to share stories of their mothers' and grandmothers' lives. After this a feminist historian came in to talk about women's struggles in those periods.

I have developed a similar process: asking women to form small groups and share stories of resistance to gender, race, class or colonial oppression in the lives of their foremothers as far back as they can remember. I then ask them to present their stories to a plenary session, using image theatre (body sculpture) to represent common images of resistance. In one session three women presented two powerful images: one was the three of them sitting on the ground, their arms locked and their heads held high in silence; the other was of them standing, each holding high a candle. Their common historical memories of resistance – as women of Jewish, Russian Doukabour and South Indian heritage – was of passive resistance and the use of fire to fight the oppressor.

At other times I have invited workshop participants to create a dance-poem, in other words, to use both words and movement to share a story about their mother, grandmother or great-grandmother. We then talk about the larger movements their foremothers were part of, or were not part of because of oppression or privilege. I have found that encouraging free movement often results in an extraordinary uncovering of memories of female ancestors carried in the bodies of the women participating.

If historical memory is recovered with the body – through movement and voice, drawing and story-telling – it is internalized at an emotional body level. This means that the memory can be re-membered at other times and places because it has become re-known at the level of the body.

Rather than dwelling solely on the impact of global restructuring on women, this work of recovering a hidden history allows women to replay it with their bodies as part of the work of generating hope and combating surplus powerlessness. For poor women, indigenous women and women of racial and ethnic minorities who have struggled for generations against a state that never really benefited them, this exercise facilitates an approach to global restructuring that sees it not as defeat but rather as a shift in the conditions of struggle.

Challenging internalized oppression

The young woman is arguing with her father. He is yelling at her that she should get a job and get off welfare. She is tearfully arguing back, trying as calmly as she can to explain why she, as a single parent with a two-year-old child, is on social assistance.

At this point the animator raises her hand to stop the dialogue. She asks the young woman to identify some of the voices that are in her head as she argues with her father. She asks her to pick some of the other members of the group to represent these voices and to shape these voices in different body positions around her. They replay the scene again, this time with all the voices 'activated' (talking aloud).

This is a scene from a workshop with anti-poverty workers that I ran with a Canadian popular theatre worker from the Alchemy Theatre Company. The exercise is called 'cops in the head', a form of theatre work created by Augusto Boal, the Brazilian activist who invented the 'theatre of the oppressed'.

Boal lived in exile in Europe in the 1970s and 1980s. He observed that, in contrast to Brazilians, most Europeans remained uninvolved in political action. He concluded that one of the main reasons for this was that people in Europe had internalized their oppression so completely that the 'cops' were in their heads.

'Cops in the head' (and all the methods of the theatre of the oppressed) is premised on the belief that the mechanisms of oppression in a society are reproduced and grounded in daily relationships: within the couple, the school, the family, the factory or office. To counter the internalization of oppression or dominance, we must first look to daily life and uncover how these mechanisms operate there.

Thus, this form of theatre provides participants with a space in which to act out a situation of conflict or oppression experienced in interpersonal relationships. Using body sculpture and the bodies of other participants, the central character builds images of the voices in her head that prevent her from doing what she wants to do. The process involves exploring the origin and history of these voices and connecting them to the social structures (school, family, religious institution) they reproduce.

The next stage of 'cops in the head' involves creating counter-voices and accompanying body images capable of altering the original dynamic of oppression. The central character learns how to replay the scene. While one person's story may be the starting-point, the collective experience of the group is reproduced in that story. The process socializes individual moments of disempowerment and creates a collective moment of power.

Because women often function primarily in the relational and inter-personal spheres, 'cops in the head' is useful in providing women with a way to make connections between the struggles of their personal relationships and larger structures and dynamics. Thus, the workshop participant who acted out the oppression suffered by a young woman on social assistance was able to replay her family drama with voices offered from the group. These included 'welfare is a right', 'raising my child is a valuable social act that needs to be financially recognized by society' and 'I am OK just the way I am'. By shifting her physical stance as well as her 'voices', the woman experienced how to think and act differently in a situation where she had felt oppressed.

Many techniques of the theatre of the oppressed are useful in work-ing on economic literacy. Sculpting, creating images of oppression, forum theatre (a play that re-creates a story of oppression after which the 'spect-actors' are asked to replay the scene, offering solutions), 'cops in the head', are all approaches that assume that working with the body can create change. In using these forms of theatre, as well as other forms of creative expression, I share Boal's belief that 'if the oppressed herself, and not a surrogate artist, performs an action, the action, per-formed in a theatrical fiction, will allow her to change things in her real life' (Boal, 1990: 40). If, as Boal believes, theatre of the oppressed is 'rehearsal for revolution', then engaging the whole person in educational work is critical for any real change.

Embodying alternatives

The animator now gives the group its next task. The women are to discuss the conditions of their struggle in ten years, that is, what their struggle will look like in the various areas they are organizing in now: health, education, housing, basic food supplies and so on. Each group is to present its conclusions in a soap opera or television advertising format.

The women are excited about this task and eagerly break into their small groups as we watch from the corner. The two of us are here in Mexico City, observing this workshop on free trade with urban poor women as representatives from Women To Women Global Strategies, a group in Canada involved in making international links between women. Suddenly the animator moves over to us and invites us to prepare a skit on where our struggle in Canada will be in ten years.

We set about our task with reluctance. Slowly we realize with some dismay that we can't envision our struggle in ten years! Not only are we unable to come up with anything now but we have never even asked ourselves this question!

This was perhaps my most painful lesson from Mexico: that I, and many of my companions, had been so caught up in a defensive mentality, always reacting to the agenda set by corporations and neo-liberal governments, that I was unable to project what the struggle would look like if we set the agenda ourselves. I remember a friend who taught me about theatre of the oppressed quoting Salverson (1993: 157-8):

> Activists ... tend to be thinkers and doers. Too much time in the emotional realm is considered frustrating, and artistic and cultural activities are frequently tolerated as add-ons, extras that get cut when time is short. But avoiding the emotional body and the unpredictable territory of play robs us of valuable information. Ultimately, neither feeling nor thinking understanding alone will take us far towards re-imaging and realizing a different world.

In focusing solely on linear problem-solving and 'strategic analysis' we had lost our ability to dream. In concentrating only on trying to influence political parties, governments and the International Monetary Fund, we had missed the possibilities for change in daily life and in the social movements that women are part of.

The task of creating alternatives must draw on a range of resources, including humour, the body and playfulness. The television skits the Mexican women presented were funny, creative and moving. In one, a TV advertisement, two women were walking down the street when suddenly one clutched at her chest and sank to the floor. Her companion immediately gave her cardio-pulmonary resuscitation (CPR) and within a few minutes she regained consciousness. Two other women appeared on the scene and gave the patient some medicinal herbs. The narrator then informed us that the women in this neighbourhood had all been trained in first aid and herbal medicine and were setting up a community health clinic.

In another, a soap opera, a housing co-operative eventually won a long struggle to receive direct credits from the World Bank for constructing their own building. A third group used a television advertisement format to present the rallying song of a coalition consisting of a teachers' union, a parents' union and a students' union united to fight educational cut-backs and demand community control of the schools. This envisioning session was then followed by an identification and analysis of the steps necessary to accomplish these conditions of struggle ten years ahead.

When I returned to visit the women's committee in Mexico City two years later, I met two women who were training community health workers in first aid, herbal medicines and body-work, a direct result of the first vision at the workshop.

What we observed in this session was women's ability to develop alternatives that were based on their concrete needs and their specific contexts and which gave them access to and control over local resources. There was a sense of practical realism here, but also a sense of hope, and a feeling that the women believed they could accomplish their dreams despite tremendous obstacles. The women's sense of their personal authority and collective power was able to develop through expressing their creativity and being free to act, draw, dance and sing without self-consciousness.

I have developed further this exercise of embodying the future by having participants dance or move to express the transition from the present to their future dream. I do this before analysis to help participants avoid the tendency to move to abstract proposals or to name actors or actions they are not part of.

I have found many helpful tools for this work of exploring alternatives in the 'creative expression method', an approach developed at the Tamalpa Institute in California in the United States. This is a group process that involves working with three levels of the self: the physical or kinaesthetic, the emotional and the mental. Participants make drawings of problem areas in their lives, enact these drawings in movement (involving the drawer and other group members), and finally use creative writing in a process aimed at facilitating the release of unconscious material and connecting the individual's inner experience to external expression (Halprin Khalighi, 1989).

Individuals may express their resolution of conflicts or identify new directions in a final dance performance; groups may express their resolution in a collective performance or ritual, an approach used extensively with groups of people suffering from Acquired Immune Deficiency Syndrome (AIDS). The creation of ritual, collective forms of expression to engage deeper meanings, allows for spiritual moments of connection and communion that can give clarity and strength to the work of transformation.

Questions and challenges

My experimentation with approaches such as bioenergetics and the creative expression method reflects one of the most significant challenges to feminist popular education: how to use, incorporate and transform healing approaches that have been developed for working with individuals. If we do not take healing work seriously, we are failing to involve the whole person in the process of transformation. This applies especially to educating and organizing around the economic conditions of women's lives, an area which is the source of much internalized oppression and emotional pain.

An issue raised by this is the relationship between therapy and popular education. I think that the type of body-work I have described here is not therapy and that there is a clear boundary that separates embodied popular education from therapy. Popular education is an education and organizing practice that works with groups and is concerned with collective problems and collective transformation. Healing work in this context is part of a larger social project. Individuals don't do their personal work in the group. If a woman's deep emotional issues are 'triggered' during group work, I talk with her outside the workshop and refer her to a trained counsellor.

The fact that participants may express feelings as a result of using their bodies does not necessarily mean that we have entered therapeutic territory. It is important for participants to tap into feelings in order to be able to move on in the process. Unlike traditional popular education which reinforced the mind–body split by disallowing feelings in the learning experience, feminist popular education facilitates the expression of feelings. When there is emotional release, physical release often occurs also and, in turn, there is a mental release that allows thought patterns to shift and open for new insight. This process is necessary for transformation.

However, the fact of the difference between feminist body-work and therapy underscores the importance of addressing questions of risk and safety when engaging the body in popular education. Many women feel discomfort with their bodies because of disability or negative body images caused by Western media stereotyping of the ideal female body. Many may feel it difficult to involve the body because of experiences of sexual abuse or assault. It is important to recognize these difficulties and to consider gentle ways of helping women to become more attuned to their bodies, for example, simple breathing exercises. It is also important to negotiate agreements at the start of group work that create a sense of a safe space and, equally, a sense that it is acceptable for participants to do only what feels right for them.

The issue of disability should be addressed directly, whether or not there is a visibly disabled person in the group. Embodying transformation is based on the idea that all bodies carry wisdom. Affirming this, in opposition to the notion that there is only one norm for a 'normal' body, is the first step in building an analysis of disability which able-bodied people need as much as the disabled. Building wholeness involves accepting our bodies as they are – fat, thin, paraplegic, old, tired, weak, infected with viruses – as part of the process of resisting the tyranny of 'the normal' and moving on to learn what each of our bodies can teach us in each of our contexts. Many exercises can be adapted for people with disabilities; new ones can be developed in consultation with those trained in movement and play therapy with the disabled.

Finally, there is the question of sensitivity to cultural differences. A Chinese Canadian woman I co-facilitate with prefers to use Tai Chi instead of bioenergetics, especially when she works with predominantly Asian Canadian groups. A South Asian women's group in Vancouver uses *bhangaraghidda* dance for energizing and revitalizing the group. In Southern India feminist popular communicators are using *Bharatanat-yam* dance forms to activate the creative energy of women for both resisting oppression and creating alternatives (Bhasin and Menon, 1983).

Conclusion

The body is much more than a tool which we must periodically wake up, energize or refuel in the educational process. Rather, it holds some of the keys to both analysis of present circumstances and identification of the future direction women can take to meet their needs and regain control over their daily lives.

An understanding of the centrality of our bodies to our daily lives, in other words, an understanding of what I have called 'the political economy of the body', allows us to find concrete starting-points for women to develop a gender analysis of global restructuring. Using certain forms of body-work that release energy, and using voice in chants, slogans and yelling, help to build a sense of authority and collective power.

Using exercises that reach back to historical memories connects women's bodies to their past and future. Processes that access deeper levels of internalized oppression, such as theatre of the oppressed and creative expression methods, function to disrupt unconscious patterns and create new possibilities for expression, vision and action. Using dance of many varieties simply to express freedom, power and joy, or lament, pain and loss, creates energy for transformation. All of these approaches contribute to building women's sense of both individual and collective agency.

Embodied feminist popular education reaches women where they live, at the level of daily life. It counters the everyday powerlessness in-dividual women experience by freeing the emotional body, breaking down the internal walls that block energy for action. On a collective level, the creation of a sense of embodied awareness and creative energy can fuel the capacity to organize and resist. If women recognize rather than ignore their bodily discomfort on a daily basis, and identify what gives them joy and passion both in the home and in the workplace, they can organize with others around this sensitivity. The body then becomes the key or sign for transforming daily experience.

Feminist popular education is defined by the way it encompasses every dimension of women's lives. Its methods integrate the emotional, physical, spiritual and mental dimensions and can be used with men as well as with women. In doing this it challenges traditional popular education to broaden its understanding of social change. Social change involves a transformation of the whole person and of the collective at the level of body and spirit. It is this combining of feeling and rationality, of personal and political realities, of private and public, of the household economy and the market economy, that makes popular education feminist. In embodying this integration we reclaim the body as a form of language, life and knowing that we have too long neglected in our work for social transformation.

Bibliography

All Africa Conference of Churches Women's Desk (1992) *To be a Woman: African Women's Response to the Economic Crisis. A Video and Resource Guide*, Nairobi.

Bhasin, K. and Menon, S. (1985) 'Workshops on Communication and Media', in Bhasin, K. (ed.), *Towards Empowerment: Report of FAO-FFHC/AD South Asian Training for Women Development Workers*, New Delhi.

Boal, A. (1990) 'The Cop in the Head: Three Hypotheses', *Drama Review*, Vol. 34, no. 3.

Doerge, S. (1992) Feminist Popular Education: Transforming the World from Where Women Stand, working paper, University of Toronto.

Ellsworth, E. (1992) 'Why Doesn't This Feel Empowering? Working Through the Repressive Myths of Critical Pedagogy', in Luke, C. and Gore, J., (eds), *Feminisms and Critical Pedagogy*, Routledge, New York.

Fernandez, A. et al. (1991) *Para Nacer de Nuevo: Una Experiencia de Educación Popular con Mujeres*, Grupo de Educación Popular con Mujeres (GEM), Mexico City.

Halprin Khalighi, D. (1989) *Coming Alive: The Creative Expression Method*, Tamalpa Institute, California.

Lerner, M. (1991) *Surplus Powerlessness*, Humanities Press, New Jersey.

Luke, C. (1992) 'Feminist Pedagogies in Radical Pedagogy', in Luke, C. and Gore, J. (eds), *Feminisms and Critical Pedagogy*, Routledge, New York.

Moser, C. (1993) 'Adjustment from Below: Low-income Women, Time and the

Triple Role in Guayaquil, Ecuador', in Radcliffe, S. and Westwood, S. (eds), *Viva: Women and Popular Protest in Latin America*, Routledge, New York.

Pineda, M. (1986) 'Feminism and Popular Education: A Critical but Necessary Relationship', *Isis International Women's Journal*.

Salverson, J. (1993) 'The Mask of Solidarity', in *Playing Boal*, Routledge, London.

3

Holding the space: gender, race and conflict in training

MICHELLE FRIEDMAN AND
COLLEEN CRAWFORD COUSINS

Relations of power and control are of central significance to any feminist (or democratic) project and by extension to any debate about the relationship between popular education and gender. How to understand such relations and how to transform them when they are oppressive is a key task for feminists. One way to explore and comprehend this slippery terrain is through rigorous reflection on practice or action. Such an approach shifts us from a mode of 'having to be right' and wanting to 'do things better next time', since each experience is valued for what it brings.

In February 1993, we[1] were responsible for organizing and running a seven-day workshop in Natal, South Africa, which focused on participatory methods for community development. We did this, in response to requests from female field-workers and researchers for 'methods to work with women', as part of the gender task group of a national network of nine service organizations focused on land and related issues, which primarily service rural constituencies.

The workshop participants were field-workers and researchers employed by the network. The twenty-six individuals at the workshop represented a diversity of experience and identities in terms of race, class, gender, age, ethnicity and urban or rural background. Diversity was also reflected in the wide spectrum of first languages and levels of formal education among the participants. Including the artist and the administrator, eleven women and fifteen men were present. The racial split at the workshop was twenty-one black people (six women and fifteen men) and five whites (one man and four women, three of whom, including ourselves, were facilitators).

The workshop was held during a period of heightened tensions within the country's political history and it, too, was marked by a high degree of conflict. There was a struggle for control of the workshop between some participants and the facilitators, in the sense that resistance to the design and flow of the workshop became more and more marked; there was conflict between men and women; and on the fifth day the process was interrupted by, or gave rise to, a field-workers' emergency meeting from which the facilitators were asked to excuse themselves. At this meeting race and power relations within the network were discussed and a committee elected to convene a field-workers' forum within the network at large. Thereafter the workshop continued more or less as planned, but with continued contestation and power plays at every level.

The workshop was an intense experience for all of us. There are probably as many stories about it as participants. For the purposes of this chapter, however, our reflection on the workshop is intended to explore two important assumptions in our understanding of gender. The first perceives gender as a central dimension of power; that is, in every society, access to power, resource flows and roles are powerfully conditioned by gender.

In South Africa today our collective view of what it is to be male and female feeds into and helps to justify different and unequal resource flows to women, different and unequal access to knowledge and power, and different and unequal rights and room to manoeuvre as social actors. This is so despite the fact that women are not passive victims of these social processes: they constantly resist, manipulate and rework their constraints in their struggle to create and appropriate space for themselves.

The second assumption acknowledges, however, that gender is always situated in a context. The problem with focusing on gender inequity in field-work, training or planning is that we don't seem to experience gender in isolation from, or before, other forms of difference in social life. Gender, race, class, culture, language, history are among identities constructed and experienced in interrelation, and each difference makes a difference to the way we experience ourselves and each other.

In this chapter, we examine our assumptions through an analysis of two central themes. One concerns the extent to which participatory methodologies address social dimensions of power. The second involves an analysis of gender in context, by means of reflection on our own understanding and learning, as well as on ourselves as facilitators in relation to the group and the wider context of the country. Our own identities were part of the dynamic we had to work with. Relations among trainers, and between trainers and participants, are part of the training terrain in gender relations and thus germane to any project of challenging subordination (see Matlanyane-Sexwale, 1994).

We begin this chapter by presenting a brief outline of why we held the workshop and why we think participatory methodologies are useful for working with women. We define some of our initial assumptions and the stated objectives of the workshop. The second section narrates part of the story of the workshop. Finally we reflect on what we think happened, and the challenges that face facilitators in such conflictual training situations.

Context

Member organizations of the network work with rural communities – victims of forced removals, farm workers, labour tenants and the residents of informal settlements – to promote social justice in relation to access to and control over land. At the time of the workshop, only one of the network members worked specifically with rural women's organizations but was keen to see this interest grow in the rest of the network.

During the 1980s the network had emphasized the rural reclamation of land and the struggle for more secure land rights. In this context, people dispossessed by apartheid legislation (whether freehold title holders or tenants, women or men) were able to stand relatively united against an external enemy, on the initiative of an emergent leadership which mobilized external support in a situation of crisis. However, the cracks between different interest groups within 'the community' were papered over, and dominant perspectives of the issues tended to emerge from a male élite, entrenched in leadership positions within organizations which seemed fragile and weakly rooted.

Now that land is being successfully reclaimed, the complex social relations in such communities can no longer be ignored by service organizations committed to principles of equity. Field-workers' abilities to facilitate negotiation between diverse interests and to develop local institutional capacity are now seen as centrally important.

Changing roles and perceptions The unbanning of the major players in the liberation movement in the early 1990s marked an important turning-point in the political culture of South Africa. Intense anti-state struggles began to give way to the politics of negotiation. In the 1980s most individuals within the network probably saw themselves as political activists, rather than development practitioners supporting the oppressed and dispossessed in their struggles, and as allied in some way or other with the broad liberation movement. Since the era of negotiations, many more workers in non-governmental organizations (NGOs) have started to think of themselves as development practitioners doing development work. They are struggling to identify and create new roles for themselves and new ways of understanding social and political process.

The discourse of development has now replaced the discourse of struggle. One reason for this is that issues no longer seem so un-equivocally clear-cut. 'The enemy' is harder to identify and there is more space for different interests (for example, those of women or tenants) to be articulated. NGO workers and political activists have had to negotiate with and serve on structures which include government officials and representatives of big business, while the protracted negoti-ation process brought to the surface the constraints on a radical land redistribution programme or on nationalizing the mines.

For some people, belief in a political formula or blueprint waned after the collapse of the Soviet bloc, opening space for a variety of strategies and approaches to liberate the energy of the oppressed. The post-colonial experiences of other countries in the region in relation to the provision of social services such as education, water and sanitation, health and transport, are likely to become more relevant.

Methodology in context   The methods that were central to the work-shop had been developed and refined in post-colonial countries in Asia, Latin America and Africa as part of a progressive rural development initiative that aimed to reverse the flow of resources away from dislocated and dispossessed rural people. The paradigm holds that, while land reform and institutional change are necessary for rural development to take place, also essential are interventions which aim to support rural people's development of 'optimal capacity for self-reliance' to discover and exert the power which is already in them for constructive action (Srinivasan, 1992: 3).

Participatory Rural Appraisals (PRAs), participatory research initi-atives, Sarar[2] 'training of trainers' workshops and field-work directed towards community action are all points along this continuum. In other words, participatory tools and methods are a necessary, if not sufficient, component of rural development.

From this perspective it is well recognized that the rural poor are overwhelmingly concentrated in the South and that women are poorer than men. The validity of indigenous technical knowledge and the value of 'listening to the people' so that appropriate solutions can be generated 'from below' are stressed. The notions of 'rural communities' and 'com-munity development' are still powerful, although approaches which concentrate on differences such as gender or class, disaggregate rural groups and recognize community development as a contested terrain.

Participatory development methodologies implicitly challenge single 'right' solutions by encouraging multi-vocality and tolerating ambiguity. In other words, these approaches recognize that the question of power is at the heart of social process; that there are many more than one right answer to every question; that anyone who holds out for only one answer probably has a particular interest in control; that both questions and answers depend on whose voices are heard; and that when enough different voices state and restate a problem we go some way towards changing things. A certain understanding of the politics of development is implicit in such an approach.

The burning necessity to resolve the 'national question' – to confront, resist and remove white domination – has tended to relegate differences among the ranks of the oppressed (such as class and gender) to second place. Although in recent years some women (and men) in positions of power and influence in the liberation movement have considerably widened the political space for the discussion of the oppression of women, many people experience any discussion of gender politics as highly divisive.

In a political tradition of mass mobilization, the unity of the oppressed has been greatly valued. Given that political division – ethnic, geographic and ideological – is rife in South Africa, and that white feminists have been prominent in raising the gender question (see Barrett et al., 1985; Beall, 1982; Bozzoli, 1983; Bradford, 1984; Cock, 1980; Cock et al., 1983; Walker, 1982), this reaction is understandable. However, this unity is obtained at the price of silencing many voices.

Elsewhere, the United Nations Decade for Women played some role in opening the space for women's voices. However, South Africa's formal exclusion from the international community meant that many of the debates and experiences popularized during the decade did not reach most South African NGO workers.

At the time of the workshop, the network, in common with many other NGOs, contained diverse views on the question of gender. Some individuals welcomed the training opportunity and were able to use it to pursue their own concerns about women and gender. Others were adamant that gender is a 'white woman's issue', an imperialist import being imposed upon them by funders. The fear was often expressed that pursuing the issue of gender oppression in rural community work would create conflict by imposing 'outside values' on communities.

The legacy of apartheid   NGOs and service organizations established during the 1980s in South Africa did not escape the apartheid legacy. The problem, as identified by field-workers at the workshop, was that most blacks in the network were field-workers while whites controlled and occupied most of the policy research and co-ordinator positions, key positions in terms of decision-making and power.

Because the origin of the workshop was the gender task group, only one of the male participants had been involved with the planning and the determination of the content of the workshop. 'Other people felt they just came to the workshop because they were asked to do so, without any background to the workshop.' These dynamics around race and power, together with the lack of communication within the network, obviously impacted on the workshop.

International context The final contextual point we will reference is the tangential relationship of South African development workers to international development debates. Participatory approaches grew out of a critique, developed in the 1970s and 1980s, of the failures and shortcomings of development approaches which had been utilized in newly independent countries. The radical absence of a popular rural development strategy backed by the state meant that the development experience of extension workers was limited in both scope and scale.[3] Because of our history, South Africans have not had these experiences.

Why Sarar? We chose to focus our training intervention on the Sarar approach for a number of reasons that are linked to our assumptions about participatory methodologies and about gender as a power relation.

As a training and development approach, Sarar claims to facilitate 'transcending behaviour'. What is envisaged is not so much a solution for every problem as facilitation of a process which aims to reverse the vicious circle of low self-esteem and feelings of powerlessness which feed into oppression and domination. Sarar aims to support the growth of self-esteem by facilitating 'learning events', which encourage people to develop their creative and analytic capacity to identify and solve problems. The emphasis, as in other participatory approaches such as PRA, is on an active 'partnership in development' between community member and outside development agent.

Implicit in this paradigm is the perception that knowledge is local, multiple, situated and negotiated, and that certain kinds of problems cannot be solved but only outgrown. Development, then, is as much about personal growth as political organization (the political is personal).

Where control, rationality, rigidity, domination, subordination and hierarchy are hegemonic ways of operating, subordinated groups struggle for space to speak or, worse, accept silence without a struggle. The seamless web of a dominated discourse denies that there is a silencing: some people choose not to speak because they have nothing to say. Although both women and men may operate in these ways, one general effect of gender domination and oppression is that women are typically awarded, or claim, less space and time to participate in the planning processes of social change and development. Depending on the social group, men defined as 'less powerful' because of race, class, language and so on, might take this 'female' role.

Participatory methods such as Sarar aim to awaken individual creativity and mobilize the resources of the group for change. Creativity awakens the courage to envision and practice new solutions to old problems.

This approach is both relevant and difficult in many rural settings where individual creativity is not particularly valued unless it is channelled into traditional forms or solutions which have survived the test of time. What is emphasized is the value of the collective over the individual, age over youth, and men over women.[4]

The Sarar approach asserts that new solutions to some of the chronic and pernicious problems of rural poverty can be facilitated by designing group-learning experiences using materials and activities which encourage people to express their feelings, attitudes and beliefs; by making the unconscious conscious through drawing, mapping, enacting, telling stories, recounting experiences and passing on information; in short, by 'holding the space' for the greater participation of traditionally marginalized and silenced people, women and men.

We therefore felt that it made sense for field-workers who would increasingly be called upon to facilitate development processes to develop a range of these skills and attitudes. The participatory, materials-based Sarar approach seemed to be appropriate in this context.

A 'resistance to change' continuum, shown in Figure 3.1, is a Sarar tool. This model suggests that people may resist change for reasons which range from inability to see the problem, to (possibly well-founded) distrust of the extension worker, fear and lack of self-confidence and self-esteem, fear of loss of power and influence, or the loss of a known evil and its hidden advantages.[5] The Sarar approach asserts that the desired change in behaviour cannot be induced by exhortation or transfer of information unless the group or individual is at the point on the continuum (5) where a certain level of resistance to change has been named and overcome. This approach also assumes that field-workers and extension staff need to work on the experiential level with these tools before using them in community work with rural people.

We entered the workshop expecting to share with the participants our understanding of and enthusiasm for some well-tried and tested materials and approaches for maximizing community participation in development processes. By holding the space for multi-vocality, we were consciously concentrating on developing skills relevant to working with power relations 'out there'. By demonstrating the power and relevance of

7 I'm willing to demonstrate the solution to others and advocate
change
6 I'm ready to try some action
5 I see the problem and I'm interested in learning more about it
4 There is a problem but I'm afraid of changing for fear of loss
3 Yes, there is a problem but I have my doubts
2 There may be a problem but it's not my responsibility
1 There's no problem

Figure 3.1 Sarar resistance to change continuum
Source: Srinivasan (1990: 162)

activities and materials that encouraged more voices to be expressed from the field, we also hoped to encourage field-workers to experiment with an approach where listening outweighs talking or leading or giving input.

With respect to gender training, we deliberately chose a neutral, inclusive focus for the workshop: how to work with marginalized groups in general by using participatory methods and visual materials. Part of the reason for this approach was that the network focuses on land struggles rather than on working with women. Many of its current staff are men and the notion of a specific gender focus is not popular with everyone.

Part of our strategy was to choose activities in which the content was appropriate to the participants' work contexts. Gender dynamics or issues were likely to emerge from a particular scenario and we would then encourage the group to debate the outcome. The advantage this approach offers is that gender relations can be contemplated in their complexity as they relate to and intersect with other social relations. The situation is not contrived and it can serve as a model for the field situation.

The workshop objectives[6] clearly reveal the assumptions we made about the efficacy of the Sarar approach in facilitating working with women.

Assumptions of participatory methods While not all participatory methodologies attempt to tackle existing social power relations, educators working for social change do so self-consciously. Workshops using participatory methodologies can provide contained venues where participants can explore and confront power relations through practical activities within the training process. Some assumptions about power that seem to operate in these contexts include:

— Power is bad when 'oppressors' have it but good when the 'oppressed' get it or win it;

— A good participatory workshop is one where participants control the process and facilitators give up power;

— Talking a lot in small groups or in plenary sessions is considered 'high' and sometimes 'dominating' participation while silence is viewed as non-participation;

— A good workshop is a happy workshop without any 'destructive' behaviour;

— Facilitators should manage the workshop in such a way as to address structural inequalities (a kind of affirmative action);

— Participants should be divided into small groups by workshop facilitators so as to create space for dominated groups (for example, separate women's groups);

— In the design of the workshop and the process of facilitation, the participants' own experience should be affirmed and acknowledged and the participants' own backgrounds should provide the content, or, as Arnold et al. (1991: 38) put it: 'start with the experience of participants; look for patterns; add new information and theory; practise skills; strategise and plan for action; apply in action; review.'

We went into the week with some of these assumptions. Struggles for power, it seemed to us, should be facilitated and made conscious, that is, explored rather than managed. Subsequently we have found ourselves questioning many of these assumptions in the light of our evaluation of the workshop.

The sections of this chapter which follow illustrate how participatory methods bring resistance to the surface and promote conflict and change. We argue that as trainers we have to support and work constructively with such moments of discomfort.

The workshop process

We followed the Sarar workshop outline (Srinivasan, 1990), although we had only seven days instead of the recommended ten for the workshop proper. This was preceded by a three-day pre-planning workshop with five of the participants, which aimed to give them more intensive exposure to the approach and the methods, to test and adapt materials, and to create a team of assistant facilitators who would support the core facilitators at the workshop. For the workshop itself, we planned to immerse participants in the creative, investigative, analytical and planning activities they would adapt and practise with community groups on field visits later in the week.

Thus, at the beginning of the workshop, the focus was on the participants' own attitudes, feelings and perceptions, with analytical and planning (intellectual and reflective) activities scheduled for later in the week. Field visits took place in the middle and towards the end of the week, to enable the participants to work in a field situation with the tools they were experimenting with. The host organization field staff had prepared the community members with whom they worked for visits from the workshop participants.

While we were designing the workshop we debated how much to debrief participants after each activity, that is, how much to allow for discussion of its pros and cons and possible field applications. Facing a severe time constraint (seven days instead of ten), we decided to concentrate on the experience rather than on reflection after each exercise. This decision was informed by the earlier decision to immerse participants in the activities first and to concentrate on reflection and analysis later in the workshop.

We tried to ensure that the workshop content was based on issues of direct relevance to the participants. As the materials were designed for use in rural areas, the participants played the role of 'community' people in some activities. Exercises to stimulate participants' awareness and understanding of themselves as facilitators and of the context in which they worked were interspersed with 'field' activities.

The issues and themes that emerged during the workshop were various and interlinked. However, for purposes of brevity we will highlight and elaborate on only two: gender and a question of ethics. While gender cannot be separated from other social relationships, for the purposes of this article struggles around gender will be a dominant focus. As to the ethics question, this was raised in relation to field trips and brought broader social power relations to the surface.

Gender struggles Perhaps because the workshop originated in the gender task group, which is comprised mostly of women, and because all the pre-planners and facilitators were women, gender was a prominent issue right from the beginning. Our first surprise was that fourteen men arrived instead of the majority of women we had anticipated. On the very first evening when rooming was being arranged, some men joked, 'Why do you want to separate the women and the men? Isn't this sexist?' When an elderly woman field-worker started the first day with the song 'Malibongwe', a struggle song which praises women, one man expressed unhappiness at having to sing this 'sexist' song. Among the expectations voiced at the beginning of the workshop were hopes for 'working better with women' and 'for men to enhance working relationships with women'. Some of the fears expressed included 'the resistance of men', 'male domination within groups', and 'gender conflict in the workshop' (see Crawford Cousins et al., 1993: 5, 6).

Moreover, we were rudely shocked to discover the degree of resistance to being there openly expressed by a number of the male participants. Fears included 'Participants are not clear about what they are doing; is the research methodology to be introduced applicable to our contexts?'; 'We will be learning nothing new here'; 'We will be learning too many rules'; 'We have doubts about the theory, practice and relevance of the tools'.

Since all the participants had received the workshop objectives before arriving at the venue, we assumed they were there voluntarily. At this point, then, we did not take this resistance seriously, or seriously enough.

The purpose of the first group activity on the first day was to stimulate individual and group thinking about community participation. In order to avoid the formulaic verbal abstractions current in NGO circles, the participants were asked to draw a picture of what community participation meant for them, to share these in small groups and then to assemble and present a group collage. All the group drawings emphasized that 'with NGO intervention, community projects emerge with the potential for involving everyone, including women' (Crawford Cousins et al., 1993: 5, 6). If there were any conflicts in the small groups over this interpretation, they were not made visible in the plenary session.

The small groups for this activity had been randomly selected and no attempt had been made by facilitators to manage the process. However, one facilitator had observed that in most of the small groups men appeared to be dominating the discussion. She suggested that for the next exercise the groups should be divided by gender into two groups of men and one group of women. She was working on the assumption (Mackenzie, 1992) that creating a separate space would be a good thing for the women participants and would also model a way of working in the field.

The next activity was a simulation of community mapping. The participants were asked to create a map of an imagined rural community, identifying problems, resources and constraints. They could choose what kind of community they wanted to map and were asked to assign themselves roles such as male landowner, female tenant, unemployed youth, widow, tribal authority, clinic sister and so on, and to contribute from the viewpoint of their role. They were also asked to observe gender relations within the community being mapped.

The facilitators noticed that in the women's group, which had chosen to map a squatter community, each individual seemed to have a clear role and activity. The group sang and hummed throughout this exercise and their map was very colourful. In the two men's groups, by contrast, there seemed to be more confusion, silencing and domination. (One of the participants commented in the subsequent plenary that he had learned what it felt like to be belittled and silenced in a group, but that taking a pen and drawing had enabled him to have a 'voice' again.)

No one in either of the men's groups chose to represent a woman for the purposes of the exercise and neither of their map presentations overtly included any information about women or gender relations. When the women's group questioned the group of men who mapped a rural community, they generated much information about women's position in traditional communities. Their interrogation also yielded an interesting debate: asked why the group had said so little about the position of women in the rural community, a spokesman answered that they had not wished to be sexist. But, said the female questioner, the map should reflect reality and reality is sexist. To this came an encoded response which engendered some male head-nodding: 'Changes must not affect the lives of the people you work with' (Crawford Cousins et al., 1993: 15).

By contrast, two individuals in the women's group chose to be men. Thus, both women and men were represented in the construction of the map and the telling of the story of the community. This was so despite the fact that some of the issues they chose to talk about, such as alcoholism, lack of crèche facilities and rejection of the use of violence to resolve conflict, are often perceived as specifically women's concerns.

In the plenary discussion some men expressed considerable anger at the division into small groups along gender lines. The facilitators were accused of having a 'hidden agenda'. One man expressed the view that 'the problems we encounter are common to all of us; it doesn't matter if I am a man or a woman farmer, it is my economic position that matters'. Another declared that 'people are happy with the way they live'. Some male participants asked why one would wish to divide a community group by gender. Was it strictly necessary? Would it not create problems? Another (male) participant suggested that it should be left to 'members of the community' to decide on division into groups and that 'structural problems' of the community should be taken into consideration.

A comment that highlights the difficulty of experiential learning in the absence of sufficient discussion came from a 'high talking', university-trained, male field-worker: 'We spent such a long time on the exercise without getting very much out of it. I would have thought it is much more important to discuss how to get marginalized groups involved.' During this exchange the black women were mostly silent, or nodded their agreement with some of the men.

We facilitators argued that dividing community members into interest groups, such as men, women, children, tenants and landowners is useful because each group brings a different experience and a different voice to the mapping exercise. The information gained by both insiders and outsiders, we said, is thus likely to be much richer. The richer the information, the better the subsequent planning exercise. In short, instead of helping the participants to process this conflict or 'edge' between opposing views, we argued for our position as correct and conclusive.

In the evaluation session at the end of the first day, one participant suggested that we 'delve deeper into existing tensions, something more fundamental is at work', and another that 'the methods being taught are irrelevant and not directly addressing existing problems in the field'. These views were contradicted by other participants who had enjoyed the activities and felt they were learning useful skills. So, from the first day, we were faced with differences within the group in relation to participants' commitment to being at the workshop.

Later that evening, in an informal evaluation session, the assistant facilitators expressed their reluctance to divide into gender groups again. Since the pre-planners were all women, they said, the women at the workshop were perceived by the men to have some informational power and advantage over them. It appeared that the men were reacting to a perceived advantaging of the women in terms of access to information about workshop activities and to the core facilitators and, on top of that, in terms of a separate small-group space.

The women pre-planners decided, given the vociferous resistance of some men to this amplification of group differences, that it would be better not to exacerbate the tensions and resistances that had been surfacing during the day. Out of respect for their feelings and judgement, the core facilitators decided against trying this form of process management or group control again. Despite their obvious enjoyment of the activity, it was clear that, for whatever reason, the black female participants either felt they had not benefited from the gender separation or were not prepared to risk the associated acrimony again.

This, then, was the first and last time we as core facilitators tried to manage the internal process of the workshop according to gender. One of us was unhappy with this decision because she felt strongly that separating the groups had been a useful exercise. In her view, the division had given the women more space than they seemed able to win in the mixed groups, and it had given the group as a whole an opportunity to surface their internal gender dynamics and make them visible. She felt that the women's response to the men was another example of women giving up power and thus losing an opportunity to develop their confidence and articulateness.

During the days that followed, many of the workshop exercises raised similar gender issues. For example, a 'balloon exercise' called on participants to analyse the situation of rural women in terms of the chain of consequences that result from any one problem faced by women. Participants were asked to construct their chains from a rural woman's perspective. Several male participants questioned this approach. 'Surely poor rural men are in the same situation as poor rural women?' 'Why do we have to do the drawing from the perspective of the woman's needs?'

The notion that social dynamics are about relations other than gender surfaced when the time came to share information about the communities which the participants were to visit for their field trips. A male field-worker used flexiflans[7] to illustrate the social dynamics of the community in which he worked. He showed the four-wheel-drive vehicle and the community committee that was constituted of men only. He described a typical meeting situation and showed how he was given a bench to sit on and how an important part of his role was to bring experts such as lawyers to meet with the community committee.

The participants then asked him many questions about general community dynamics. In evaluating the use of this tool, one participant (a man) felt that flexiflans did not allow 'the real story' about social dynamics to emerge. Another participant (a woman) argued that the flexiflans had highlighted the gender set-up typical of rural areas and inquired: 'If these are not social dynamics, what is?' (Crawford Cousins et al., 1993: 28).

The point to emphasize here is that the activities worked brilliantly to bring many layers of gender dynamics to the surface. However, we lost the opportunity to process these dynamics as they were surfacing within the group. We did not have enough consciousness, analytical understanding or technique for processing 'edges'. We tended to respond in one of two ways: either we would argue our position as correct and conclusive (as above), or we would mentally note the comment and the dynamics, but let the 'edge' go by unchallenged. For example, when a participant said 'changes must not affect the lives of the people you work with', we were so surprised to hear this articulated by a professional agent of change that we made no response. Also, we were frozen by the mixture of feelings in the room, which included the high level of tension, the men's anger and the women's fear.

In retrospect we might have explored the participant's position more fully by encouraging him to articulate and take on the position of the gender conservative as openly and fully as he could. Further, we could have explored all the positions on the continuum of resistance to change by encouraging people to articulate (give voice to, enact, feel) the different stances in relation to this issue. We might also have encouraged people to move between these positions on the continuum as the resonance changed for them. In this way, the gender conservative would have engaged with other positions at the level of feelings.

On reflection, we saw that we could have used the resistance to change continuum as a container for the intense feelings generated by the power struggle and thus fear of conflict in the workshop. When, as facilitators, we hold the space and thereby support all positions so that thay can be deeply felt and publicly expressed, in dialogue with each other, then the energy of the conflict shifts. Changes within the group and within the participating individuals occur. This is one way of working with resistance and of deepening insight without being didactic. As facilitators, we need to have the skills and confidence to face our fear of conflict and our desire to control a politically correct right answer (Mindell, 1993; Summers, 1994).

Field trips   The second theme we reflect on in some detail here has to do with the ethics of field trips. This activity played a critical role in allowing broader social dynamics and power relations within the entire group as well as within the smaller groups to surface.

The workshop design included two field trips. The first was planned to allow the participants to familiarize themselves with the area, to make initial contact with community members and to discover key issues or problems around which a workshop could be facilitated later in the week. The second was designed to give participants an opportunity to practise and field-test what they had learned. The workshop venue was chosen because it was close to a number of communities with which the host organization worked. Given the size of the group, we (facilitators) decided that the participants should divide into three groups (self-selected on the basis of criteria agreed together) for the field visits. Much of the preparation for the field trips would be carried out in these three groups.

On the first day, when the programme overview was presented, one of the men questioned the morality of the proposed field trips, arguing that it was 'unethical to use communities for our own ends, as if they are laboratories'. During the discussion that followed it was clear that this objection resonated strongly for some participants. A later slot in the programme had been allocated for a briefing on relevant dynamics by the field-workers familiar with the communities, and it was agreed to hold over the debate until then.

The initial reconnaissance field trips took place as planned. One group came back and reported slight embarrassment at having to explain its presence in the area. A group member felt that she had experienced a role reversal ('I'm usually the one who demands that outsiders explain themselves'), but the group none the less had arranged with the people they had met to return on the weekend to facilitate a workshop that would feed into ongoing community work in that village. The second group did not have much to report because they said the community members they had visited had been busy collecting their pensions.

The third group felt hesitant about returning for a further field trip. Their spokesperson said that they were extremely anxious about abusing the members of the community and were uncertain of the value of the exercise. In any event, it was likely that a funeral would take place on the day of the second field trip and this would resolve the ethical dilemma for them. However, he then attempted to involve the whole workshop in the dilemma: he said that the only appropriate way to tackle it was collectively and called on the big group to make a decision 'in a unified way' not to return for a second field trip.

At this point we facilitators intervened. We had recognized that this particular power play, as we saw it, was coming to a head and had decided that it should be tackled head-on. We saw ourselves as refusing to let the power of a few men automatically dominate over individual choice in the powerful name of the collective. Thus one of us made (an equally powerful) counter-move by saying that at a participatory training methods workshop no one should feel forced to do something he or she did not wish to do. She suggested that each individual reflect and make his or her own choice about whether to participate in the next field trip.

This threw the large group into confusion. Some people were clearly unhappy about making individual choices ('Don't undermine!') and pushed for a collective decision. (In retrospect we saw that by asking for an individual choice, we had also awakened the ghost of white divide-and-rule tactics.) The group compromised by deciding to caucus in their field trip groups and to come to a small-group decision.

After a short caucus in small groups, two groups returned to report to the plenary that they had decided they would go back to the field on the appointed day. The third group announced that individuals within the group had strong differences of opinion and that they were still debating the issue. Their answer depended on whether they could resolve their ethical dilemmas and find a tool that was appropriate for the existing situation in the community.

This group, having surfaced its internal differences, worked very hard over the next few hours to come to a unified decision. In the end the group decided to go to the field and designed a new material, an adapted mapping exercise, which looked at land-use options with the group of women they had arranged to meet. They were proud of their achievement and felt that by holding their positions and going through a fierce struggle they had worked through the issue.

Of the other two groups, one contained three female field-workers (including two of the pre-planners). This group had been keen all along to go to the field and planned an ambitious series of activities that would feed into an ongoing community water project. The group seemed to be experiencing some internal power struggles but these were not made public.

The third group had agreed to the field trip but in fact made no attempt to plan activities. When the facilitators visited this group it appeared that the two female members were sitting on one side while the men were discussing other issues. At the planning report-back, this group's spokesperson criticized the workshop methods as 'top-down and academic' and expressed strong reservations about using the activities and tools they had experimented with in the workshop. He reported that the group intended an investigatory visit only. They would take cameras to 'document' the community and planned to hold informal discussions with community members.

The fifth day had been set aside for the groups to prepare the activities and materials they would need for the field trips on the sixth day. While the ethics of the field trip had been a contentious issue from day one and had become a way (for some people) of raising reservations about the workshop as a whole, it became clear by the end of the planning report-back that the process was blocked in some way, and that the gap between what was being said inside and outside the training room was becoming too painful for some participants to bear.

Thanks to strong facilitation and the courage and persistence of two of the participants (a woman and a man),[8] it became possible for the group as a whole to own to the fact that many people had strong issues beyond the workshop that were being discussed as if the problem were the workshop itself. It was agreed that, since feelings were running high, it was appropriate for the facilitators (as official representatives of the network? as whites 'in authority'?) to leave the rest of the group to discuss what these underlying problems were. A time-frame for the discussion was agreed and the three of us left the room.

We returned to a report-back in plenary which identified structural problems and power relations problematically linked to race within the network.[9] Most blacks in the network, said the rapporteur, were poorly paid field-workers while most researchers and co-ordinators, key positions in terms of decision-making and power, were white. The structural problems and lack of communication within the network, interacting with race-linked power relations, meant that many of the current participants had not been involved in planning or determining the content of the workshop. 'Other people just came to the workshop because they were asked to do so, without any background to the workshop.' The group had produced a memorandum which listed these problems and had mandated two representatives to take these questions forward to a national field-workers' forum. It was further decided that, despite these problems, the workshop should continue.

As it turned out, neither of the planned community workshops was successfully held in the end. One was indeed cancelled because of a funeral; the second because all adults in the community were called to an emergency tribal meeting.

Analysis of workshop dynamics

The disturbers This was the name we later gave to those men who resisted the workshop, who struggled with us to control the workshop, and whose contribution has been the most valuable to us in reflecting both on the workshop and on the role of 'the disturber' in other contexts. It was this experience of conflict, which could not be ignored or papered over, which continues to have value for us. In a way it is the heart of this chapter.

We deliberately used materials and methods to evoke feelings, attitudes and beliefs in the workshop. Also evoked were the disturbers and the shadow, which will be discussed below. At one point in the workshop, participants were asked to brainstorm what activities were implied in the concept of 'participation' at a workshop. One of the disturbers mentioned 'destroying' as a workshop activity. At the time this contribution evoked slightly scandalized laughter. In retrospect we saw that he was not only acknowledging his own important role, he was simultaneously giving recognition to the shadow side of 'good' participation, namely, actively 'destructive' participation.[10]

The shadow In common with other participatory approaches such as PRA, Sarar does not problematize or theorize the shadow side of creativity and participation. However, during the workshop we found the concept of the shadow useful. We met this concept in Jungian psychology where the shadow is described as those parts of the individual which, as a result of socialization and particular family experience, have had to be denied, suppressed and split off because they were unacceptable. The child must have love or die, so she willingly performs these mutilations. Indeed, normal socialization is impossible without splitting the 'good' from the 'bad' and identifying with the good.

The trouble with the shadow – and the shadow is always trouble – is that when it is split off from our 'good' selves, we become unconscious that it is a part of ourselves and project it on to others, as if we were projectors and other people blank screens. Thus, we meet our unacceptable and hateful selves in others.

At a deeper level the shadow is personal, but it can be socially manipulated to fall on to particular groups. In South Africa black people carry the collective shadow of white people. White South Africans have been encouraged to project all that is hateful and frightening about themselves on to black people.

However, Jung maintained that the way to the self is through the shadow; that is, it is by naming and taking back what we have projected on to others that we become healthier, even whole. Because we are able to acknowledge more of ourselves and because we are investing less energy in repression, we are able to live more powerfully and authentically.

The shadow, then, is terrifying but also deeply attractive. While it can be collectively mobilized, it seems to be essentially personal, the product of a personal history and experience. We noted that each one of the facilitators tended to be hooked into projection by different elements at the workshop. For one of us, challenges to control were the most threatening and unacceptable. For another, it was the need to mother and the rage engendered by rejection ('ingratitude') that were hardest to bear. For the third, lack of acknowledgement and affirmation generated feelings of devaluation and worthlessness.

During the workshop we three facilitators supported each other in acknowledging and naming the deep feelings aroused in us, so that we were less inclined either to project our trouble-making and aggressive feelings on to the participants, or to be hooked in turn into identifying with a shadow-carrying role. We helped each other to recognize, on the basis of strong feelings of identification with one party or another in a conflict, when we were falling into a projection. When we were unsuccessful, the group let us know in evaluation sessions: 'facilitators should be less emotional' was the comment from one participant.

To the extent that we succeeded, we were able to contain our fear and anger at what we perceived as negative and threatening behaviour towards ourselves and others; to refrain from using the power we had as facilitators to control, punish and hit back; and to become more able to see the complexity of the dynamics at work.

The differences within the group included differences of race, gender, age, class, education, language, political and religious belief, as well as motivation and interest in being at the workshop. Being cooped up together and working hard in an uncomfortable venue for a week with materials and methods specifically designed to evoke feelings, attitudes and beliefs, was difficult for all of us. In this context, unifying factors which could explain and direct uncomfortable and troubling feelings on to others were very attractive.

As whites in authority, we three facilitators provided a focus for black rage at political oppression. As women, in alliance with some of the other women at the workshop, we were targets for resistance and attempts at domination by some of the men. And yet, even with these ready-made hooks, the group was too diverse for any projection to stick consistently: there were too many other struggles and differences within it.

Older women were impatient with the attitudes of young men; women in general expressed, in private and in the workshop evaluation, their anger at male domination; those who had chosen to attend the workshop for professional reasons were impatient with those they saw as closed from the start to the opportunities the workshop offered; the more political elements doubted that there was any value or relevance in participatory, developmental methodology at a stage of the South African struggle preceding majority rule; some of the men complained about the fact that all the facilitators and pre-planners were women and said they feared a 'hidden agenda'; the more practical were impatient with the intellectual 'high talkers'.

The emotional demands on facilitators in a workshop of this sort are enormous. Mackenzie (1992: 88) argues that the facilitator should not take sides. She should let all voices be heard and should merely manage the process of discussion. She should not get emotionally hooked into issues and does not always need to be right. We would add that it is useful also to avoid being swept away or frightened by the issues; to welcome the disturber elements and create space for gossip to be publicly aired; to refrain from defending against attack but rather to hear it and to be open to its symbolic meaning.

What do we as facilitators have to do to enable us to perform what seems an almost impossible task? Shared values and a common commitment to a growth-oriented approach helped us to maintain the shared task of facilitation during this difficult week. Through the process we were able to build our own associative strength and self-esteem and tap into hidden resourcefulness. There was sufficient trust to enable us to challenge as well as support each other.

However, the shadow side of our relationship as facilitators was that its very strength often created an us-and-them situation. (The rapporteur commented on more than one occasion, 'You three always look as if you are caucusing.') In addition, certain duties and responsibilities each one of us would have taken on as a matter of course as individuals sometimes slipped through the net of our collectivity; for example, each one of us alone recognized the importance of a detailed individual needs assessment, but as a triangle we 'lost' that knowledge.[11]

We were also sometimes guilty of taking sides and giving cues to participants; that is, we found it very difficult not to identify with the women (against the men) in gender conflicts, and we often gave cues to various participants by means of encouraging nods and sympathetic murmurs. Such practices add to already existing structural power and strengthen the resistance against it. In other words, by identifying and siding with the women, we unconsciously encouraged male paranoia and men's urge to control. We did try to process what was going on, both in terms of group dynamics and our own feelings, but this processing was confined to the facilitation triangle and could therefore be seen as shoring up the facilitators' power.

Reflections

In the battle for control of the workshop that raged throughout the week between ourselves and the group of male disturbers, questions relating to the ethics of the field trips, the relevance of the materials and the agenda of the white facilitators continually resurfaced and prevented any prospect of a smooth process. The long working days and the different perspectives within the group built up a great deal of tension. As facilitators we were acutely aware of the very real time limitations on the process, as well as the danger of trying to rush, bully or stampede the participants into the next step. We kept scrapping activities we had prepared and constantly re-examined what to give up on and what to insist was important.

In seeking to understand the dynamics of the workshop, it became increasingly impossible to ignore the broader context in which it was taking place. At a national level, whites were still in power but negotiating to share power with the liberation movement against a backdrop of increasing crisis, violence and chaos, particularly in the areas where the black poor lived. Within the network, it was clear that black people were sensitive to racism within the organization. Race dynamics could not be kept out of the workshop.

Looking back at the workshop from a distance, its main lessons continue to resonate powerfully. We learned that participatory methodologies do indeed hold the space for marginalized and silenced voices to emerge, and that we need to know how to work with all the voices that emerge. We learned that disturbers bring important information to the group, and that we need to learn how to welcome and integrate them, whoever they may be. We learned that conflict is not negative, that the energy it brings to a situation is the motor of differentiation and change, and that we need to learn how to work constructively with it.

If the primary process or focus of the workshop was learning about participatory methods and tools, the secondary process was the exploration of race and gender dynamics. We learned that, of the two, gender is the more disavowed at this time. The focus of the workshop was on tools for working with gender and yet, at the moment when gender dynamics surfaced most overtly and powerfully (at the end of the mapping exercise, when women and men had been working in separate groups), the edge in the room generated fear and we failed to recognize this as a major opportunity to reflect on gender and power in an experiential way. We thus missed the chance to help the group explore these dynamics and process them. In short, we failed to welcome consciously and work with the creative aspects of the conflict in the room. Although we processed some of these issues within the triangle of the facilitators, our process excluded the participants and helped to maintain an us-and-them situation. In the end, the facilitator's consciousness and tools have to be good enough. At the time, ours were not.

We understand far more clearly than before that the broad context is present in the workshop space ('out there' is 'in here'). Also clearer is the fact that the dichotomy between field-worker and community member is only one point on a continuum: that is, the dynamics and issues of the training room are likely to be reproduced in the field, in the new ministries and within NGOs themselves if we continue to develop our participatory methods and tools. Didactic methods suppress dissenting voices, conflict and, ultimately, creativity.

When we reflected on the workshop and tried to understand what had happened and why, we were forced to ask ourselves why we had not followed our own basic workshop rules. Why had we been so inflexible with the Sarar package? Why did we not do careful individual needs assessments? Why did we not take more account of what we knew about the role of field-workers and the changing political and developmental context? (We failed, for example, seriously to engage with the place and status of developmental approaches in the participants' work.)

Our decision to spend less time on debriefing and reflection also helped to block the processing of conflictual experience. We had a tight structure which we kept changing as we went along, but we did not really negotiate the changes and in this way we held on to control. We had a curriculum as well as a methodology because we were answerable to the network as a whole, rather than to the individuals who attended (who, it became clear, because of their status within the network and in society were not in a position to choose not to attend). If we hold that meaningful popular education must be negotiated with adult learners as equals, what stance do we take in relation to issues of power and control in the organizations (and communities) within which we work?

We have come to understand that power in terms of facilitation and group processes is in the relation betweeen structure (control) and open-endedness (formlessness), and in the issues of fear, containment and resistance that both these poles arouse. We have also come to see that the essence of 'holding the space' lies in the ability of the facilitator to abandon her structure and follow the energy in the room. How to integrate this insight and work with content, curricula and focused objectives (rather than in groups whose focus is primarily process itself) is our current challenge.

Notes

An earlier and longer version of this chapter was published as a working paper by Olive Information Service, Durban (see Crawford Cousins et al., 1994).

1. The facilitator 'we' in this chapter refers to the two authors and the third facilitator, Tessa Cousins (see Crawford Cousins et al., 1994).

2. Sarar is an acronym which stands for self-esteem, associative strength, resourcefulness, action planning and responsibility. Low self-esteem can lead to feelings of powerlessness which feed into oppression and domination. People build up self-esteem by realizing through experience that they have the creative and analytic capacity to identify and solve their own problems. Group work can help each individual to find his or her strength and to develop the capacity to act together. Each individual is a potential resource to the community. The method seeks to develop the creativity of groups and individuals in seeking solutions to problems. Change can be achieved only if groups plan and carry out appropriate actions. The responsibility for follow-through belongs to the group, not to the agency.

3. On the whole, the approaches of the South African state and agribusiness have not been intended to involve or serve impoverished rural dwellers, but rather to create a rural middle class. The few more 'popular' rural development projects were marginalized and only ever impacted on very few people.

4. In southern Africa over the last hundred years young women have felt pushed as well as pulled to the space opened up by life in town (Beall, 1982), or to become traditional healers who create around themselves a sphere of power and authority.

5. The process psychologist Mindell (1989) has described resistance to change as occurring when a person comes up against an interiorized cultural edge, that is, an unconscious barrier to doing or thinking differently from what has been inculcated as good, appropriate, decent behaviour since early childhood. While we all intuitively know this, it is very interesting to go through a 'resistance to change' exercise ourselves when the issues are not cut and dried. Try something like: the really dangerous drugs are tea, coffee and alcohol, so we should concentrate our entire health education budget on dissuading the youth from abusing these drugs (Crawford Cousins et al., 1993). When it comes to really threatening cultural edges such as the rights of women, such exercises can help us to understand and differentiate people's responses.

6. The objectives of the workshop were approached from three points of view: understanding, attitudes and behaviour. In terms of understanding, the goals were for participants to understand more about:

- Different meanings of participation
- When to use what methods
- Resistance to change
- Constraints and opportunities facing rural women
- Field-workers' role as facilitators of learning
- Exploring the roles of, and relationships between, research and field-work in projects.

In relation to attitudes, the objectives were for participants to:

- Recognize that community members, and women in particular, are sources of resourcefulness, creativity and knowledge
- Experience increased self-esteem and confidence in themselves
- Feel excitement and enthusiasm for high-participation activities
- Increase their self-awareness of their own style
- Have increased confidence in the process.

The objectives in regard to behaviour were for participants to:

- Use these tools to increase the participation of women and other marginalized groupings in the field, in organizations and in planning
- Have experienced using the tools
- Become more process-oriented and less directive, less controlling
- Be more sensitive to women's position
- Decrease the percentage of their talking in interactions in the field
- Use creative, investigative methods.

7. Originally designed as an alphabet for illiterates, flexiflans are perhaps the most open of the artist-made materials. They are a set of small, jointed human figures and props cut out of card and assembled and painted to resemble the men, women and children of the local community in which the field-worker is working. People are invited to use the flexiflan representations of people, houses and other props to start narratives.

8. Today, several years later, the leadership qualities of these two people have been formally recognized in their positions as chairperson and vice-chair of the network.

9. There was no mention of gender problems within the network.

10. According to reports, some of the disturbers have gone on to use the workshop methods and materials in the context of their work, and have found them to be exciting and valuable.

11. Colleen felt that, as the external consultant, she had no control over or contact with the workshop participants; Tessa felt that, as an already frantically busy affiliate worker, this was not her role or responsibility but rather Colleen's and Michelle's; and Michelle felt that Colleen and Tessa, who were familiar with the Sarar methodology, would have pushed for a needs assessment if they had thought it necessary.

Bibliography

Arnold, R. et al. (1991) *Educating for a Change*, Between the Lines and Doris Marshall Institute for Education and Action, Toronto.

Barrett, J. et al. (1985) *Vukani Makhosikazi: South African Women Speak*, Catholic Institute for International Relations, London.

Beall, J. (1982) *Class, Race and Gender: The Political Economy of Women in Colonial Natal*, unpublished MA thesis, University of Natal, Durban.

Bozzoli, B. (1983) 'Marxism, Feminism and Southern African Studies', *Journal of Southern African Studies*, Vol. 10, no. 3, April.

Bradford, H. (1984) '"We are now the Men": Women's Beer Protests in the Natal Countryside, 1929', unpublished seminar paper, University of the Witwatersrand, Johannesburg.

Cock, J. (1980) *Maids and Madams*, Ravan Press, Johannesburg.

Cock, J. et al. (1983) 'Women and Changing Relations of Control', in South African Research Service (eds), *South African Review One*, Ravan Press, Johannesburg.

Crawford Cousins, C. et al. (1994) *Holding the Space: Explorations of Power and Control in Training and Development*, Olive Information Service, Avocado Series, 6/94, Durban.

Crawford Cousins, C. et al. (1993) *Participatory Methods*, report of workshop held for National Land Committee affiliates at Kwazamokuhle, Natal, 8–14 February.

Mackenzie, L. (1992) *On Our Feet: Taking Steps to Challenge Women's Oppression. A Handbook on Gender and Popular Education Workshops*, Cace, University of the Western Cape, Bellville.

Matlanyane-Sexwale, B. (1994) 'The Politics of Gender Training', *Agenda*, no. 23.

Mindell, A. (1993) *The Leader as Martial Artist: An Introduction to Deep Democracy*, HarperCollins, New York.

Mindell, A. (1989) *The Year I: Global Process Work*, Arkana, London.

Srinivasan, L. (1990) *Tools for Community Participation: A Manual for Training Trainers in Participatory Techniques*, Prowess/UNDP Technical Series Involving Women in Water and Sanitation, New York.

Srinivasan, L. (1992) *Options for Educators: A Monograph for Decision Makers on Alternative Participatory Strategies*, Pact/CDS, New York.

Summers, G. (1994) *Conflict: 'Gateway to Community'*, unpublished PhD thesis, Union Institute, Cincinnati, Ohio.

Walker, C. (1982) *Women and Resistance in South Africa*, Onyx Press, London.

4

From a seed to a tree: building community organization in India's cities

SHEELA PATEL

Educational and organizational strategies must go hand in hand if the process of mobilization of the poor is to be comprehensive, sustainable and capable of delivering lasting change. The further challenge of building gender issues into these linked organizational and educational processes has become central in discussions on development. Both practice on the ground and theoretical debates around activism need to explore ways and means to ensure women's participation. As adult educators urging recognition in educational and organizational processes of the roles women play, we have to examine ways to incorporate new practices and paradigms in institutional arrangements.

Naila Kabeer (1994a) defines institutions in terms of rules, practices and resources. Institutions operate according to official norms and practices working in tandem with informal values, procedures and practices. These rules enable some members of the institution and constrain others. Institutionalized practice, or the particular manner in which things are done, allows recurring decisions to be made with an economy of effort. Institutions are sites of production, management, distribution or exchange of resources which may be material (food, assets), human (labour or skills) or intangible (information, contacts). Finally, institutional rules, practice and resources together determine how power and authority are distributed among the membership.

This chapter focuses on the Society for Promotion of Area Resource Centres (Sparc), describing how it has developed its organizational and educational programme over the last eleven years. Most of the processes described evolved from intuitive choices. In almost all instances, these choices were corroborated after the fact in terms of theory or sufficiently articulated insight, almost as though we had made our coat and subsequently acquired a peg to hang it on.

It is difficult to balance the demands for ongoing activism with the need to share experience around process. While both are important, the urgency of ongoing work often obliterates the need to strengthen one's vision and confirm one's intuition in interchange with others. The poor women with whom we work often express a similar dilemma. Why bother with seeking acknowledgement for what we do when there is so much to be done? Thus, just as we seek to facilitate women from poor communities to take time to think and reflect on their achievements; to share their experiences; to create a knowledge base in order to help each other; to take charge of their own lives, state their priorities and demand their place in development; so, we as educators now seek forums in which to share what we know and encounter others whose experience can strengthen our own.

Small beginnings

Sparc was started in 1984 by twelve people who became the founders of the organization.[1] We were either full-time or volunteer workers at a neighbourhood centre in the inner city of Bombay which provided a range of services to poor families. We had all been influenced by the women's movement which emerged in the 1970s and radicalized by the changes occurring in India, including the impact of rapid urbanization and migration to the city of very poor families.[2] Those of us who worked full-time tried hard, within the institutional constraints of the centre, to design meaningful programmes that would do more than merely engage women as consumers of the services we delivered.

An important influence on our thinking were feminist critiques of development strategies which failed to address the structural factors underlying and perpetuating the exploitation of poor women. We learned the need to distinguish between women's 'condition', material factors such as low wages and poor access to health-care, and their 'position', the social and economic status of women relative to men.

Women who came to the centre to procure resources on behalf of their families began to take advantage of the space created for them to reflect on their lives and explore their own and each other's aspirations. Almost immediately there were signs that this process was helping women to learn from each other's experiences.[3] An alliance between poor women and some of the centre staff began to emerge and demanded a change in the centre's decision-making structures, and in the roles and relationships of staff and neighbourhood women in the organization's programmes.

While some of us rejoiced, the rest of the organization refused to explore new possibilities. The choice forced upon the 'rejoicers' was either to accept the limitation imposed by the centre, restricting our explorations to one programme, or to leave the organization to seek an alternative way of working. We chose to leave and set up Sparc, taking with us a clear picture of how we did not want to operate.

In retrospect, we have seen how our experience is reflected in the debates taking place around women and development. We have seen that our intuitive choices around the design of institutional processes and the development of educational and organizational strategies resonate with feminist perspectives within mass organizations, especially rural mass movements. Indeed, we see in retrospect the clear impact of these perspectives on our own 'intuitive' thinking.

Feminist scholars, of whom Ester Boserup (1970) is an early example, have shown how social and gender relations are shaped by the production forces of capitalism. They have elucidated the ways in which structural inertia and change impact on women's lives; the integrated or interlocking nature of the way different forms of oppression operate; and the double or triple burden involved in women's often unacknowledged work in the family and community, in addition to their income-generating work.

The politicization of large numbers of women in mass-based movements since the 1970s and their dissatisfaction with 'the women's question' has led to their increasing participation in specifically women's movements. However, the women who constitute the mass base of the women's movement differ fundamentally from the women involved in past and present urban, middle-class women's movements in their refusal to confine their concern to gender inequities, their insistence on community and class struggles as well.

The challenges for us as we began Sparc were to locate what we wanted to do, design an institutional framework for it, and make it sustainable. Locating it was simple. We wanted to work in the urban context. We could see that existing urban interventions were designed not to facilitate organization among the poor but to mollify small numbers of poor people with palliative services. We wanted to be involved in creating organizational processes which belonged to the poor and could be used by them to serve their interests.[4] This approach, by and large, is one that has evolved in rural areas. Describing the emergence of a women's movement in India around 1972, Gail Omvedt et al. (1988) note that it had the same dialectic of a rural and toiling people's base and the interaction of middle-class urban intellectuals.

The empowerment paradigm

The concept of women's empowerment appears to be the outcome of several important critiques and debates generated by the women's movement, while the roots of the concept of empowerment *per se* lie in popular education as developed in Latin America. The concept arises, to some extent, from the insight that the meeting of such material needs as food, health-care, fuel and water is a necessary but insufficient condition for enabling women to meet their strategic needs: to abolish the sexual division of labour, end male control of women's bodies and generally establish political and social equity for women.

As to the meaning of the term, for the purposes of this chapter I will define empowerment in terms of its goal, as a process aimed at transforming existing social relationships, particularly as they affect the most oppressed women, those disempowered also on the basis of class and race. In this regard, Sen and Grown (1987) refer to the need for transformation of structures of subordination through radical changes in law, property rights and other institutions that reinforce and per-petuate male dominance. Batliwala (1994) usefully points out that 'empowerment' contains 'power', defining this as control over material assets, intellectual resources and ideology. Thus, empowerment can be understood to imply a process of gaining influence in decision-making over the distribution of material resources, knowledge and the ideology governing social relations.

Empowerment, then, is both means and end, a process and the result of process. The goals of women's empowerment are to challenge patri-archal ideology, transform structures and institutions that reinforce and perpetuate gender discrimination, and enable poor women to gain access to and power in relation to the control of both material and information processes.

A point often missed is that women's empowerment also liberates and empowers men, on both material and psychological levels. First, women greatly strengthen the impact of political movements in terms of their numbers, energy, insight and leadership capacities. Second, women's struggle for material resources and knowledge also benefits men and children, family and community. Third, women's empowerment frees men from the role of oppressor and opens up the possibility of relationships with women based on shared responsibility and mutual respect.

The quest for empowerment must also be seen as related to the reality that demand for change does not arise spontaneously from the conditions of subjugation. It must usually be sparked off by a realization that those conditions are unjust, and such a realization must often be facilitated. A key role of the external activist therefore lies in giving women access to a new body of ideas for changing self-image and inspiring action.

However, if this is to be a sustainable process, it must involve more than a few women. Otherwise traditional power structures will ostracize and isolate the few who deviate from the norm. Society changes only when large numbers of women are mobilized and an empowering process must therefore involve the organization of collectives.

Thus, the process of empowerment is a spiral involving changing consciousness, locating areas for change, planning strategies, acting for change, analysing outcomes, changing consciousness again. It is a process that affects everyone involved – activists, the collective, the community – and it cannot be top-down. All involved must play a role in shaping it.

Practising empowerment

Working with this notion of empowerment, we wanted to ensure women's participation in the organizational arrangements of Sparc from the outset. We saw women's participation as both a means and an end.

Although women in India are relatively powerless, they are not totally without influence. They have seized power within families or seized control where they could, and attempted to exert influence from their positions as workers, mothers and wives. However, the prevailing patriarchal ideology promotes values of submissiveness, sacrifice and obedience which undermine attempts at assertiveness.

Women's primary role as caretakers of families persists, regardless of their wage-earning status. Yet the official view of poverty among women is that it is a technical problem resulting from their being unemployed, illiterate or poorly skilled. Rarely recognized are the social, reproductive and economic relationships that structure the conditions faced by poor women and channel them into the informal economy and subsistence sectors.

Thus, our view was that women could be mobilized initially in relation to their family and community needs. We felt that poor women would reject an approach whose focus was exclusively or even largely on themselves. What we envisaged was a process beginning with women's existing aspirations for their families and communities and moving gradually, through a growth in skills, resources and confidence, to an exploration of their own aspirations. Finally, we hoped to facilitate the development of strategies for persuading families and communities to see the potential for alternative development processes in which men and women were equal.

We decided that we would locate the project within a specific geo-graphical area to start with. Within that area we would begin to work with the poorest communities, initiating dialogue with the women of those communities. We would create the conditions for us to get to know each other, and together we would identify their critical priorities and begin to help them seek ways to meet them. We hoped that this approach would ensure responsibility for 'solutions' by the women themselves, since they would be the people within the communities who would operate them and pass benefits to others.

In accord with these decisions, in 1984 we began what developed into an intense relationship with women from pavement settlements in Byculla, a municipal district of Bombay. The initial interaction was a difficult one because we as middle-class women, usually perceived by poor women as providers of either services or unsolicited advice, now sought a different relationship. The process of building this relationship transformed all of us and created the foundation for the educational process of empowerment which is now the basis of Sparc work in both urban and rural communities.

The women of Byculla identified secure shelter as their most critical need, an area in which none of the professionals working for Sparc at that time had any knowledge. However, rather than being daunted by this lack of expertise, staff and Byculla women alike were galvanized into exploring the entire issue. As a result, not only Sparc staff but also the 600 women who participated in the process became aware of why poor people receive no official assistance in obtaining shelter in cities. We also began to understand the kind of mobilization that would be necessary to change this situation.

At the end of this first cycle of 'training', the women of Byculla agreed that the process had both built solidarity and given them the means to understand their situation as nothing else had. Together with the fact that the process had been 'theirs', these perceived gains created a confidence among them which is impossible to describe. They decided there and then to create an organization called Mahila Milan, which means 'women together', with the aim of providing back-up to women in other settlements who were trying to change processes within communities in order to access resources. Acquiring ration cards, negotiating with hospitals and police, gaining admission for their children into schools and so on ceased to be daunting activities for women who had started their own savings and loans programme and begun, with the slogan 'from a seed to a tree', to deposit funds for housing into a bank account.

As important as this visible sense of empowerment was the fact that their families, menfolk and even husbands began to see the advantages of transformation in the lives of the women. This attitude was facilitated by the fact that the approach to the housing problem had been developed

by the women themselves, for their communities, and without any suggestion that this was an exclusively women's affair. Women's collectives
in various slums led the way in deciding the extent to which they would
challenge existing norms governing women's roles and behaviour in
communities. It was a combination of wanting changes to occur and
knowing how to cope with their impact. No one was in a hurry and
Sparc staff never set the pace.

A wider alliance

Just as individual challenges can easily be crushed, so can the
struggles of small local collectives. Empowerment must lead to the
formation of mass organizations of poor women at regional and national
levels. Strategic alliances need to be formed, and it is important that
they include men. In 1987, the National Slum Dwellers' Federation
(NSDF), led predominantly by men and representing people living in
the slums of twenty-four cities throughout India, began to show an
interest in what Sparc and Mahila Milan were doing. NSDF had been
established in 1974 but it was seeking to incorporate elements of sustain-
ability into its successful community mobilization strategies. This Mahila
Milan and Sparc were able to provide, and the three organizations now
work together on all issues affecting the urban poor.

NSDF helps people living in informal settlements to organize themselves into federations around common issues, often the need for land.
Within each settlement, Mahila Milan facilitates a process for helping
the women to understand the linkages between their survival needs and
how cities function. Most of these women are illiterate migrants from
rural areas and, until they build connections with other women and
learn urban survival skills through participating in the Mahila Milan
process, suffer from both isolation and a sense of powerlessness. Gradually, as the process develops, powerlessness gives way to a confidence
about participating in community decision-making. The male NSDF
leaders play a very important role in this progression, helping men in
informal communities to move from stereotypical roles of domination
into collaborative strategizing with women. Each federation is then
assisted to pursue whatever goals it has identified.

In consequence, local federations which earlier had only men as
members of their decision-making bodies now increasingly seek the
participation of women. Another significant development is that all assets
and resources which the federations gain through their struggles and
negotiations are managed by a women's collective appointed by each
settlement for this purpose. Several important gains for women flow

from this. First, their roles as community managers are acknowledged and formalized; second, they develop the skills for operating in the public domain; and, third, family and community assets are increasingly owned officially by women, with the consent of the men.

Today, poor women in urban India have a choice. They can take on roles as members of Mahila Milan in fulfilling community management roles, or become trainers of other women, or they can move into the NSDF work of advocacy, lobbying and negotiating. Federations all over India are very closely connected to each other. They participate in each other's training programmes, share experience and lend their support to partner federations involved in negotiation with the state. As a result, the alliance between NSDF, Mahila Milan and Sparc represents a critical mass of mobilized urban poor who merit serious consideration in any intervention contemplated in relation to the cities.

Papers published by Sparc document these processes in detail, supporting the view that a decentralized network is the organizational form with the most potential for sustaining the participation of women over time. Other literature on women and development emphasizes the related need for flexible organizational forms and functions in organizations serving poor women, since sheer survival remains both their most pressing concern and a massive drain on their time and energy.

This chapter must pass over such considerations, however, to maintain its focus on the creation of an educational and organizational process which had its beginnings eleven years ago.

The process

The process began with the exploration by two groups of women of life and survival strategies, evolving into the creation of conditions for making that exploration process the fuel that drives the engine of the alliance between NSDF, Mahila Milan and Sparc. Sparc can say today that it has facilitated the institutionalization of its own intervention, on the one hand, and, on the other, provided the basis for a mass urban movement of the poor. The aims are equity in resource allocation in the cities, and participation by poor people in solving not only their own problems but also those faced by the city, in which they demand a role as key stakeholders.

This educational process follows a simple path. It begins with knowing all the people who are stakeholders in a situation, beginning with yourselves as individuals and as a group. It is important to know what you can and cannot do and, similarly, to assess what significant outsiders can and cannot do.

The next step is to identify and understand the problem that needs to be addressed, including the set of key ingredients that must be encompassed by a solution. This approach enables those who face a problem to contribute to the design of a solution, including an assessment of the skills, resources and strategies they possess which they can contribute to the process. It also reveals what they do not have and need from the outside.

Once these steps have been taken, the alliance facilitates the setting up of negotiations for those resources identified as needs by the community, and provides assistance of various kinds right through to the execution of the solution envisaged by the group. In return, those communities thus assisted second members to serve as alliance trainers in communities new to the alliance.

The women from the pavements of Byculla, who began to work with Sparc in 1984, are now part of a 500-strong cadre of alliance trainers who work not only in India but also in other Asian countries, including Laos and Cambodia, and as far afield as South Africa. They work with poor people, particularly women, sharing experiences and helping them to design their own strategies. Within India itself, increasing recognition of alliance members as actors in the urban context makes them difficult to ignore. Yet they remain committed to the primary work of supporting poor communities in designing their own development processes. Making the poorest women in urban settlements the key trainers and innovators means that, as both women and pavement dwellers, they are central to the mobilization process.

Given that the resources to which the urban poor seek access lie with the state, especially in the Indian context, mobilization for change necessarily involves a relationship with state structures. Little work has been done on women and the state in India (Chanan, 1988) but studies in the Western context suggest that the relation is an antagonistic and uneasy one. Women fight to keep the state out of their personal lives on issues of reproduction and sexuality, yet they must seek resources from and co-operate with state agencies on such issues as child-care and health. Women see the state as a complex entity encompassing a multiplicity of agencies with both complementary and contradictory aims. The policies emanating from this distant complexity, even when genuinely intended to accommodate the realities of women's lives, inevitably create problems, since they are designed and implemented by a bureaucracy with no provision for participation by the women they are meant to serve.

The Indian state has been characterized as omnipresent and highly interventionist in social and economic change. Today, however, it is seen to be ineffective in dealing with issues of poverty. State development programmes and policies, although apparently focused on poverty alleviation, in reality fill the pockets of middlemen (Rudolph and Rudolph, 1987). The resultant declining legitimacy of the state has been instrumental in providing space for the rise of grassroots mass movements in which women are involved in large numbers (Sen, 1990). Nevertheless, it is to the state that the marginalized must turn in their struggle for resources and against injustice (Wood, 1987).

The relationship between non-governmental organizations (NGOs) and the state in India has not been studied systematically but it is one characterized by a mixture of hostility, confrontation and selective co-operation. Across India, organizations focusing on work with women have emerged with explicit goals for alleviating poverty. Among the needs identified by them as crucial are the generation of resources, the addressing of inequities and the seeking of alternative paths to modernization and state-led development.

While the resource mobilization school argues that large centralized organizations are the best means for dealing with the centralized structures of the state (McCarthy and Zald, 1987), the experience of activists in the field of women and development is that more flexible, decentralized organizational structures deliver better results for the women themselves (Beneria and Roldan, 1987; Boserup, 1970). The strategy of the Sparc, NSDF and Mahila Milan alliance, which draws on both approaches, is: act locally and negotiate globally.

This strategy has emerged from the praxis of education and social action as hundreds of communities seek equity in access to resources and demand negotiations on the development roles of state and civil society. As precedents are established and local solutions forged, they become a resource for the alliance network. The entire alliance stands behind each embattled community: assisting organizational activity within each settlement, setting up women's collectives, providing training for negotiations and assisting in the follow-up.

Empowering strategies

There is no magic formula or fail-safe design for empowerment. Nevertheless, experience does suggest that empowerment strategies must intervene at the level of women's condition while also assisting to transform their position. In other words, they must address practical and strategic needs simultaneously. With this in mind, and with reference to the conceptual model elaborated by Batliwala (1994), a number of elements and stages necessary to a process of empowerment can be identified.

First, educational interventions must be designed both to challenge patriarchal ideology and to enable poor women to gain greater access to and control over both material and informational resources. These two goals may be addressed sequentially or concurrently, depending on the particular context.

Second, an organization concerned with facilitating women's empowerment must begin by locating the geopolitical region (urban or rural) in which it wants to work, and identifying the poorest and most oppressed women in that area. Activists among these women then have to be trained and this training is critical. It must impart to activists an awareness of the structures and sources of power, especially in relation to gender, and it must equip them with the skills necessary to mobilize, while also learning from, the women with whom they plan to undertake consciousness-raising. In general, female activists are preferable, since they are in a better position to initiate the empowerment process with other women, notwithstanding differences in class, caste or educational background.

Third, activists in the field should encourage women to set aside a separate time and space for themselves – as women seeking empowerment rather than as passive recipients of welfare or beneficiaries of programmes – to question their situation collectively and develop their critical thinking about it. Women should be assisted to examine themselves and their environment in new ways, to explode sexist misconceptions, to recognize their strengths and to develop positive self-images. Such forums should enable women to evolve from a collection of individuals into a cohesive collective. At the same time, activists should also help the women collectively to claim access to new information and to begin to develop a critical understanding of the ideology of gender, the systems and institutions through which it is perpetuated and reinforced, and the structures of power governing their lives. This is the process that expands women's awareness beyond their condition to their position.

With a growing consciousness and collective strength, women's groups can prioritize the problems they would like to tackle. They begin to confront oppressive practices and situations both inside and outside the home, and gradually to alter their own attitudes and behaviour. This often includes changing their treatment of their girl children and asserting their reproductive and sexual rights. In the course of both individual and collective struggles for change, women also build skills relating to collective decision-making, accountability and action. This may include forging new strategies and methods, such as forming alliances with other groups of exploited and oppressed people, or involving sympathetic men from their own communities in their projects.

Another vital element in the empowering process is the acquisition of practical skills that enhance women's individual and collective autonomy and power. Activists or NGOs working with women can do much to assist them to gain competence in such areas as vocational and managerial know-how, literacy, numeracy and basic data-collection techniques for conducting their own surveys. Thus equipped, women's collectives begin to seek access to resources and public services independently, demanding accountability from service providers, lobbying for changes in laws and programmes that are inaccessible or inappropriate, and negotiating with public institutions such as banks and government departments. They may also collectively set up and manage alternative services and programmes, such as their own child-care centres, savings banks or schools.

Finally, collectives operating in villages or neighbourhoods may form associations at local, regional, national and even global levels. Such expansion of collective strength obviously extends the effectiveness of challenges to existing power structures and relations. At the same time, it takes the process of empowerment to its logical conclusion, with women confident, skilled and collectively strong enough to take on responsibility for the well-being of society as a whole.

Conclusion

Such a process of empowerment demands political space. As Batliwala (1994: 127) notes:

> Grassroots experiments in empowerment have made considerable headway since the mid-1980s but it is clear – at least in South Asia – that they have a long way to go. One obvious reason is the absence of a democratic environment. An empowerment process of the kind outlined here is impossible without democratic space for dissent, struggle, and change.

She points to another difficulty: the fact that the term empowerment has been co-opted by planners and policy-makers, creating the potential obstacle of 'empowerment' stage-managed by the state. She warns also of the over-simplification of some approaches, which tend to equate gender discrimination with blatantly oppressive practices such as child marriage, dowry demands, wife-beating, bigamy, polygamy and curtailment of food, education, employment and mobility for women. The result is a focus on some of women's practical needs but a neglect of the underlying strategic issues.

The organizing and consciousness-raising approach outlined in this chapter has 'come somewhat closer to a holistic strategy of empowerment', according to Batliwala (ibid.). However, it 'still needs to solve many methodological problems before the complexities of the social construction of gender and the ways in which family, class, caste, religion and other factors perpetuating women's subordination can be changed.'

Looking back at the work of Sparc over the last decade, it is clear that we have come a long way but also that we have a long way to go. What we have achieved is the creation of an empowering process, rooted in communities of the poor, in which women play a central role; a process which now incorporates the organizational and educational capacities to reproduce itself. The next decade will test the potential of this process to evolve while it expands its reach to face the enormous challenge of urban poverty in India.

The survival and growth of this process of empowerment depends as much on the political situation in India as on the internal health of the organizations involved. At present, the state's ineffectual response to the resource needs of the poor, combined with the ongoing conflict between and within political parties, helps, ironically, to create the space the process needs to flourish. Nevertheless, our hope of facilitating the emergence of new leaders, rooted in the most needy communities and able to participate in and influence political life at the highest level, will remain a fragile vision unless we are able to maintain the current rate of expansion of the process.

Notes

1. These founders were Leena Bakshi, Srilatha Batliwala, Mona Daswani, Celine d'Cruz, Prema Gopalan, G. A. A. Britto, Mona Saxena, Sheela Patel, Rajesh Tandon, Shabbir Soni, Kamal Wadkar and Indira Kotwal.

2. Migration from rural areas remains the main reason for the growth of cities in Asia, especially India. For example, urbanization continued to swell the population of Bombay until 1991, when the census showed a decline in this trend for the first time. All over India, as national economic programmes influence development, villages are becoming small towns and small towns are becoming large towns. The result is increasing numbers of landless and displaced agricultural labourers and artisans. In the 1950s and 1960s the tendency was for rural men to come to the cities to earn cash to supplement the subsistence farming maintained by their wives and older adults in their home villages. The trend since the late 1970s has been for entire families to migrate to the cities.

3. Welfare programmes represent the main intervention for the urban poor in India. Trade unions, which have always played a dominant role in urban life, focus on the organized sector, ignoring the large numbers of people outside it who are not amenable to mobilization by the same strategies as the formally employed. Therefore the urban poor have remained isolated, exploited and marginalized from mainstream development in cities. Betrayed by the recurring empty promises of political parties seeking their votes at election time, their

main interaction with city and state institutions is facing demolition squads sent to clear the land they squat on for some other development.

4. City bureaucracies, which allocate resources and disseminate information in ways utterly unknown to rural people, have largely ignored the presence of poor people within the cities. As a result, larger and larger parts of Third World cities operate outside city regulation, with families squatting on land belonging to someone else (often the state), working in the informal sector and creating micro-systems and survival mechanisms of their own. This phenomenon is on the increase, making a mockery of city planning systems and development and land use strategies. For instance, Bombay has a development plan on paper which does not acknowledge that squatter settlements occupy 25 to 30 per cent of supposedly vacant land, or that only 12 per cent of the adult city population works in the formal sector. As a result, services such as housing, water supply, electrification, health-care and education are not delivered to poor people, who often have no idea how to gain access themselves.

Bibliography

Batliwala, S. (1994) 'The Meaning of Women's Empowerment: New Concepts From Action', in Sen, G. (ed.), *Population Policies Reconsidered*, Harvard University Press, Cambridge, MA.

Beneria, L. and Roldan, M. (1987) *The Crossroads of Class and Gender: Industrial Homework, Subcontracting and Household Dynamics in Mexico City*, University of Chicago Press, Chicago.

Boserup, E. (1970) *Women's Role in Economic Development*, Allen and Unwin, London

Chanan, A. K. (1988) *Socialization, Education and Women: Explorations in Gender Identity*, Orient Longman, New Delhi.

Heston, (1990) 'Poverty in India: Some Recent Policies', in Bouton, M. and Oldenburg, P. (eds), *India Briefing*, Westview Press with the Asia Society, Oxford.

Kabeer, N. (1994a) *Reversed Realities*, Verso, London.

Kabeer, N. (1994b) 'Gender-aware Policy and Planning: A Social Relations Perspective', in Macdonald, M. (ed.), *Gender Planning in Development Agencies: Meeting the Challenge*.

Kolhi, A. (1990a) *Democracy and Discontent: India's Growing Crisis of Governability*, Cambridge University Press, New York.

Kolhi, A. (1990b) 'From Majority to Minority Rule: Making Sense of "New" Indian Politics'.

McCarthy, D. and Zald, M. (1987) *Social Movements in an Organizational Society: Collected Essays*, Rutgers University Press, Brunswick, NJ.

Omvedt, G. et al. (1988) 'Women and Movement Politics in India', *Asian Survey*, Vol. XXIX, no. 10, October.

Rudolph, L. and, S. Rudolph (1987) *In Pursuit of Lakshmi: The Political Economy of the Indian State*, University of Chicago Press, Chicago.

Sen, G. (1990) *A Space Within the Struggle: Women's Participation in People's Movements*, Kali for Women, New Delhi.

Sen, G. and Grown, C. (1987) *Development Crises and Alternative Visions: Third World Women's Perspectives*, Monthly Review Press, New York.

Wood, (1987) 'Reservation in Doubt: The Backlash Against Affirmative Action in Gujarat, India', *Pacific Affairs*, no. 60, Fall.

5
Education for liberation? Two Australian contexts

KATE PRITCHARD HUGHES

Like many other women working in the field of education, whether it be adult, secondary, or tertiary, I am interested in the ways in which the educational process intersects with social change. In particular, as a feminist teaching in an Australian university, I am concerned with the connections between a specifically feminist politics and the role which education can play in the development of societies with a commitment to social justice. This role, of course, is one that involves individual students and the ways in which they act within their community. Exposure to feminist education can be the first time women come into contact with ideas that challenge them to make connections between their individual situations, those of the women they know, and society in general. As a feminist educator, it is my role to facilitate the making of these connections, and to generate within the women I work with the desire and ability to engage critically with their community and to transform it through social action.

In this chapter, I begin by outlining the educational model which informs my practice as a teacher. Then I discuss two educational programmes I have worked on which use this educational model, but with two very different groups of students.

Feminist pedagogy: theory

Like feminism itself, feminist educational theory is a collection of different strands of thought too numerous and complex to outline here. For my purposes, I shall concentrate on what has been termed the liberationary model (Maher, 1987). This model does not take as its starting-point the notion that women have inherent qualities which mark them out as distinctive thinkers, but rather sees women as part of the oppressed who share a particular way of seeing the world and acting within it. An aspect of this relational mode, which has been outlined by Freire (1972) and has particular relevance for feminists, is a lack of self-confidence and self-esteem: an internalization, if you like, of the diminished value accorded by mainstream culture to those seen as marginal.

Much of the inspiration for this educational model has, indeed, come from the Brazilian Paulo Freire and his work and writing developed in Central and South America. Liberationary pedagogy can be characterized as a process by which individuals come to see and understand the structures which stand between them and what Freire (1972) calls being 'fully human'; that is, unexploited and whole. Becoming 'fully human' is foremost a process rather than an end result. For women, it might mean a number of different things according to the context in which they find themselves: for those living in circumstances of poverty or violence, it could mean being involved in resistance and attempts to transform the conditions underlying those circumstances; for middle-class women, it might mean being economically independent of their partners. Yet whatever changes are made in individual lives, it is important to bear in mind that transformation does not stop there, that such changes are linked to those within wider society.

Feminist education or pedagogy from the outset involves 'providing students with the opportunity to develop the critical capacity to challenge and transform existing social and political forms' (Giroux, 1991: 47). Perhaps we should add 'individual forms' to this formulation. It includes a process in which co-learners isolate what is regarded as 'natural' in their society, and investigate whether or not it can be transformed. Freire calls this 'problem-posing' education and his methodology requires the group members to determine what matters to them in their own concrete situations, what constitutes a problem for them. Co-learners then look critically at the problem they have identified, asking such questions as: What are the structures which support it? Is it linked to any other problems? Who benefits from its existence? How can the group work to change it?

Central to this educational process is the notion of conscientization: the development of critical consciousness which facilitates understanding of the operation of power structures. Crucially, conscientization is thought to develop in concentric circles (Freire, 1972: 75), beginning with the learners themselves and then moving to locate the learners within gradually widening contexts: within a community, a society, a nation and so on. To take a specific example, a group might focus on the problem of domestic violence perpetrated by men on women. The group might investigate why it occurs, what legitimacy it is given by the community, the power relations between women and men generally, the purpose such relations serve in the life of a society and who benefits from them. Finally, such reflection would be followed by action designed to transform such relations. Knowledge in this model is defined by its purpose (Maher, 1987) which is to promote social change. Thus, it is not immutable but negotiable, defined as worthwhile knowledge by the co-learners themselves.

At this point, I would briefly like to make a distinction between conscientization as outlined above, and the consciousness-raising which has been so important to the women's movement. Both are concerned with the release of 'subjugated knowledges', knowledges which are generally seen as unreliable, perhaps, or subjective and therefore emotional. They are often knowledges which arise from oppression: those of the mother, the midwife, the housewife, the psychiatric patient (Sawicki, 1991: 57).

Although the speaking, or liberation, of subjugated knowledges is seen as critical in empowering the oppressed in both consciousness-raising and conscientization, it has been argued that consciousness-raising tends to limit itself to the examination of gender without looking at other oppressive structures with which gender is linked (see Allman, 1988). In other words, consciousness-raising might well empower women on an individual level and develop the critical capacities mentioned earlier, but unless the critique feeds into social action for change which moves beyond individual awareness, the structures which maintain oppression remain intact.[1]

Maher (1987) suggests that the liberationary model I have discussed can achieve three things. First, it can help women understand their oppression systemically so that individual experience and individual understanding are linked to the structures within which they exist. Second, it recognizes and acknowledges the connections between power within and outside the classroom. In other words, through the development of conscientization, it might well be that power relations between the teacher and the student, and between the students themselves, become obvious. Such differences might not be at all palatable to the feminist educator, but to reflect upon them and to investigate their supporting structures is a process which can lead to knowledge and, potentially, change. Finally, it can link women's experience with that of other oppressed groups, and explore the intersections of gender and other axes of identity such as race, class, ethnicity, age, sexuality and so forth. This is possible precisely because the liberationary model develops the understanding of the bridges between oppressive structures and discourses, rather than an understanding of gender alone.

Feminist pedagogy: practice

The linking of gender with other forms of oppression has been particularly important for me and the women with whom I work. These women come from the community which surrounds the university in the west of Melbourne, a working-class area with high rates of unemployment. The university is only six years old and, until recently, had a policy of attracting 85 per cent of all students from the surrounding community. Because the area is both economically and educationally deprived, this meant that the community had access to such an institution for the first time.

Perhaps it would be more appropriate to speak of 'communities' here because one of the remarkable things about the west of Melbourne is the large number of different ethnic groups that live there. Most came after World War II when there was a 'white Australia' policy and migrants were enticed from various European countries – Italy, Britain, Greece, Malta, Yugoslavia, Turkey – with the promise of a better life. With the end of the 'white Australia' policy in the 1970s, migrants were attracted from countries seen as less desirable, such as those in South-East Asia. Some of these communities have lived in the western suburbs since the 1950s and the establishment of the university has enabled their children to gain access to tertiary education, but also enabled older migrants to undertake various kinds of education themselves.

This is because the university offers courses at different levels, from community education through to post-graduate degrees. There is an articulation programme in place which enables students to enter the institution at any level and to use each course completed as the entry qualification for the next level. The Community Education Unit offers literacy, numeracy, English as a second language, basic science, programmes for women, study skills and bridging programmes designed to articulate students into certificated TAFE[2] courses or into tertiary education. I have taught women, for example, who came to the university for a literacy course and articulated through a bridging programme called 'Preparation for Tertiary Studies' to gain entrance into a degree course. One has just graduated with a Bachelor of Arts in community development, another is finishing an Honours year for her Bachelor of Arts, majoring in the politics of the Asia–Pacific region.

As is perhaps obvious from these remarks, the success of the articulation process has been measured in terms of the number of students who move successfully from community education to tertiary education. In the case of many women I have taught, this movement has brought them tremendous benefits in terms of a sense of empowerment, self-confidence and the possibility of economic independence. These are individual benefits, and no less meaningful for that, yet to what extent are these benefits fed back into the communities from which the students come? Do they simply offer the potential for individual women to move out of their communities and into mainstream, middle-class Australian society?

It was this consideration of the connection between individual and community benefits that a university education can provide which led me to think critically about my own practice as a teacher, as a facilitator of 'the opportunity to develop the critical capacity to challenge and transform existing social and political forms' (Giroux, 1991: 47). In order to outline the theory and practice which have become part of my role as a feminist educator, I will focus on two groups. First, a course taught in the Community Education Unit entitled 'Communication and Assertiveness for Women' and, second, a post-graduate unit in the Master of Arts in women's studies, both of which used the Freirean model outlined above in order to generate not only individual but also community benefits.

'Communication and Assertiveness for Women'

The women who enrolled in this course were mainly in their thirties and forties, tended to be married with school-age children and, with the exception of one who came from Hong Kong, belonged to the first wave of migrants to Australia. Most worked part-time as part of the paid workforce or full-time within the home. Most had left school in their teenage years and had not had any contact with education since then. They came to the course looking for the opportunity to develop their education and, they said, to do something for themselves rather than for anyone else. They chose this particular course because it covered an area they felt comfortable with – communication – and some of them thought it might be a good starting-point for further study.[3] Others felt the need to meet new women in their neighbourhood, and to become more assertive. About fourteen women were enrolled.

I planned the programme for the first week only. My rationale here was to ensure that the students had their expectations met, in the first instance at least. The name of the course itself unfortunately carried with it both the implication that women have a deficit (in this case an inability to communicate or assert themselves effectively), and a promise that, at the end of the course, the students would be able to communicate and assert themselves every bit as well as a man might. In other words, the title implied that the individual prospective students had individual failings which the course would set to rights, and it was within these expectations that the course was set. This 'deficit' could be seen as a gender issue, but also one related to students' ethnicity, since many spoke English as a second language (that is, were bilingual or even multi-lingual in some cases) and came from communities which did not have a large purchase on mainstream Australian culture.

We began by introducing ourselves and playing some games designed to relax us and to focus the class on themselves: their hopes, their pleasures, their families, their disappointments. Following this, we focused on the variety of roles they played in their lives, both in terms of relationships (mother, lover, wife, grandmother, daughter and so on) and in terms of activities (cook, taxi driver, family counsellor, teacher, playmate, laundry-maid, cleaner, accountant and so on). We then explored the gender differences between the ways in which they, and men, spend their time, and in the status given to various gendered activities.

We went on to discuss communication in a general sense, by examining methods of communication, and concluded by posing the question: 'Why are there gender differences in the way we communicate?' This session was structured and controlled by me at the outset but, towards the end of the three hours and with the aid of small-group activities, I began to withdraw from the role of educator and to speak much less than at the start of the class. As a corollary, the learners spoke more. The session ended with an evaluation and a plan for the following week's class.

In the subsequent seven weeks, the content of each class was controlled by the learners. In the light of this, the students analysed the ways in which they communicated and the factors which determined those modes. They went on to discuss how their partners and children communicated with them, and why the communication took the form it did. This produced what Freire (1972) has called a 'generative theme': what is male power? We analysed how male power operated in their lives, in society as a whole and for what purpose. Much of the analysis was discussion-based, in other words conducted through dialogue.

At the start of each week I would provide an activity intended to be stimulating and to provide a means for focusing upon the issue at hand. Alternatively, each person in the circle would report on the intervening week and the ways in which they had communicated and been communicated with, looking at whether intervention (or breaking the communication rules) meant resistance which was not only temporarily useful, but effective in the long term. In other words, whether individual actions like this could lead to social change.

This process seemed very close to the Freirean model. It was conducted as a dialogue, the students generating knowledge which evolved in concentric circles beginning with themselves and ending with society as a whole. Over the eight-week course, there was a process of conscientization rather than consciousness-raising, although some of the introductory sessions where we shared what had happened in the preceding week could be viewed as the latter.

The process can be termed conscientization, I believe, because the students did not stop at their own lives, but systematically analysed the relationship between their communication system and its function in the maintenance of patriarchy. As a result, the students reported in the course evaluation, there had been changes in the way they communicated, how they viewed the world, and in their relationships with their families and communities. The learners said that the course had met its objectives in the personal sense of improving communication and assertiveness, and had empowered them in the sense that their confidence had increased, as had their understanding of the constraints which structured their lives. A number of these women then applied for admission to the Bachelor of Arts as mature-age students.[4]

At the end of the course, the women decided to continue meeting each week at each other's homes. I offered to provide what assistance I could in terms of information they might require for discussions and/ or community actions. They went on to meet regularly, for discussions for the most part, but also for campaigns in the community which were often co-ordinated by a local community centre offering such things as self-help groups, consumer awareness education, classes in literacy and numeracy, exercise classes and so on.

It could be argued, then, that 'Communication and Assertiveness for Women' generated for the participants an increase in both their sense of their own agency and their individual confidence, enabling them to go on to make changes to their lives which were beneficial to them. It was not difficult to trace these changes as their teacher: one saw them enrol in other courses and discover their intellectual prowess. It is more difficult to assess the impact of these changes on community life but it is clear that they did feed into the life of the community: the women's activities within the community increased as they engaged in social action around a number of issues, and reflected upon this action in their weekly meetings.

'Gender and Education'

This was offered as a fourteen-week unit in the Master of Arts in women's studies. The students who enrolled in it came mainly from the western suburbs of Melbourne and were primary and secondary school teachers, social workers, nurses, workers with people with disabilities, a rape crisis worker and two actresses. They worked full-time on the whole, were also in their thirties and forties, and came from a variety of living situations and ethnic backgrounds. Most enrolled in the course for a combination of personal and professional reasons: they were interested in feminism and also felt that a higher degree would be useful in terms of their careers, particularly in gaining promotion.

'Gender and Education' ran for two hours in the evening straight after a seminar called 'Feminist Theories and Critiques' which I taught very formally, delivering a seminar paper, followed by a paper by a student and/or discussion. The curriculum was tightly controlled by me, not open to negotiation, and student assessment, also non-negotiable, consisted of one 3,000-word essay and a seminar paper. In other words, the seminar course was taught in a conventional, 'banking' mode which Freire (1972: 46-7) outlines:

1. The teacher teaches and the students are taught.
2. The teacher knows everything and the students know nothing.
3. The teacher thinks and the students are thought about.
4. The teacher talks and the students listen – meekly.
5. The teacher disciplines and the students are disciplined.
6. The teacher chooses and enforces his/her choice, and the students comply.
7. The teacher acts and the students have the illusion of acting through the action of the teacher.
8. The teacher chooses the programme content, and the students (who were not consulted) adapt to it.
9. The teacher confuses the authority of knowledge with her/his own professional authority, which s/he sets in opposition to the freedom of the students.
10. The teacher is the subject of the learning process, while the pupils are mere objects.

Conversely, it is possible for the tutor to dispense with each one of these ten characteristics and to replace them with a learning environment in which knowledge is seen as something which can be produced by all, is neither owned by the tutor nor delivered to the students, and can help the co-learners understand and transform oppressive structures. Similarly, as a result of this different approach to knowledge, it is possible to blur the boundaries which divide the learners from the tutor so that everyone, being engaged in the same educational process, is seen as a co-learner, and orthodox notions about classroom discipline, order, or authority are replaced by an environment of collaboration and mutual co-operation. It was with these understandings in mind that 'Gender and Education' evolved.

The contrast between the learning environments of the two courses was engendered by me for two reasons. First, since the Master of Arts in women's studies was running for the first year at the university, it was important to ensure that the unit dedicated to feminist theory and critiques conformed to the orthodox university model of knowledge transference, that it developed a reputation for quality in the university's own terms. Second, I wanted the course participants to have two pedagogical models to compare. I felt that this comparison would be facilitated through the very different pedagogical environments, and through enabling participants to decide on the format of their written assessment and their submission dates for the 'Gender and Education' course.

These are some of their observations about this comparison in the course evaluation:

—The up side of this is the discussion that came from all of that, which I don't think would have happened in a more structured class. The sorts of things we talked about which were really relevant to people's lives, I think came out of 'Gender and Education' rather than 'Feminist Theories and Critiques'.

—I think in 'Gender and Education' we did more looking for solutions to problems that women face than in 'Feminist Theories and Critiques'. 'Theories' presented us with views of women's oppression and didn't particularly talk about feminist solutions to those problems. Whereas when we were talking about things that were important to us, we would say 'this is a real problem' but we always tried to come up with some kind of solution and never more, I think, than when we were talking about the rapist.[5]

—All of us were wondering, 'Why do women have to be so scared of one man?'

—(KPH) That would be an example of what Freire talks about: looking at your individual response to something, or experience of something, and asking 'What function does that have in wider society?' It's not an accident, it's purposeful and it has a relationship to the society that you live in.

—I think some of our politics were far more challenged in 'Gender and Education' because our initial response was all 'how horrific clitoridectomies are'. I still think they are, but I was at least challenged to look at it in a different perspective, beyond that just of my culture making statements about another. For example, the sex trade in South-East Asia: who determines appropriate sexuality? I think there were issues there that were challenging the way we saw things, even if in the end we agree or disagree. It was a sense of 'I didn't really think of it that way'. I think that was quite powerful.

As I did in 'Communication and Assertiveness for Women', I started 'Gender and Education' with a plan. In this case, I prescribed Paulo Freire's *The Pedagogy of the Oppressed* (1972) and in the first four weeks

we discussed some of Freire's key terms, such as dialogue, conscientization, generative themes, praxis, banking education and so on. It was
structured like this in order to enable the participants to reflect on the
class itself and to aid the development of a productive learning environment for us all. As can be seen from the evaluation comments above, I
was quite explicit about linking what we were doing with Freire's work.
This differed from the approach I took with 'Communication and
Assertiveness for Women' where, although we discussed the way the
classes were conducted and I was explicit about my aims, I did not ask
students to read Freire directly because they would have found it quite
difficult and alienating. Instead I paraphrased it for them, and extracted
the key issues as I saw them in terms of their eight-week course.

After the first four weeks, we began to dialogue and to generate the
themes which were of concern week by week. After each session we
decided what the following week's programme would focus on and I
sent the participants some background reading material. The course
evolved in the following way:

Week 5: Visit from Sheila Wilkinson, professor of women's studies at
York University in Canada, and seminar on 'The Chilly Climate for
Women in Academia'.
Week 6: Genital mutilation. Women in Islamic societies and Western
perceptions of them.
Week 7: Evaluation of the course so far. Discussion of the academic
requirements and my role as educator. Homosexuality. Moral dilem-
mas faced by women whose friends' partners are having affairs.
Week 8: Transsexualism, transvestites and masculinity.
Week 9: The sex trade in South-East Asia. The impact of the HIV
virus and AIDS.
Week 10: Library research for assignments.
Week 11: The serial rapist at large in Melbourne and the impact he was
having on all women. What individual women, and society, could do
for protection and to curb his activities.
Week 12: Whether rape and the threat of rape was used systematically
in the community to subjugate women. Discussion of a case study of
a community in North Queensland in which rape was practised in a
highly organised way by the men.
Week 13: Pornography and its links with sexual violence.
Week 14: Course evaluation.

As in 'Communication and Assertiveness for Women', the course
developed its own momentum and direction, and each week determined

what it was we should look at the following week. Here are some further observations from the participants about this process:

—(KPH) Why do you think we wanted to talk about sex all the time?
—Maybe we don't get enough opportunities. We just don't get the opportunity to open up in groups. It's a socially taboo thing, people just don't want to talk about it.
—It's got to do with body image, hate.
—It's the basis of our oppression.
—(KPH) Do you think that in the context of all this post-structuralist kind of stuff about what do women have in common, that we sort of homed in on our genitalia?
—We didn't talk about our genitalia that much. We talked about men's genitalia more than ours.
—(KPH) We talked about genital mutilation, rough sex, the sex trade in South-East Asia, a lot of cross-cultural stuff and also home-grown stuff about being knocked around basically, sexually. Transsexualism – can someone born a man ever be a real woman – is it about genitalia?
—I don't think that talking about things like rape and assault are actually talking about sex, they're talking about oppression, and the link to sex is not really what we are talking about. We're talking about what it is that makes us feel oppressed and scared.

The point made by the participants about 'Gender and Education' is that the learning environment, which depended on the generation of dialogue, was one in which connections were made between the individual and society generally. The scope was there to develop a relationship between action and reflection, not only in terms of how the course itself operated, but in terms of social action. Most of the women worked in the areas of social services and education, and they all believed that the philosophy of the course, the skills that they had learned during it and the praxis they had developed would inevitably feed into both their personal and professional lives.

Less time has elapsed since the completion of this course, so it is more difficult to assess what long-term results it might have. In the short term, the Master of Arts students are interested in seeing the philosophy of the course incorporated into the other units they are to take, and in discussing this with the staff involved.

Individuality, power and oppression

At the start of this chapter, I outlined a teaching model which is thought to achieve three things. According to Maher (1987), these are: an understanding of individual oppression and its links with wider structures; an acknowledgement of the power relationships within and outside the classroom; a linking of women's experience with that of other oppressed groups. Can we say that these were achieved in these two programmes?

First, I think that in both cases course participants came to an understanding of the connections between individual and gender oppression. In 'Communication and Assertiveness for Women', this came about through looking at each person's situation and the constraints which operated to stop them from achieving what they wanted to achieve. Some of these were personal (for example, attitudes of family members and the communication of these) and some were structural (lack of education because of early marriage, sexism). Gender oppression was expressed as a dynamic which linked the personal and the structural.

In 'Gender and Education', the participants were less interested in discussing their personal situations. This might have been because they were studying gender at a more academic, theoretical level. But, as can be seen from the generative theme(s) which evolved, sex (in the broadest sense of the word) was seen as a key way in which individual women, women as a group in Melbourne, and women throughout the world were, to some extent, controlled. The lack of personal input about sex and sexuality was replaced, I believe, by the testaments of those in the group who worked in the area of sexual assault or as family-planning nurses, and could report to the group on the ways in which sexuality in a patriarchal society affected the women with whom they came into contact: hence, our consideration of the ways in which rape and sexual assault operated systematically as a means of social control.

Second, were the power relations within and outside the classroom laid bare? In 'Communication and Assertiveness for Women', it was more difficult for me to withdraw from a didactic role. I think the reasons for this were complex but related to the relative lack of confidence of the participants, the shorter length of the course and the fact that, as an Anglo-Australian, I had greater power than the students both culturally and economically. This is, of course, the case. Similarly, the students enrolled in the course in the hope that they would learn useful skills from me as a representative of the dominant culture, and my withdrawal from that role was not particularly welcomed by some of the group members.

With this in mind, I was much more circumspect about my teaching in that, although I withdrew from being an authority who wielded explicit power over them, I responded nevertheless to their requests for information to which I had access. I saw this as a more than necessary part of the development of self-directed learning in the participants, and part of the power differential between them and myself arising from both our ethnicities and our classes.

These differentials in class and ethnicity were not as clear in 'Gender and Education'. Furthermore, participants in this course had studied both Freire and feminist epistemology (in 'Feminist Theories and Critiques') and so, it could be argued, had the intellectual tools with which to approach the reduced role I was at pains to adopt. In the evaluation, the students reported that this had not been a completely successful manoeuvre, as the following comments make clear:

—I was just thinking of the first part of the evening, when it was structured and you were obviously in charge of what was going on, and then you suddenly say 'It's got to be different!' 'OK, we say, 'it's going to be different,' but as soon as there was a lull we all waited for you to say something because you were still there.

—I think, too, it's just assuming that you have more knowledge than I do on certain things. It's like 'How can I justify myself raving on for ten minutes when I don't really know what I'm talking about?' There are obviously others here who have more knowledge on certain subjects than myself but because of your position I look to you.

—(KPH) I think it depends on what type of knowledge we are talking about because, for example, when we talked about the sex trade in Thailand, that was a week when I was holding the fort because it's probably traditional knowledge which I might have been privy to. However, remember a couple of weeks ago when we were talking about the serial rapist? The dialogue was hopping about between what you could do to not get raped, what this person was doing, how the media were handling it: it was a general dialogue about rape really, and then we delved into issues like what makes men do that. In that sort of scenario, I think that any authority I have has gone completely.

—But somebody else took that over! We still turned to someone who had more knowledge – Helen.

—We did that a number of times. We did it with Helen when we were talking about sexual violence. But when we got stuck we turned back to you again. If we knew someone had more knowledge, we would rely on them to take over but as soon as we got stuck it was back to you again.

It was suggested, therefore, that there was a 'hat' of expertise which was passed around among the group members according to the topic under consideration. What changed was exactly who got to wear that hat and, in our case, it was shared, although I was seen to wear it more often than most. The reasons for this are not completely clear. Among them might be, as was suggested, that it was difficult to make the transition from the 'banking' model which had been operative in the previous seminar. Also, it must be acknowledged that I did have considerable power over the students which arose from my professional position and the fact that, at the end of the course, I would be assessing their work. Nevertheless, these were issues which were discussed during the course and, I believe, were problematized, if not solved.

The final question which needs answering is whether in respect of both courses it is possible to say that the participants were able to make clear links between women and other oppressed groups. I think the answer to this is 'no' for 'Communication and Assertiveness for Women' and 'yes' for 'Gender and Education'.

In the former, much of the work we did centred on gender. Many were coming across the notion of gender itself for the very first time and were most interested in exploring its complexity and its impact on their own lives, on the lives of the people they knew and on their communities. As one participant in the 'Gender and Education' course noted, the women were in an environment which gave them permission to explore issues and feelings which usually were considered taboo: in this case it was not sex but gender oppression, particularly within families. For the most part, the participants were interested in exploring gender in their own terms, but also drawing upon my 'expertise' to help them answer such questions as 'Do men and women think differently? In which ways?'

The point is that there was resistance to broadening the dialogue to include other oppressions, especially those related to ethnicity. As I mentioned earlier, the students came mainly from non-English-speaking backgrounds and were long-term migrants in Australia. Their interest in their children entering university, and in their own entrance to education, was linked, I believe, to a desire to participate in mainstream Australian culture in a more than peripheral way. Thus, their interest was in acquiring not only the ability to speak and write English very well, but also to be involved in the production of cultural capital, which means having a university education and an 'Australian' point of view. In this context, the women actively resisted discussions focusing on their ethnic background, or using ethnicity as an axis of identity. This was said quite explicitly at times: 'That is about the old country. We live in Australia. We are Australians.' What they were resisting was being identified as marginal, peripheral or 'the Other' (De Beauvoir, 1972). They wanted to be people seen as mainstream.

But it was different in 'Gender and Education'. The difference can be accounted for in at least two ways. First, the participants in this course, despite their ethnic backgrounds, saw themselves as mainstream. Some of them were, in fact, the daughters of early European migrants who had been successful in the Australian education system and thus perceived themselves as already 'owning' some of that cultural capital, and able to accept or reject it as they pleased. Second, through their study of feminist theory, they were well acquainted with the material dealing with ethnicity, race, class and sexuality from a feminist perspective. Consequently, because of their interest in their own ethnicity and its intersections with gender, and their theoretical consideration of these issues, they can be seen to have made links between women's experience and that of other oppressed groups. Indeed, the 'other oppressed groups' discussed were those to which they felt they belonged.[6]

To summarize, then, it seems to me that the educational model used with these two quite different groups of students was largely successful within its own terms. Where it fell down was in relation to issues of ethnicity rather than gender, the subject positions of the students themselves (whether they saw themselves as mainstream or not), and their power in relation to me.

Such a measurement of the success of a programme leaves unaccounted for the question of whether it led to social action. It is not a question I feel I can answer with any degree of certainty, beyond recounting that the women from 'Communication and Assertiveness for Women' continue to be active in the community, and some of them are completing degrees. Similarly, those from 'Gender and Education' continue their post-graduate studies and continue to inform their working lives with feminist practice.

Conclusion

I began this chapter by outlining the theory that has generally informed my practice as a feminist educator. Through the discussion of two different educational programmes for women, their similarities and differences, I hope to have shown how theory and practice have been linked, and the importance of flexibility in this linkage.

In this, I am indebted to feminist theory which has as its base a reflexivity, an ability and a desire constantly to critique itself; an approach to theory as non-monolithic but rather something much more organic and eclectic. Similarly, I am indebted to Freire's action–reflection dialectic, which impresses on one the need constantly to reconsider one's practice and to make it better than it was. This is a hopeful and optimistic dynamic.

As I have indicated, the most difficult part of evaluating these programmes is determining their long-term effects, not for each individual student necessarily, but for the life of the communities in which they live. Perhaps one can take heart from the closing comments of the 'Gender and Education' students:

—(KPH) I think we should close up now. Is there anything that you want to say? Any other issues we haven't covered that need to be? Are you all going to come back after the holidays?

—Just for the camaraderie! Not for anything else!

Notes

1. In my own practice I have found this movement from individual awareness to cultural transformation the most difficult to generate. This might be due to the nature of the institution in which I work (a university) rather than an inherent difficulty, because it is not an institution which has a focus on 'really useful knowledge' or on community outreach.

2. TAFE stands for Technical and Further Education, offering a range of certificated courses in subjects ranging from computing to community development.

3. One of these women is currently finishing a BA with a major in women's studies, an interest generated through this course.

4. Mature-age student entry involves demonstrating the capacity for successfully undertaking tertiary-level study. The only other requirement is to be over twenty-one years. For a description of a similar approach at Neighbourhood House in Melbourne, see Foley (1991).

5. During the period of the course, there was a serial rapist at large in the community.

6. In the publicity for the post-graduate programme in women's studies, we emphasize the focus on the intersections of ethnicity, class, race, sexuality and gender. This has especially attracted students from non-Anglo cultural backgrounds.

Bibliography

Allman, P. (1988) 'Gramsci, Freire and Illich: Their Contributions to Education for Socialism' in Lovett, T. (ed.), *Radical Approaches to Adult Education: A Reader*, Routledge and Kegan Paul, London.

De Beauvoir, S. (1972) *The Second Sex*, Penguin, London.

Foley, G. (1991) 'Radical Adult Education', in Tennant, M. (ed.) *Adult and Continuing Education in Australia: Issues and Practices*, Routledge, London.

Freire, P. (1972) *The Pedagogy of the Oppressed*, Penguin, London.

Giroux, H. A. (ed.) (1991) *Postmodernism, Feminism and Cultural Politics*, State University of New York Press, Albany, NY.

Maher, F. A. (1987) 'Inquiry Teaching and Feminist Pedagogy', *Social Education*, March.

Sawicki, J. (1991) *Disciplining Foucault: Feminism, Power and the Body*, Routledge, London.

6

From activism to feminism to gender and development work in the Philippines

CAROLYN MEDEL-ANONUEVO

The demands of building and sustaining social movements are so immense that the rich experiences the process involves are often not written about and therefore cannot be learned from by others. This is particularly true in the area of popular education, where there is an ongoing need to present to as many people as possible an alternative framework that addresses their diverse problems. At the same time, there is a need continuously to develop and implement political education courses for cadres and activists involved in education work. This dual task is complicated by the fact that actors in social movements cannot work only for transformations in consciousness but must also develop a broad range of training programmes with the capacity to equip both the broader population and education activists with particular skills.

Success in this kind of work tends to be measured in terms of the numbers of people reached and the kinds and levels of programmes offered, perhaps in response to the social movement goal of maximum out-reach. However, the experiential richness of the process of developing and implementing programmes is often left undocumented, since educators are so immersed in their work that taking time out for collective reflection on their tasks becomes a luxury. Among the pressures on educators are the urgency of developing and providing education and training programmes for the growing numbers of people joining the movement; the need constantly to re-examine formulations in relation to changing realities; and the need to balance our roles as agents of change through reflection and assessment of how our work in the social movements is changing not only the lives of others, but also our own.

In a sense, therefore, this chapter represents an attempt to address the educator's dilemma in relation to finding a space to think about her work. As an activist and educator in the Philippine social movement for almost twenty years, I felt that by reflecting on my experiences I could provide a stimulus for others to reflect, react or criticize, in the hope that this would contribute to the process of providing support to each other.

I also recognize that writing about individual experiences has both its purposes and its limitations. Its major purpose is to make public formerly private reflections that can then be elaborated and therefore enriched. Its major limitation lies in its partial nature, the fact that an individual cannot adequately reflect a collective lived reality.

Having learned in the Philippine women's movement to value accountability, I ask myself to whom I am answerable as I write of my experiences. In the end, I realize that there are different layers of accountability: to the broader social movement that has initiated me into the world of activist politics; to the women's movement, which has further strengthened my commitment to societal and individual transformation; to the Centre for Women's Resources (CWR), where I worked for almost ten years and where I gained most of my experience in feminist education work; and to my husband and children, who had to cope with my long periods of absence yet supported me in their own way. In the final analysis, however, my accountability in writing is to myself, particularly since I see this chapter as a reflection not only on my experiences in education work but also on my life.

Feminist work

I started to work as a researcher at the CWR in the latter part of 1984. Established two years earlier to gather materials on women, provide resource persons and help build women's organizations, the CWR had broadened its work to include research and more systematic education programmes. I remember the first series of research surveys we did, in partnership with women's organizations, on the conditions of women workers, students and urban poor women, and the effects of militarization on women. While the primary objective of these studies was to assist in organizing women, I think they also performed an important function in making us understand that the life conditions of women across classes were far more nuanced than our class analysis would explain.

In 1985, centre staff started writing 'How Do We Liberate Ourselves? Understanding Our Oppression Towards Our Emancipation'. This was an education module that we labelled 'basic women's orientation' and we intended it to be used to clarify the particularities of women's conditions and their history in the country. In a way, it was a response to the focus of existing education modules which neglected women and had class as their main thread of analysis, whether they were general education modules on the problems of Philippine society, or sectoral modules for workers, peasants or the urban poor.

'How Do We Liberate Ourselves?' consisted of four parts: understanding our bodies and our selves; understanding the societal conditions of women and the laws in the country; history of women's oppression and the basic problems of society; and organizing women for change.

As one of the writers of the module, I remember that we agreed to start with ourselves and, more specifically, with issues relating to sexuality. This was one of the most under-developed areas in popular education at that time, yet one of the most powerful in helping women to understand the different mechanisms of patriarchal control. We then proceeded to review the different socializing agents which have been instrumental in reproducing the stereotypes that continue to affect the way women think of themselves, as well as how they are treated in society. This meant analysing the family, the educational system, the church and mass media in regard to their portrayals of women.

The second part of the module allowed the women to move from an understanding of their individual life stories to an understanding of both the similarities and differences in the conditions of women from different classes in Philippine society. Discussion of the various laws that have discriminated against women was included to show how the legal system perpetuates discrimination against women in our communities.

Working from the premise that one can understand the present only if one has examined history, the next segment of the module looks at how written history has largely ignored women's contribution to the development of society and their role in the different nationalist struggles. Since Filipino women are rendered invisible in the chronicles of the past, it is no wonder that the varying roles they have played through time are not valued. Aside from looking at history from a women's perspective, this part of the module also examines the three basic problems commonly discussed in activist education, namely, feudalism, imperialism and bureaucratic capitalism, with the addition of patriarchy as another basic problem plaguing women.

The final part of the module looks at the importance of organizing among women and at a variety of strategies for bringing women into organizations. The goal of this section is to show that after gaining an understanding of one's oppression in the present and how it is rooted in the past, it is crucial to translate insight into concrete action for change through collective efforts.

The module reflects some of the principles and approaches of the broader social movement tradition. First, it underlines the importance of historical and class contexts; in other words, the notion that events need to be interpreted as the unfolding of an historical process, and people understood in relation to their class backgrounds and interests. Second, it is concerned with analysis of the basic problems of Philippine society. Third, it emphasizes the value of organizing in societal trans-formation, highlighting the fact that co-ordinated efforts by politically conscious agents achieve more than isolated individual efforts. Finally, the module reflects the high regard of the social movement for the collective, in contrast to the liberal view of the importance of the individual.

However, the module also diverges from the social movement approach, most significantly in its treatment of gender as 'primary contradiction', at the same level as class rather than a secondary conflict. Consequently, such issues as sexuality, understanding our bodies, how different agents of socialization have shaped women's lives, and women's double burden are considered political and part of the focus for change. The module includes a feminist interpretation of history instead of the usual 'progressive' history which renders women invisible. Finally, it views patriarchy as a basic problem of society, of the same order as feudalism, imperialism and bureaucratic capitalism.

At that time, such analysis was considered radical, especially in a movement which valued ideological unity. Some considered our work divisive because it alienated male activists. When women started talking about sexual harassment or sexual inequality within the movement, rather than focusing on class oppression, men and some women were distraught. Our analysis was criticized as lacking sharpness or being full of holes. Some asked for proof for our assertions. A few tried to engage us in more theoretical debate on the issues.

The effect of these criticisms was one of creative tension, stimulating both evaluation of existing education programmes and experimentation with new education content and forms for women. 'Trained' in the collective reading of the prescribed works of Mao Zedong and com-mentaries on the national situation mostly drawn up by men, we had to shift to a strategy of providing space for women to think about their day-to-day realities and reflect on the relationship between poverty and gender. Using women's own lives as the starting-point allowed us to examine the nuances of women's problems seldom captured in orthodox macro-economic and political analyses. The challenge for us was how to relate the lives of the women to the larger national picture.

Discussion with other feminists, reading feminist materials produced both inside and outside the country and, more importantly, doing our own research on the particularities of the so-called women question helped us to meet this challenge. Feminist content contributed to the success of our education sessions but equally important were innovative methods, both those we had invented and those adapted from other education modules.

It is difficult to pinpoint which of the different groups in the social movement first started using popular education methods. Suffice it to say that when we began in 1985 to think about creative ways to present our educational modules, we were able to draw on the experience of theatre groups, peasant organizations and community-based health programmes. These groups did not describe their work as popular education but it was popular education none the less.

We were explicit in our use of popular education methodology and it formed an integral part of our education programmes. In fact, its creative and fun-filled approach to evoking women's experiences and making these the focus of educational sessions concretized for us the principle that 'the personal is political'. Three exercises in particular have proved extremely useful, not only in helping women participating in the sessions to reflect on their lives, but also in assisting me, as an educator, to understand the range of possibilities among women.

The first is an adaptation of the 'life story session', an exercise which involves participants in drawing a life line or map of their lives as women. Instead of narrations focusing on class origin, which has tended to be the approach in educational work lacking a feminist orientation, this adapted exercise enables women to get in touch with their own symbols during the process of reflecting on their lives. Living things commonly emerge as symbols. For example, a woman may compare herself to a tree taking root, a symbol which facilitates a connection with another woman who may talk about herself as a flower, one that could bloom beautifully if cared for adequately. Fruit or grains of rice are symbols that emerge often in work with rural women.

During the discussion in small groups that follows this exercise, participants gain insights into both similarities and differences in their lives. They also often realize at this point that much of their life experience is rooted in the fact of being women, rather than or as much as their membership of a particular class. In some instances, women immediately see how gender and class intersect and interact in shaping their lives.

The second exercise I have found particularly useful is one called 'the favourite part of my body' which is used to introduce the session on sexuality. Participants form a circle and take turns to move into the centre of the circle. Each then identifies the favourite part of her body by naming it and touching it at the same time. She also explains the reason for her choice. The rest of the women then repeat both her gestures and what she has said.

In the Philippines, where there are strong taboos against both touching and discussing women's bodies, this exercise produces a lot of laughter and discomfort. The discussion that follows is used to process these feelings, starting with a question about how participants felt during the exercise. It is common for women to remark that it took time for them to identify the favourite part of their bodies because they are not used to such questions. Women will also frequently describe initial feelings of discomfort about touching a part of their bodies, feelings which are eased by the experience of other women breaking the taboo. Many report that the exercise gave them a sense of regaining contact with and appreciating their bodies.

The third exercise I want to mention as particularly useful involves content analysis of different print media, an exercise aimed at facilitating understanding of socialization. The women work in small groups, looking through a variety of women's magazines or comics and discussing the ways in which women and men are portrayed. They then cut out a selection of these pictures and arrange them in a collage to represent the themes they have discussed. This forms part of a presentation to a plenary session of the whole group. It is usual for three themes to emerge in these presentations: popular notions of beauty for women and for men; representations of 'sexy' women and men; and the societal roles assigned to women (housewives) and men (breadwinners).

In the discussion that follows, women are able to see the subtle but powerful ways in which the media shape our perceptions, whether of our own bodies or of our roles in society. The fact that such messages impact on all people regardless of class, since all are exposed to the media, facilitates an understanding of the process of socialization and this assists women to reflect on the multiple factors that simultaneously shape their own lives.

It has become clear to us in our education sessions that evocative methods should be balanced with inputs and discussions aimed at synthesis. We have observed that some popular educators do not go beyond evocation of life experiences, omitting the inputs and discussion which, in our experience, give women the space to ponder the structural context of their individual situations. For our part, while we acknowledge the importance of the individual's experience and knowledge, we believe also that it is vital for women as a group to gain access to the contextual and analytical information necessary for an understanding of how gender oppression operates and impacts on the lives of women everywhere. For many women in the Philippines, our education sessions provide the sole access to this kind of knowledge. In balancing evocative sessions with inputs on such issues as the contest for control of women's bodies, laws that discriminate against women and the invisibility of women in patriarchal history, we hope to show women that learning is not only fun but also involves a range of emotions as well as the use of reason.

In addition to variety of method, we have found variety in the size of working groups an important factor in the success of our module. It is important that women should be given opportunities to work on their own, in pairs, in small groups and in plenary. This range allows women to experience inward reflection, to listen to themselves and to others, and to have the experience of being listened to. It is an approach that accords value to both the collective and the individual, instead of the exaltation of the collective that is usual in social movement education, as is the dismissal of any focus on personal experience as 'individualistic'.

Another important principle revealed by experience is that if one pays attention to the creation of a supportive atmosphere, learning goes on happening beyond the confines of actual education sessions. For example, when programme schedules include sufficient free time, the themes of working sessions are explored further by participants, but in an unstructured and informal way. It is interesting to know that relationships and sexuality are among the most popular topics in these exchanges 'after hours'.

As more and more women attend our education sessions, we find that new needs are being created. We receive requests for training for trainers, leadership training, training for organizers, training in feminist participatory research, assertiveness training. This escalating demand persuades us that there is growing recognition of the benefits offered by a feminist approach and that there is a need to explore and develop a greater range of applications for this approach.

In reflecting on the education work of the CWR, it has been useful for me to think in terms of its impact on four levels: in the broader social movement, among grassroots women, for the women working at the centre and for myself. In terms of the broader social movement, I would like to think that our work at the CWR has contributed to a broadening and deepening of political consciousness. Until the emergence of feminist theories and praxis, the social movement laboured under an ideological homogeneity which accorded primacy to class. But there is now increasing recognition of the fact that gender is a vital consideration for both social analysis and political consciousness. The same developing understanding in the social movement holds in relation to race.

As far as women at grassroots level are concerned, I often ask myself about the value of our education work to them, given that survival is their primary concern. In the end, however, they themselves always provide the answer: our work is important because it offers them the space to reflect on their lives, to learn that others share similar experiences to their own, and that there are other ways of living and thinking about life. The knowledge they give and receive from each other during the sessions affirms the value of what they know, and this in itself is empowering. The sheer provision of a space for coming together is valued by these women, who often have no other experience of 'time out' for reflection and discussion. For many it is the first step towards regaining control of their lives.

For women employed at the centre, a major gain from our work has been experiencing that education is possible in many forms. Apart from learning from the rich life experiences of women participating in our sessions, CWR workers constantly learn new things and new ways of doing things as we respond to numerous requests for training. In addition to learning on the job, staff members can also attend education or training sessions offered by the CWR itself and by other institutes or organizations. They also participate in 'exposure trips' or visits to rural areas and urban poor communities which are aimed at ensuring that CWR programmes are not out of touch with the realities of the lives of grassroots women.

Informal discussions, during lunch for example, as well as structured discussions on national as well as feminist issues help to ensure that we are updated on political developments that form the larger context of our educational concerns. Attendance at seminars and conferences in other countries provides us with the opportunity to share our work and to learn from the experiences of other women's organizations. Participating in rallies and demonstrations helps us to keep our educational work in perspective, as one of a variety of ways of working for women's liberation and the social transformation that must involve.

For me personally, our work at the centre has had an enormous impact. While it was often very hectic, I enjoyed my time there primarily because of the education with which it provided me. Ongoing interaction with grassroots women reminded me constantly that my privileged middle-class position was not shared by the majority of women. It also kept me exposed to and inspired by the strength and example of women who do not allow the daily struggle for survival to pre-empt participation in the larger struggle for social change.

It was not only the content of their life stories which influenced me but also the processes we underwent together. Brief and quick as they were (basic education courses at the CWR usually last for two to three days), the education sessions never failed to make a vivid impression on me, compelling me to reflect again and again on my identity, my relationships, my limitations and strengths in relation to the movement, and even my understanding of life.

However, our education efforts also raised a few questions. Why were they focused on women? How long were these education efforts going to last? How was our education work related to ongoing development initiatives? These questions were answered, at least in part, by a phase of our education work which I have labelled 'gender and development' work.

Gender and development work

When the four-day people's uprising finally ousted Marcos in 1986, activists were divided in their reactions. Many felt uncertain about the future. Others were pessimistic, doubting that there would be any meaningful change. Most saw reason for hope and I was among them, although I remained critical of the economic policies of the new Aquino government and of its subtly militaristic tendencies. I saw that a space had opened and believed it could be opened further if we worked on it.

Alternative development programmes and projects, considered subversive by the Marcos regime, were being discussed openly and in concrete terms. As the possibility of genuine development programmes increased, so funding agencies which had supported the education work of non-governmental organizations (NGOs) started to float the idea that perhaps it was time for education work to give way to more concrete, development-oriented projects. NGOs and quasi-NGOs mushroomed to take advantage of bilateral development aid which poured in to support the so-called new Philippine democracy. At the same time, women internationally had begun talking about gender and development, or making development work gender sensitive, and so-called Women in Development (WID) policies were being formulated by many mainstream and alternative development agencies.

Towards the end of 1986, the Organization of Dutch Volunteers, which was involved in development projects in different parts of the country, asked the CWR for assistance in making their work more women-oriented, this being a demand in their own country. We proposed and then conducted a small study of selected development projects to assess to what extent they were biased against women and how they could be improved. While the study was limited in scope, we were nevertheless able to profile a heterogeneous Philippine population practising particular culturally-based discrimination against women. One of our recommendations was that these findings should be presented to the relevant NGOs and that our basic women's orientation module should be presented at the same time.

While this strategy worked in the beginning, we realized later that our module needed fine-tuning if it was to be appropriate to the particular context and needs of NGOs involved in development work. As I saw it, the challenge was to find the broad outlines of a framework that had yet to be articulated in concrete development work. Our approach was the same as it had been in developing the women's basic orientation module: we drew on our existing knowledge, looked at other models, talked to the NGOs, adapted what had been written and learned on the job, and explored the nuances that arose as we began to conduct our first development-oriented gender-sensitivity sessions.

In the beginning, our objective was to help NGO workers to realize that even alternative development work can be detrimental or discriminatory to women. The first step was to awaken awareness of the fact that women are often left out of development projects. This led to an exploration of how deep-seated or embedded gender bias is, and recognition that development projects taking pride in being alternative were far from immune to this bias. One of the problems we discovered, together with NGO workers, was that communities targeted for development projects were seen as homogeneous blocks of people, with the result that the particularities of women's needs were invisible.

As we talked of the double burden women carry, shouldering total responsibility for domestic work and child-care in addition to agricultural work and/or income-generating work, and the ways women have been socialized into stereotyped roles, it became clearer that alternative development projects were reinforcing these roles.

In the workshops we would ask NGO workers a series of questions, the first one being whether women were involved in their projects. If women were involved (and often they were not), we asked what kind of activities women were involved in and to what extent they participated in the planning of activities. It was distressing how often women were excluded. For example, although women take responsibility for a lot of agricultural work in the Philippines, as elsewhere in the world, they were excluded from one project because it was a 'farmers' project'. In another case, they were not included in development activities because they were busy with such income-generating activities as raising pigs and sewing. Where women were involved in development projects, it was only in their implementation. Planning was a male affair.

The more we became involved in gender-sensitivity sessions, the more

I realized that we still had a lot of spadework to do. We had to become more concrete if we were to offer viable ways to make development work gender sensitive. It was not enough to make NGO workers aware of gender bias in their projects; we also had to work together to discover alternatives, and this was difficult in the beginning. Many would remark that they had enjoyed the sessions and learned from them, but the question of how this new knowledge could be applied in reality remained unanswered. For example, what could be done about an income-generating project that was needed for the survival of the family, yet reinforced stereotyped roles for women?

As we read the works of other feminists and WID practitioners, we discovered terms that could help us to find answers. For example, Maxine Molyneux's (1985) analysis of practical and strategic gender needs was useful in clarifying that immediate and short-term needs have to be addressed without losing sight of the more long-term changes that are required. Different models of gender analysis, for example, Moser and Levy's gender planning model (1986), gave us valuable insights into the concepts that could be applied, although we realized that we would have to apply them critically, since they had been developed from a certain perspective and for particular usage. In a way, our work consisted of continuous small experiments: we were constantly trying to put together what we already knew with information we were gathering to help focus and sharpen our work.

As was the case in relation to our basic orientation module for women, we realized that we needed to evolve other building-blocks or support courses to sustain our efforts in the gender and development arena. For instance, as we talked about the need to gather gender-disaggregated data as a prerequisite for gender-sensitive development work, we also had to offer training in how to do participatory gender-sensitive research. As we pointed to gender bias in the organizational structure and dynamics of NGOs, we had to offer the skills relevant to gender-sensitive organizational development so that NGOs themselves could take further the process of unravelling the entrenched male culture that marginalizes women even in alternative organizations. In the initial phase, our efforts were *ad hoc* and reactive, but the CWR is now in the process of writing up the basic modules for work with development NGOs, as well as systematizing and refining what has been started.

There is a huge demand for gender-sensitivity or gender and development workshops. While women's groups have played an important role in problematizing the issue of gender in development work, the major impetus for this demand for training workshops has been the requirement of funding agencies for gender sensitivity in both projects and organizations themselves. This has been our experience at the CWR at least, and, for me, it posed three important questions.

The first question is this: if, by running workshops, we are fulfilling a funding agency requirement, are we not acting as a conduit for the imposition of a particular framework? Second, to what extent are our education efforts going to be shaped by the gender and development discourse that has become fashionable in the NGO world, especially given the fact that workshops for NGOs earn money for the centre? Finally, problems and doubts notwithstanding, how can all these gender and development sessions assist in the transformation of gender relations and opppressive societal structures?

In relation to the first question, I think it is important to remember that the women's movement has been responsible for establishing the importance of gender in development efforts. The fact that funding agencies now require gender sensitivity in NGOs and development projects is, in fact, a step forward for women. I have therefore come to think of gender-sensitivity workshops as effective strategies for translating our feminist vision of gender-sensitive development into concrete practice. While initially a requirement imposed by donor agencies, these workshops can become the means for instilling in NGO workers a genuine concern about redressing the oppression of women.

As to the second question, the real issue is how to prevent a reductionist, cynical or mechanical approach to gender-sensitivity workshops. The danger, on the one hand, is that funding agencies and NGOs may fall into the trap of viewing such workshops as among the technical requirements automatically included in development proposals and packages. On the other hand, the danger for the women's groups who provide such training is that its capacity to attract funding can begin to dwarf considerations more germane to the work itself. The solution, it seems to me, is to concentrate on a process of clarifying our vision of gender-sensitive development. However, finding a way to ensure that gender-sensitivity workshops enable women's groups, NGOs and women in communities to work together at this process of clarification, remains a challenge.

The answer to the last question, about how these workshops can assist in social transformation, is intricately related to the articulation of this vision of gender-sensitive development. Visions have practical consequences and the kind of vision we articulate will determine, for example, whether we consider it necessary to distinguish our own development efforts from mainstream initiatives like those of the World Bank, multilateral agencies and government agencies which have appropriated our discourse on women's empowerment. Another way of saying this is to point to the need to be clear about the relationship of our own development efforts to those of mainstream organizations, and how this relationship is operationalized in communities. To what extent do we work with government agencies, which are not as homogeneous as we used to think and in which both former activists and alternative development language are now well placed? How do we differentiate mainstream market-driven realities from ours, when there is a demand for our education work in the market and it is there that we find opportunities for being self-reliant? How do we balance our gender-sensitivity work, which earns the centre a considerable amount of money, with education work with grassroots women for which there is less and less money? Who among our educators should be working in gender-sensitivity workshops and which of us should focus on basic women's orientation?

As I look back on our experiences, I realize that we seldom had the opportunity to begin to work out the answers to these questions, although they lurked at the back of our minds as we faced the immense demands of being comprehensive in addressing women's issues. The day-to-day pressures of our education efforts and our daily lives as women prevented us from reflecting on and assessing our work adequately in relation to our vision. The fact that the vision itself is not fixed but has to be constantly negotiated and re-created only adds to the need for this process of reflection.

As I ponder now on such questions as where our education efforts are leading, what kind of society we want in the future and who will provide the framework for social transformation, I realize that there can be no fixed answers. Models and the frameworks they are based on need constant reformulation if they are to remain adequate for the reality of change in our lives, change which regularly defies formulaic prediction.

When I look back on almost twenty years of education experience, I think that this is the most important lesson I have learned. There can be no fixed way of doing things, particularly in work that has to do with changing consciousness in the hope of transforming society.

Our work at the CWR necessarily involved experimentation, adapting old ways to new realities, borrowing from others, and constant reflection, demonstrating that education is essentially about creating and re-creating alternatives. While it might be convenient to imagine that there are fixed approaches, frameworks or systems that can meet all situations, in reality there is no formula for transforming the minds and lives of the people. This being the case, those involved in the project of social transformation must constantly improvise and revise not only the ways we do things but also the questions we ask and the issues we address.

So, for instance, United States imperialism and the Marcos dictatorship were the issues around which activists rallied in the 1970s. Today, while we have not dropped the discourse around American imperialism, nor forgotten that authoritarianism exists at all levels of society, issues that have moved to the foreground of our concern include the negative effects of structural adjustment programmes and the rising fundamentalism in our society.

It is in this context that I would like to examine what I think are two of the key issues that educators should consider in their work: power and identity.

Power and identity

Inequality, oppression and domination are terms that are familiar to activists but the notion of power as the core of problematic relationships at both macro- and micro-levels is more recent. This understanding of power comes largely from the feminist movement, with its early insight into the fact that 'the personal is political', and has also been elaborated by Michel Foucault.

Unequal power relations between classes or between the state and the people is, again, a familiar idea. Far more problematic is the assertion that unequal power relations also characterize interactions between activist husband and wife, for example, or between educator and workshop participants, or between NGO development worker and target community, or between leaders in the social movement and their followers, and even between feminists themselves.

It is not easy to talk about power, whether one is in a powerful position (as an educator, for example) or relatively powerless. Another difficulty is that power is constantly shifting. I can be powerful as the head of an organization but virtually powerless as the World Bank imposes its adjustment policies and wreaks havoc with my fixed budget, for instance. The questions which arise include which situation of unequal power relations needs to be addressed most urgently, which is most amenable to change, and how to deal with different sites and levels of power.

In the past, the notion of empowerment seemed to be the mechanism for dealing with power as a core issue. We knew and explained to those participating in workshops that power has economic, political, psychological and social dimensions, as well as individual, community and societal levels, and thought that this was sufficient. Now I realize that this is only the first step towards understanding how power works and, more importantly, translating that understanding into changes to our own practice in as many ways and at as many levels as we can. This means addressing both global power relations, such as with the World Bank and religious fundamentalism, and smaller power relations, such as those within organizations, families and couples.

The question is how to transform our learned way of behaving in terms of 'power over' others, into behaviour based on notions of 'power within' and 'power with', while at the same time maintaining awareness of the structural bases and manifestations of power. To my mind, this is where the issue of identity becomes important.

It seems to me that we need to emphasize that women are not only victims of unjust societal structures and poverty but also agents of change, whether at the level of making choices in their everyday lives or in organized action aimed at confronting macro-structures. This entails questioning dominant messages such as that women are passive or suited to certain roles. Our education work should provide an environment in which women can reflect on this whole matter of identity, unpacking those aspects imposed by society and examining how they preserve such imposed identity in themselves, as well as in other women. More importantly, our work should aim at enabling women to realize that they have the power to reclaim their authentic identities.

However, in a movement where societal structures have been the primary focus of analysis, it is not easy to insist on the importance of identity, particularly since it is commonly understood to refer to a suspect individualism. For instance, I have often heard that looking for one's identity or searching for one's self is a preoccupation of women in the Northern countries. Our feminist sisters from the North, so it is thought, have the luxury of being able to reflect on such matters because they are not saddled to the degree that we are with family, organizational, community and survival responsibilites.

While I would be the first to agree that the issues we take up should be based in a particular context and in specific needs, this does not mean that we should exclude the possibility of raising in our discussions (at the right moment) such fundamental issues as identity. In fact, it seems to me that differing views on the importance of examining identity issues reflects one aspect of the difference and relationship between practical and strategic gender needs, or short-term and more long-term goals.

I therefore consider identity a fundamental concept that can help us to clarify our vision of a transformed society beyond the broad strokes of our ideals and hopes. It is a concept that encourages more nuance, leading to questions such as: What kind of persons will live in this transformed society? What kind of relationships will they have with each other? What kinds of families will they live in? What roles will women play? How do we ensure the nurturing and caring capabilities of both women and men?

Of course, these are not original questions. They have been asked and continue to be asked, not least by women in social movements. But I think the point is that we need to be constantly reminded that our vision should involve ongoing creation and re-creation, in respect of detail as well as the big picture, and that part of this creative process involves juxtaposing what we imagine and hope for, with where we are currently. The persons we are now and the persons we may become are crucial poles of this creative and visionary process.

Another way of talking about this is to point to the need to examine the gap between our most cherished beliefs and hopes, and the reality of current limitations in ourselves and in our actions. As Foucault puts it: 'At every moment, step by step, one must confront what one is thinking and saying with what one is doing, what one is.'[5] In a real sense, this is the crux of our education efforts: to provide the environment in which members of communities, particularly the women, are able to participate in a dialectical process aimed at transformation. A critical part of this process, which is essentially about exploring ways and means to realize our vision of social justice, is the building of a sense of ourselves as agents – agents with the capacity to transform both our individual lives and identities and the society within which we live together.

Bibliography

Molyneaux, M. (1985) 'Mobilisation without Emancipation? Women's Interests, the State and Revolution in Nicaragua', *Feminist Studies*, no. 11, 2.

Moser, C. and Levy, K. (1986) 'A Theory and Methodology of Gender Planning: Meeting Women's Practical and Strategic Needs', DPU Gender Planning Working Paper no. 11, London, University College.

7
Understanding difference differently: a Canadian view

RIEKY STUART

There are two ways to have a discussion about gender issues in development. One way generates heat, the other generates light. Learning how to plan a process that maximizes the potential for learning and attitudinal change, and thus for increased gender equity, has been both an intuitive and a reflective process during ten years of teaching adults at Coady International Institute. At the root of what I have learned is the importance of differentiating between challenging people's values and attitudes and exploring how these values and attitudes are constructed differently. The former generates 'heat' in the form of active and passive resistance, defensiveness and anger. The latter helps people to explore their own understanding in a less threatening atmosphere and has greater possibilities for both learning and attitude change. The former constructs the adult educator as adjudicator of 'right' and 'wrong' values among the participants. The latter encourages individual and collective exploration of how 'right' and 'wrong' are constructed through socialization and life experience.

In this chapter, I relate an example of feminist adult education which tries to explore difference differently, generating light rather than heat. The day-long programme that I describe takes place at Coady International Institute, a Canadian training centre for development workers from Asia, Africa and the Americas. The institute is part of a long tradition of adult education for personal and community development, viewing adult education and group action as a key tool for addressing social injustice.

While it is only one small example of efforts at the institute to 'do' feminist adult education, the day-long programme represents an initial exposure for Coady participants to gender issues. I chose to explore it here because it is offered when the group is very new, and because the diversity of the group in terms of age, culture, gender, language, class and race presents a challenge for effective feminist adult education.

The institute ties together its six-month diploma programme in social development with several activities involving the student body as a whole. These are designed to provide an over-arching framework for the diploma and to build opportunities for reflection and community building. The first of these activities, after a one-week orientation to familiarize students with each other, the programme, the campus, the town and the climate, is a three-week workshop on adult education. The purpose of the workshop is to provide an opportunity for building community and sharing background and experience among the participants, as well as exposing participants to the practice and theory of 'emancipatory adult education'.

The approach to this workshop is eclectic, drawing from popular education as developed in Latin America and Canada as well as from other adult education movements around the world. The workshop is designed to be highly participatory and experiential, and includes processes for individual and collective reflection.

The theme of the first week of the workshop is 'What is emancipatory adult education? Sharing backgrounds'. The instructor encourages participants to use drawings, sculpture and drama to reflect on the nature of adult education they have experienced and practised along a continuum from banking education to popular or emancipatory education. Often participants have had a range of experience with formal and non-formal adult education and there are differences in philosophies and ideologies among them, as well as differences in the scope of what they know as adult education.

Gender is infrequently included among the oppressive relationships identified spontaneously by participants in this initial week, because it is so deeply internalized that it is rendered invisible. When it does emerge in a drama or drawing, it may generate resistance or embarrassment from both women and men, because there is no common understanding or vocabulary for talking about relations between women and men, or because those raising the issue are seen as 'blaming men'.

Thus, a day is set aside in the second week of the workshop to introduce gender issues from both an emancipatory adult education perspective and in relation to their relevance to development. The purpose of the day is to introduce gender in a way that encourages listening and dialogue among participants, that gives a vocabulary and a validity to talking about gender relations and development, and that identifies the central issue as the inequitable social construction of gender relations. This day is an introduction for all participants and is intended as an invitation to pursue this issue in other courses and learning opportunities.

Gender in the adult education workshop

The theme of the second week of the workshop is 'frames of analysis'. Participants are asked to look at current issues in development from a variety of perspectives. The objective is to facilitate the realization that there is no 'right' analysis and no 'prescription': development workers need to encourage the articulation of various kinds of knowledge and perspectives in order to generate sustainable and acceptable solutions. This means including traditional knowledge and modern expertise, the perspectives of women and men, and the constraints and potential of the natural environment as well as of the human beings involved.

To begin the week, the instructor brings in a camera and asks someone to volunteer to take a photograph of what is happening in the group. When someone tries, the impossibility of the task is revealed: one photograph cannot capture what is going on. With about sixty participants seated in a large circle, certain people become central to the picture, while others may be left out. How does one choose the foreground or focus of a circle? In any case, the photographer will not be in the picture.

Sometimes a subsequent volunteer photographer will try to arrange people in a group. Someone will say that this is not what is happening in the group, the photographer is changing it. Not infrequently, someone will suggest rigging the camera high up in the ceiling so that everyone will be in the picture and the circle will be maintained intact. But, another will challenge, all you will be able to see is the tops of our heads and our shoes: that will not represent accurately what is happening in the group. In any case, someone will note, a picture is static, while what is happening in the classroom is dynamic: sometimes serious, sometimes funny, sometimes with one central happening, sometimes with many different foci. One person may be bored or sleepy, while another is engrossed. How can all that be captured in one photograph? A video-camera would be better, although the camera operator would choose what to video-tape and what to leave out. A video made with a static camera would be very boring, as well as incomplete.

The instructor then draws the attention of the group to empty picture frames hung suspended in various parts of the room. Participants are asked which frame will give the most accurate view of what is happening in the room. The obvious conclusion follows that accuracy will depend on what one is trying to capture: that no frame or perspective is hegemonic.

The instructor then explains that the second week of the workshop is aimed at examining development from a variety of perspectives or 'frames', none of which is complete in itself, and some of which seem to have more (or less) authority and validity. The purpose of the week is to make the frames – the values, perspectives and assumptions which underlie particular understandings of the world – visible and open to question, comparison, discussion and analysis. This exercise serves as an introduction to the week and as a conceptual tool which participants and instructors can use to deepen and problematize comments which emerge.

The first frame participants examine is traditional knowledge compared to expert knowledge. The second frame is the current concept of development project planning and implementation. For each of these frames, participants are exposed to case material, through a video, a written case study and role play. They are then asked to articulate the frames (values, assumptions, perspectives) which are implicit in the examples, to identify the strengths and weaknesses of the frames and to compare the examples to their own experiences.

The third frame examined is gender. The instructor names this as the frame to be discussed during the day and defines gender as the socially constructed relations between women and men, giving several examples. This definition remains abstract for the moment, as participants are divided into mixed groups of ten or twelve to work through a case study or simulation of a development project called 'Manomiya'.

'Manomiya' means woman farmer in the Hausa language of West Africa. The case study unfolds through a board-game played with a set of cards designed to portray what frequently happened in large-scale agricultural intensification projects in West Africa. The case study was developed by British returned volunteers and is based on a series of in-depth studies of the gendered impact of West African agricultural development projects (Palmer, 1985). Participants are given the role of rice farmer (with better land) or mixed farmer (growing vegetables and working on rice production as well). The case study takes the two groups of farmers through four seasons: two before the development project intervention and two after.

There are many clues in the case study to indicate that the mixed farmers are women and the rice farmers are men. The rice farmers, for example, pay the taxes, join the co-operative and have leisure time. They purchase watches and bicycles with their profits. The mixed farmers perform all of the community labour, such as cooking and child-care. They pay health costs and contribute free labour to the rice farmers.

As might be expected, the development project – an irrigation scheme – unbalances what had been an unequal but viable arrangement. Before the development intervention, the mixed farmers did more of the work but there was a mutuality of obligations. After the development intervention, the mixed farmers' labour contribution to the rice crop doubled, with two crops per year, while the rice farmers' labour input remained static as their land preparation labour was mechanized. In consequence, mixed farmers had insufficient time to grow vegetables for the table and for sale. All profits from the rice went to the rice farmers.

In repeated sessions of the game, a number of common themes emerge. Participants' anger and suspicion is most often directed at the government representative who introduces the project, rather than at the relations between themselves. When mixed farmers do question why they donate free labour to the rice farmers, and attempt to renegotiate, the relationship is invariably understood by the participants as a class-based rather than a gender-based arrangement.

At the end of the game, the person playing the role of the government representative asks why the mixed farmers don't talk to their husbands, the rice farmers, about their unhappiness with the development project. Most participants are surprised by this question. Those who listened to the internal clues and the initial introduction, and who 'suspected' that the mixed farmers were women, either kept silent or were not heard in the group.

In the debriefing, the invisibility of gender relations is a major issue. Women participants who protected the privilege they experienced as rice farmers and male participants who 'discover' their position as women have an opportunity to reflect on gender relations from a different frame. The difficulty of renegotiating traditional roles and relationships without a clear understanding of the frame becomes visible: the injustice was within the power of the community to redress, but the inertia of traditional values is seldom seriously challenged.

The social construction of gender relations takes on a more grounded meaning in the debriefing, as participants reflect on the similarities and differences in the division of labour and responsibilities between women and men in their cultures and in Hausa culture. They ask themselves how and why these roles and responsibilities are assigned: who benefits and who pays?

After lunch, the participants are grouped by region and, where such groups are large, further subdivided by gender. The groups are asked to share some common proverbs and traditional sayings from their cultures about women and men, and to pick three to share in the subsequent plenary session. Once these are listed, participants look for commonalities and differences. Many of the sayings warn men about women, or reinforce the superiority and dominance of men in the culture. Sayings about women which are positive tend to praise women's reproductive work or submissive behaviour.

Participants often note that the sayings no longer have wide support in their cultures: they are viewed as out of date or irrelevant. Yet these are the cultural artefacts that they have internalized; more balanced or contemporary sayings have not stayed in their memories.

In the second part of the exercise, participants are asked to return to their groups and rewrite the statements to represent the kind of gender relations they would like to see. A list of examples of the original and transformed sayings that emerged in the 1993 course follows:

Behind every good man there is a woman.
Behind every good there is a woman and a man.

A man works from sun to sun, a woman's work is never done.
We work from sun to sun and still have time for fun.

Heaven is under the feet of a woman.
Man and woman make heaven.

A woman's knowledge is limited to the kitchen.
A woman's knowledge is open to the world.

No means yes when a woman speaks.
No means no.

A woman's place is in the home.
Half a moon for a woman, half a moon for a man.

Finally, students are asked to reflect individually and to identify and discuss the advantages and disadvantages of maintaining current unequal gender relations for women and for men. In 1990, some participants argued that both women and men gain some advantages from current, unequal gender relations. Women, they said, gained security, protection, a degree of certainty and freedom from sole responsibility for children. Men gained feelings of superiority and more freedom, income and status.

Disadvantages identified for women included less power, less control over their futures (greater uncertainty) and a heavier workload. Men were perceived to be disadvantaged by not having the joy of spending much time with their children, suffering from superiority complexes (and the stress and competition that accompanies them), and bearing the burden of responsibility and risk taking.

However, there was considerable debate about the analysis presented and many participants challenged the factual basis of these conclusions. Some asked, for example, 'Which women get security from their relations with men? What is the nature of that security and what is its limitation and its price?' Also questioned was the frame of the reporters, in terms of gender, class and culture. (Is this the way men perceive it? Is this true only for the middle class, only in particular cultures?)

The workshop session on gender ends with the instructor presenting the debate as a further opportunity for learning: exploring the relationship between individuals' differing gendered perceptions and social reality is an important way to make one's own frame more visible.

Evaluations of the gender session in the adult education workshop have been very positive. Among the comments in 1990 was this: 'The session sparked spontaneous applause from the participants. It was interesting, informative and was an eye-opener to many.' Another participant noted: 'Discussion on gender differences in values and attitudes was challenging and sensitized participants to the issues.'

Reflections on the programme

This initial day of feminist adult education is designed to encourage participants to think about new issues in new ways. For many of the participants, especially men, it is the first time they have given serious attention to the construction of gender and gender relations. Our aim is to whet their appetites for further learning and to encourage an examination of unquestioned beliefs and attitudes.

Judging from the immediate response elicited from participants, both women and men find the day a positive experience in that it enables them to 'see' relations between women and men in a new way, a way that is helpful and engaging. Both men and women find it fascinating to explore gender differences and similarities in a supportive environment.

One of the factors which assists this process is the experiential nature of the Manomiya case study, which gives participants a common experience from which to explore and clarify their own feelings and understanding. In the discussion of the case study, there is a great deal of empathy about the feelings participants report: the frustration of being a mixed crop farmer, the guilt or ambivalence (or pleasure) of being a rice farmer. Even if the interpretation of the case study is debated, there is friendly laughter and empathy about the personal feelings the role playing engendered, encouraging exploration and reflection.

In the session on cultural sayings, participants are not asked to quote sayings to which they personally subscribe, but merely ones which they remember from their cultures. This distancing again permits a more critical stance by the individual, as does the collective analysis of all the sayings. Without such an environment, it is an activity that often leads to easy stereotypes and clichés which anger and silence the women or men they are aimed at, and often reinforce beliefs instead of allowing them to be examined critically.

An example of such stereotyping took place in the 1993 afternoon session described above, when a group of men generating cultural sayings came up with 'No means yes when a woman speaks'. A number of the women participants were outraged when this went up on the board, as they felt it endorsed sexual violence against women. They were angry at the men who generated the saying, an anger evident in verbal and non-verbal reactions around the room and in heated discussions during the break. It was as if the men in the group had invented the saying, rather than naming it as a cultural artefact.

In the second round, when groups were asked to transform the sayings, several male and female groups revised 'No means yes when a woman speaks' to read 'No means no'. This again established common ground and allowed a more insightful and dispassionate discussion of the origins and purpose of the original saying.

While it is easy to maintain a positive atmosphere with a relativistic approach, pursuing a goal of social justice implies that some frames are more likely to lead to just outcomes than others. A goal in the gender session is to help participants speak honestly of their perception of gender relations and use their articulation to question the construction of their personal beliefs, values and behaviour. An atmosphere conducive to such questioning is not possible when others are judging or blaming the speaker.

Creating an atmosphere of non-judgemental mutual inquiry is a separate activity from determining how to transform relations for greater justice. Combining both in one session presents both a conceptual and a pedagogical challenge (Brookfield, 1993: 66). Razack's (1993) conclusion is that trying to share differing perspectives (in her example, sharing personal experience through story-telling) is not as effective as trying to understand the world-views of different participants and how they were constructed. The experience at the Coady Institute supports this view.

The methodology used in the gender workshop under discussion is to try to understand the frame or world-view expressed in one case study and in the traditional sayings and proverbs of differing cultures. Participants can then analyse how their personal frames are similar to or different from those examined and can do so both collectively and privately.

'Seeing' the frame in the exercises makes both the relativism and the permeability of their own frames visible. Transforming the traditional sayings is the activity which requires the students to move from exploring frames and how they are constructed to expressing their values about appropriate gender relations. The examples of transformed sayings which the participants produce are clearly informed by gender values different from those underlying the traditional sayings. Participants themselves determine this direction, although it may well be at least partially shaped by peer pressure and their understanding of the facilitator's expectations.

During the diploma course, we try to model and build an atmosphere which encourages respectful behaviour and discourse between women and men in a number of ways which are described later in this chapter. The six-month programme gives participants an opportunity to try new ways of relating and to receive various kinds of feedback. Follow-up with a number of participants in their home environments shows that some do give greater importance to gender equity in their personal lives and their work upon their return. The classroom work, and the culture of the Coady community that we try to create, together reinforce the potential for sustained change, as long as there is consistency. If we teach gender equity and model paternalism, if we teach respect and condone harassment, the chances for sustained personal change in attitude and behaviour remain small.

One of the factors that makes an exclusive focus on gender relations difficult is that everyone acts out of a number of frames at once: gender, race, class, personal experience, age, sexual orientation and so on. Gender is only one part of what determines an individual's outlook and action in a specific situation. Further, whether gender, class or something else predominates may vary over time and place for the same person, even in similar situations.

One of the strengths of the approach described in this chapter is that it presents gender as one of several frames to be explored, and the relationship between the frames is one of the areas that is questioned. This approach helps participants to compare and weigh gender as one factor among others, and allows them to draw their own conclusions about its relative strength and similarity to other frames.

The day-long programme provides participants with a common experience and a common vocabulary for further work on gender issues. It also gives institutional sanction and 'space' for participants to continue learning about and questioning gender relations in the Coady community.

In our experience, however, unless such subsequent work is well facilitated, it may result in misunderstanding and conflict. On several occasions, mid-term and final evaluations have criticized Coady staff for raising issues of gender relations, saying that this resulted in problems among the students. On closer examination, what seems to happen is that expectations about non-sexist behaviour on the part of both men and women are raised through classroom sessions and if sexist ideas or actions surface and are challenged among the students, the atmosphere of inquiry changes to one of judgement, resulting in conflict.

In part this may be because institute staff have not clarified a common understanding and approach to gender issues, resulting in some inconsistency in the way both community behaviour and gender and development issues are dealt with. In part it may be because the students cannot themselves make the shift from speaking and hearing from their own particular perspective, to examining and articulating the sources of that perspective.

Over the years, we have experimented with adding other related topics to the session on gender, but have concluded that allowing time for deeper reflection and exchange on introductory elements is more useful than trying to cover more territory. Since the students at this point in the programme are still learning to hear each other, because of language, cultural and life experience differences, taking the time to explore a limited number of issues deeply is judged to be more effective by both participants' and facilitators' evaluations. In consequence, for example, we cut out of this workshop a discussion of power and resistance and also dropped an exercise aimed at understanding symptoms and causes of the maintenance of gender inequality.

The day-long session, as it has developed over the last seven years, meets the institute's needs as a preliminary introduction for women and men to gender relations in adult education. It encourages comparisons and self-questioning, raises the question of justice in gender relations, and seems inclusive enough to be interesting to both feminists and traditionalists. While it is only one day of a six-month course, it is an important first step, in tandem with other efforts at the institute, towards incorporating a feminist voice in our adult education.

From the particular to the general

Several larger issues emerge when one tries to understand what works and what doesn't in feminist adult education. The first is the need to understand more clearly what ideological assumptions underlie definitions of feminist adult education.

In Chapter 1 of this book, Shirley Walters defines feminist adult education as adult education which deals explicitly with the inequality between women and men. She makes a distinction between feminist content – the nature of gender relations – and feminist process. The latter includes attention to feelings as well as ideas, learning based on experience, and critical attention to the 'voice' of the adult educator as well as those of the participants (see also Arnold et al., 1991). Feminist process, Walters argues, is an accepted part of any adult education activity, while feminist content is frequently excluded.

While this may be so, it is not sufficient to look only at issues of process and content in feminist adult education. Education dealing with the inequality between women and men varies greatly in its under-standing of the reasons for such inequality and in its prescriptions. Therefore it is important to elaborate distinctions in the ideological approaches taken by feminist adult educators and to situate a particular approach.

Some feminist adult educators emphasize and reinforce 'natural' characteristics of women or men (Faludi, 1991: 326). This may be reflected in depictions of women as less violent, more capable of dealing with feelings and more nurturing than men, for example. While this may be true statistically, it begs the question of the cause – social or biological – and the wide range of differences to be found among individual women and men. Some men may be nurturing and some women domineering, for example, thus belying facile generalizations. More importantly, an assumption of innate gender differences is the basis upon which patriarchy has been constructed. Feminism's aim should not be to pose matriarchy as an alternative to patriarchy. Re-placing a belief in the superiority of 'masculine' attributes or activities with a belief in the superiority of 'feminine' attributes or activities creates neither justice nor liberation for women or for men. Alternatively, a feminist adult educator may wish to depict women as the victims of male domination. This is a powerful approach for organizing women to take action. It allows them to name their personal unhappiness as socially caused by men and by patriarchy (Kardam, 1991: 9). However, it may be counter-productive if women do not feel themselves to be victimized, or do not identify themselves as primarily oppressed because of their gender (for example, if they feel age or racial oppression is dominant in their lives). In addition, this approach often generates anger and hostility from men, as they may feel personally blamed or attacked.

Yet another approach taken by the feminist adult educator may be to focus on the gendering process. This approach implicates both women and men in the creation of domestic and societal structures which have advantages and disadvantages for both, but more evident disadvantages for women (see, for example, Ehrenreich, 1983).

A final approach comes disguised as academic 'neutrality': an effort to understand the biological and sociological creation of sex and gender, without explicitly considering the educator's own values and location, and with implicit intent of personal or social change. This kind of feminist education can generate resistance, as illustrated by the negative reactions of some students to the values implicit in some women's studies courses (Lather, 1991).

The approach most consistent with teaching difference differently is to explore the social and biological construction of gender in a way that situates the feminist adult educator as one of the explorers; that attempts to locate the ways and means by which we experience, value and understand gender, in order to view them critically. I present gender as primarily a social construct, created and maintained by women and men. It constrains both women and men, but women more so. Exploration focuses on how frames of understanding, or world-views, are constructed rather than on their content only. Looking at how development initiatives can challenge or reinforce an unjust social construction of gender relations offers concrete ways for participants to shape their future interventions. A second issue that emerged in my attempt to understand what works and does not work in feminist adult education is whether and to what degree this approach complements or fits in with the 'emancipatory adult education' for development workers practised at the Coady Institute. This question needs to be placed in context if an answer is to make sense.

Historically, the institute grew out of efforts led by the Extension Department of St Francis Xavier University in Maritime Canada to combat local poverty and exploitation by organizing adult education (through kitchen meetings) to promote self-help co-operatives and credit unions. Fishermen's co-operatives, consumer co-operatives, agricultural marketing co-operatives and credit unions flourished from the late 1920s, attracting outside development activists who wanted to learn from the 'Antigonish Movement', as it came to be known.

Moses 'M. M.' Coady, who headed the Extension Department during this time, believed in building personal capacity through adult education and in the use of collective action for social and economic betterment (Coady, 1967; Laidlaw, 1971). When he died in 1959, the institute was established to train people from other parts of the world in the principles and practice of the Antigonish Movement. Over time, the institute has learned from the experience of other movements and efforts for social change and today provides training for development workers grounded in values of social justice, principles of participatory adult education and a belief in the importance of building people's organizations as a basis for sustainable social change.

As a development training institution, the Coady International Institute views sustainable development as an holistic process with a number of dimensions. At the personal level, individuals need the material, intellectual, moral and volitional capacity to develop themselves. At the community level, organizations and processes are required for mobilizing resources and energy for collective benefit. At a structural level, the institutions of the society, the nation and the globe need to be transformed so as to serve and benefit the individual and the community equitably. On the level of the environment, people's use of both re-newable and non-renewable resources must be sustainable. Finally, at the level of culture, the beliefs, values and expressions of a group of people need to embody respect for and empowerment of individuals and communities.

In designing curricula and pedagogy at the institute, staff take the position that training effective development workers requires critical reflection and change in the attitudes, values, capacities and behaviour of the development workers themselves, as well as in the people they work with. The institute's goal is to assist in building capacity for development organizations to empower the disadvantaged for greater social justice. Critical thinking is seen as essential for creating sustainable social change: values must be generated from within, they cannot be imposed.

One way of building this capacity for critical thinking is to begin with a recognition of the differences between participants as men and women, old and young, resident in urban and rural areas, coming from poor and middle-class backgrounds and from Africa, Asia and the Americas. The approach is then to exploit the rich variety of perspectives and ex-periences of the participants as a keystone for learning. Brookfield (1988: 1) describes critical thinking as 'calling into question the assumptions underlying our customary, habitual ways of thinking and acting and then being ready to think and act differently on the basis of this critical questioning'. Interaction with a community of peers as varied as the Coady diploma participants provides a rich opportunity for fostering critical thinking, but also carries the risk of deepening mistrust, re-inforcing communication barriers and hardening existing attitudes. An approach that maximizes potential for a positive outcome is to explore difference differently: to build a learning situation where the understand-ing of how difference itself is created becomes the site of exploration.

It is in this context that questions about the role of feminist adult education must be asked, in particular, how it relates to an understanding of what constitutes good development. I want to argue that it can and should play a central role in the training of development workers.

Every human being has experienced both biological and social categorization and formation as a man or as a woman. Everyone who teaches and studies at the Coady Institute is implicated as an actor in the creation, transformation or maintenance of gender relations. A very deep sense of identity and powerful emotions are attached to sexuality and gender. The dynamics involved in understanding one's gendered self-perception and how one is perceived by others as victim or villain, passively accepting the status quo or actively struggling for change, provide a powerful lens for examining all relations of power and domination. Relations of power and inequality are the heart of development work, and feminist adult education can help us to examine the construction and maintenance of dominance of all kinds.

Equally important is a corollary: we cannot claim to be active in the struggle for social justice unless we also challenge the injustice based on gender inequality.

A third large issue that emerges from an examination of the role of feminist adult education is the need for consistency between what is taught and what is practised. Learning about the social construction of gender and exploring the implications of increased equity between women and men in the 'gender class' cannot be divorced from what is taught in other courses, or what is experienced in daily life at the institute. Therefore, an important part of reinforcing learning is the creation of an environment which enables new behaviour and the application of new attitudes.

This task of creating an enabling environment is tackled at the Coady Institute in a number of concrete ways. We actively recruit women students and provide positive support to them during their stay at the institute. We have established clear policies against sexual harassment and act on complaints. We encourage men and women to share weekend cooking chores. Everyone does his or her own laundry. Gender dimensions of various development issues are explored in all courses, from macro-economics to project planning. Lecturers model and reinforce respectful behaviour across gender as well as race, class and cultural divides among students.

Putting all of these supportive mechanisms in place has taken time, energy and much discussion. As a result, the institute is becoming an easier and more useful place for women, and also a place for women and men to struggle with new understandings of how to transform gender relations in their lives and in their work.

Bibliography

Arnold, R. et al. (1991) *Educating for a Change*, Between the Lines and Doris Marshall Institute for Education and Action, Toronto.

Brookfield, S. D. (1988) *Developing Critical Thinkers*, Jossey-Bass, San Francisco.

Brookfield, S. D. (1993) 'Breaking the Code: Engaging Practitioners in Critical Analysis of Adult Educational Literature', *Studies in the Education of Adults*, Vol. 25, no. 1, April.

Coady, M. M. (1967) *Masters of Their Own Destiny*, Formac, Antigonish.

Ehrenreich, B. (1983) *The Hearts of Men*, Doubleday, New York.

Faludi, S. (1991) *Backlash: The Undeclared War Against American Women*, Crown, New York.

Kardam, N. (1991) *Bringing Women In*, Lynne Rienner, Boulder, CO.

Laidlaw, A. (1971) *The Man from Margaree*, McClelland and Stewart, Toronto.

Lather, P. (1991) 'Framing the Issues' in Lather, P. *Getting Smart: Feminist Research and Pedagogy with/in the Postmodern*, Routledge, New York.

Palmer, I. (1985) *The Nemow Case*, Kumarian Press, Hartford, CT.

Razack, S. (1993) 'Story-telling for Social Change', *Gender and Education*, Vol. 5, no. 1.

8

'The creaking of the Word': a feminist model?

ASTRID VON KOTZE

Women have many different difficulties. Some of them are exploited by their husbands. They are beaten for nothing because they have no strength to fight. At home they have no right to talk: they must sit down and listen to their husbands. They must agree even if their husbands are telling them wrong things because they paid lobola for them and bought them clothes. They have no right to own anything in the house – cattle, goats and even the land must be written under the name of the man. Even the children belong to their fathers ... There are no laws protecting women ... Many women are exploited by their employers. They do not earn enough money because they are women ... There are not enough political and other structures for women. That is why they are always left behind. There is no woman leading any organization but women are the majority in our country. Even the unions have few women in leadership positions. (Mahlaba, 1992)

Beauty Mahlaba's experience is that of so many other black working-class women in South Africa and elsewhere in the world: treated as a minor with no voice of her own, she feels exploited at home and in the world. Left to raise three sons by herself, she lost her factory job as a result of cut-backs and in 1991 lost her home when her house was burnt down in a wave of political violence. She now lives with her sons in a shack in a war-torn informal settlement on the outskirts of Durban. In order to survive economically she started her own sewing co-operative and, since the workshops described in this chapter, has become a founder member of the Self-Employed Women's Union.

Her writing tells the story of black working-class women's daily struggles for survival in a world of patriarchy, racism and capitalism. Through her writing she wants to urge other women to tell their stories and to join the struggle for women's rights in the home, at work and in society. But she also wants to reach her male comrades and friends who, engaged in the struggle for liberation, forgot that 'a nation is only free when its women are free'.

Walters (1991) has outlined briefly the different strategies and avenues adopted by women in South Africa for challenging their subordinate status and positions. In recent years a number of historical, sociological, political and even literary books have given a voice to those nameless people whose labour has kept this country going. However, in order to gain a full perspective on the perceptions and experiences of those workers, particularly the women forced to occupy the lowest place in the social hierarchy, it is crucial that they themselves should record their experiences and the strategies they adopt to resist both their personal and more objective subordination, exploitation and oppression.

This chapter describes a series of creative writing workshops that were part of a culture course situated firmly within the struggle for political, social, cultural and gender change in South Africa. It examines whether the workshops could be viewed as a model of feminist educational methodology, both in their approach to creative productivity and in the impulses they generated in learners and facilitator. Alongside considerations of methodology, the chapter describes another struggle: one of conscience in which I, as the facilitator, was constantly torn between my commitment to creative practices in the struggle for new cultural productions in South Africa, on the one hand, and my role as a feminist challenging sexism and stereotypes in creative writing, on the other.

Charting the field

Mahlaba wrote the introductory lines of this chapter when she participated in the course, which was developed and run in 1990 by cultural activists associated with the Culture and Working Life Project (CWLP) in response to demands by workers and their unions. In essence, three factors gave rise to the course: culture as an expression of working life and people's creative power, culture as a tool for reclaiming traditional art forms and inventing new ones, and culture as a 'weapon' in political and labour struggles.

After 1985, inspired by the performances of such people as Alfred Qabula, Nise Malange and Mi Hlatshwayo,[1] workers rediscovered their cultural and artistic potential. They asserted their creative powers by organizing choirs and drama groups and encouraging their favourite *izimbongi* or praise poets to perform from political and workers' platforms. Increasingly, workforces engaged in disputes with management began to publicize their struggles through story-telling of various kinds: one group of dismissed workers used the successful campaign waged with the help of their play as a springboard for forming a more permanent drama group.[2]

With this surge in the celebration of cultural expressions, workers and activists looked to traditional art forms for inspiration. The CWLP articulated this new interest in campaigns: the creation, development and control of cultural productions reflecting the context of changed social, economic and political pressures had to be in the hands of the people rooted in that culture. This is a crucial principle, particularly in the face of years of colonialism and cultural imperialism which saw the culture of black South Africans relegated beyond the margins of culture to a tenuous existence as 'tribal art'. The consequences have been incalculable. As Afro-American Adrian Piper notes (Lippard, 1990: 7): 'Cultural racism is damaging and virulent because it hits its victims in particularly vulnerable and private places: their preferences, tastes, modes of self-expression, and self-image.'

When the Congress of South African Trade Unions recognized cultural productions as potentially powerful tools for unifying workers and raising awareness, it began to take seriously workers' voices calling for culture to be placed on the agenda of every meeting and gathering. However, this explosion of creative energy needed to be harnessed and shaped, and the CWLP was overwhelmed with requests for assistance. Demands for help with drama, music and writing projects far exceeded the number of available skilled cultural activists.

The culture course, incorporating creative writing workshops, was one response to this crisis. It was also a way of ensuring that the values of the dominant culture in South Africa would be challenged at the creative, artistic level as well as at the strategic, political level, and it fed self-consciously into the struggle for democratic change in the country.

The aims of the course were to develop the creative skills of worker poets, artists and performers, and to provide training in organizational and educational skills. In the process it was hoped that learners would assert both their critical, analytical faculties and their imaginative spirit to create images and stories, sounds and dances which would reflect the daily reality of working people. This clearly political aim was linked, for the majority of course participants, to a desire to strengthen their particular union. Their active commitment to the political, labour and personal creative struggles was an ever-present element of the course.

The focus of the writing workshops was to be the production of texts which would capture workers' lives and histories.[3] The targeted readership was primarily other working-class people. The curriculum did not have an explicit feminist perspective: if anything, the facilitators (women) were concerned that their feminism should not alienate conservative and/or male participants. However, this remained an area of tension for facilitators throughout the course: the need to challenge accepted stereotypes and conscientize around gender issues clashing with the need to maintain a position of minimum interference while serving the expressed interests of participants and their unions.

The workshop process described here was run twice, with two different groups. In both cases there were seven participants of whom three were women, in the first instance, and two in the second. All were factory workers. While all lived in urban townships around Durban, the women particularly had strong links with rural areas. The preponderance of men over women in both groups had the potential of creating dynamics in the class that favoured the male majority; however, as I will argue later, the process itself functioned to counteract this.

My involvement in the process described here arose first and primarily out of my practice as a cultural activist working in the labour movement in South Africa. This work is fed by my belief that when people employ their creative imaginations and energies, they can contribute significantly to the transformation of both their subjective existences and the broader social and political structures. However, as a woman I am constantly aware that on both the personal and strategic levels, women's needs have been subjugated to the broader political and economic struggles in the country, and that unless decisive action ensures a truly democratic development, women will still find themselves at 'the bottom of the pile'.

In deciding on an appropriate process for the workshops, I relied more on my experience in cultural workshops in art, drama and writing than on theories of popular education or a specific articulated feminist position. From the visual arts I borrowed the need to focus clearly and to simplify an image, sometimes by extracting its main components. Drama taught me improvisational techniques and the skill of invention on one's feet under pressure. My work in grassroots educator training involves constant exercise in critical reflection on learning processes, with an emphasis on working towards emancipatory impulses through analysis and understanding. I believe it is this very combination of lateral and linear thinking that both underlies feminist methodology and produces the kind of memorable narrative published in *Umkhumulansika*.[4]

The approach is rooted in praxis: it grew out of everyday life and the particular practices necessitated by oppositional work under the repressive apartheid regime. This included theoretical debates and readings which remained largely oral because radicals were excluded from the academy. For my part, a participatory workshop approach was also inspired by the philosophy of Paulo Freire and descriptions of Ira Shor's (1987) utopia workshops. Thus, I chose for the writing course a mode of interactive learning through dialogue and exploration, underpinned by what Giroux (1992: 125) calls 'the discourse of possibility'. What might make such a participatory, experiential process of learning a model for feminist writing workshops will be explored later in this chapter.

The process

The writing process of the course goes through a number of different stages: from individual experience expressed predominantly through a non-linguistic medium, to the collective construction of arguments and counter-arguments, to experience of a dialogue based on power relations and diversity of standpoint, and finally to the creative, imaginative writing process which allows (but does not compel) participants to translate and mediate their personal experience into a more general third person or fictionalized story.

It begins with the context of culture and working life, the combination of creative speech and productive work: women in production telling stories about daily lived experience, often with a didactic message. The process draws on the tradition of women as story-tellers, as a force for maintaining histories and heritage, as social educators and healers. Speech and productive activity usually go hand in hand. As Trin T. Minh-ha writes: 'Making material, spinning and weaving is a euphonious heritage of wo/mankind handed from generation to generation of weavers with the clapping of the shuttle and the creaking of the block – which the Dogon call "the creaking of the Word"' (quoted in Lippard, 1990: 71). The image created on the loom and the stories painted in words go together as much as production and speech. Furthermore, in oral cultures the spoken word carries a particular importance. People create and re-create themselves through action and telling: 'Like a candle the 'I' lights up only in the activity and is extinguished at other times. But not dead. With the retelling of the story, the candle comes to glow again' (Illich and Sanders, 1989: 72). Thus, the context of creative writing or story-telling workshops seems an appropriate starting-point for the emergence of a methodology in the mould of popular feminist education.

Naming[5]   Writing begins with an inspiration or a stimulus. The workshops that were to produce texts to challenge oppression took the word 'discrimination' as their starting-point. It was a word deliberately chosen for its strong emotional effect and yet its openness to different interpretations.

During the process of elucidating the term we searched less for examples and experiences than for linguistic clarity. Acknowledging that certain words might mean different things in other languages drew attention to the fact that 'we think in terms of "languages" as self-contained systems of communication that may be compared with one another, but only in the context of their separateness' (Illich and Sanders, 1989: 62).

English is only a convenient medium of communication in a multi-language group, but not necessarily the dominant language. Searching for the approximate word in participants' home languages and struggling for an appropriate expression when the exact word could not be found was useful, as it could call attention to possible reasons for the existence of a word – and the experience it labels – in one language but not another. We asked such questions as: Do the approximations have the same connotations? What are the values attached to the words? For example, could the word 'discrimination' be applied to anything other than a negative practice? Do participants' mother tongues have a more differentiated terminology? What does this mean?

As a learning activity this discussion drew attention to different systems of communication and values, as the focus on differences between participants' perceptions and understandings invited us to look at our own socio-cultural backgrounds with fresh eyes. In creative terms, the discussion helped to conjure up images and ideas. In consequence the ensuing task, which restricted discussion to a minimum in favour of communication through visual means, was accomplished fairly easily and participants used verbal communication for the co-ordination of collective drawing in small groups, rather than to discuss images and representations associated with the word 'discrimination'.

Drawing This task required participants to work in groups of three to four people and collectively to prepare drawings around the word 'discrimination'. The tools supplied were large sheets of newsprint and pens and crayons of different colours. I imposed no time limit but indicated that participants would be expected to present their pictures to each other, explaining and elaborating on drawings. I acknowledged the tension the task created: most participants had little or no experience with drawing and suffered from 'performance anxiety'. I explained that works of art were not expected and emphasized that it was crucial for everyone in a group to contribute to the drawing and not rely on the confidence and/or skills of any one member.

There are numerous accounts of how educators have used drawing as a useful non-linear mode of learning, and how a process that favours the right side of the brain is more intuitive and holistic than left-brain processes.[6] Introducing drawing into 'serious' learning means asserting the value of approaches other than those involving linear, analytical thinking. It implies that there are other ways of tackling problems and that these may be more imaginative, playful and, in the end, more productive. Indeed, psychology often uses drawings to access deep-seated attitudes and beliefs and can lead to a revelation for both learners and facilitator when unarticulated views and values come to the surface.

The choice of drawing as a start to a writing workshop is based first on the need to create a 'product' which can become the basis for further work. Second, drawings are a useful medium for a multi-lingual group, particularly if some participants have had only a basic level of formal education and consequently lack confidence in expressing themselves in writing. Thirdly, and importantly, drawing invites participants to go beyond hollow words which have lost their meaning as a result of over-use or misuse.

Many of the participants in the culture course were leadership figures used to operating in public forums. Many exhibited a tendency to be prisoners of slogans and jargon, the 'language of struggle'. Words such as 'unity', 'equality' and 'non-discrimination' tripped off their tongues fairly easily. Indeed, the facile use of such terminology has been evident even in capitalist enterprise and among members of the old apartheid government, as they adopted the positive-sounding words of democratic forces in order to signal 'change'. However, if asked to elaborate on the meaning of these words in the concrete terms of daily experience, many people have problems. What is the colour of 'equality'? What is the sound of 'freedom'? The drawing activity asks participants to generate pictures, concrete images. It throws them back on concrete lived experience, stories and feelings rather than speeches and campaigns.

Drawing collectively rather than individually has the advantage of allowing individual participants to 'disappear' in the general picture. The collective experience, in which each participant takes risks but also receives respect, generates a support structure for all. The collective drawing moves the experience described away from the personal or individual, generalizing it into an issue that becomes common 'property'. The final product of the drawing is owned by the whole group and the group will later decide collectively which images to select from it, and how to turn what started as an essentially creative process into an educational one.

In other workshops I discussed the importance of such collectively generated visual narratives. In the creative writing workshops under discussion, however, I failed to realize the educational potential of the experience, since I used the process to stimulate creativity rather than deliberately to construct impulses for reflection and learning.

Telling The presentation of drawings generated much laughter and led to a general release of tension. More importantly, it deepened participants' understanding as it offered them a chance to ask questions. A wide range of interpretations, responses and viewpoints were introduced for discussion and the notion that some might be 'right' or 'wrong' or more or less valid was entirely absent. This openness was crucial for dialogue and provided an entry into a deeper examination of the concept of discrimination. Questions asked included: What are the power relations represented in the pictures? Who is exercising control? Who suffers? And, more generally: Where does discrimination come from? Why does it happen?

Participants then wrote individually about 'discrimination'. They could choose to do free writing or to use the drawing as a starting-point. In most cases the memory of the drawing and ensuing discussion was fresh in people's minds and writing came easily. The texts represented participants' thoughts and ideas and, when read out subsequently, were useful indicators of the general level of awareness and consciousness in the group.

> This kind of life [in the hostel] was very difficult. Because at home I live with my wife who does everything at home. But now everything changes. Because I left my family I am the only person responsible for cooking, washing my clothes and dishes and cleaning the room. After work I am tired but I have to cook for my supper. Because I don't want to cook I have to eat bread and tea.

Themba Khumalo's text is an example of writing which displays little concern for women's position beyond their traditional roles as caretakers of men. When it became obvious that he was unaware of the anger his text aroused in women participants, they challenged him. How had this experience in the hostel changed him and had he also transformed his relationship with his wife back home as a result of it? Had there been a shift in roles now that he had not only become a skilled caretaker but also had felt the pain and strain of being solely responsible for the upkeep of a home? Did he ever think, when he demanded a cooked supper after she came home from work, about how tired his wife must feel?[7]

In this case, the challenge was taken up by other course participants but it offers a clear example of the ambiguity in the role of a facilitator with 'two agendas'. As a feminist, I wanted to push the discussion towards maximum understanding of gender; as a cultural activist (and it was in this role that I had been asked to facilitate the course), my concern was primarily the production of texts. I worried that too much critical interference could freeze or silence the writer.

My intervention took the form of asking participants to compare the texts produced by two other participants. Both dealt with the rural areas. The first, written by a male, described his longing for his rural home where he held a respected position, was treated 'like a man' and enjoyed the power accorded to an important person. In the city, by contrast, his job as a labourer denied him basic dignity: he was called 'boy' and felt emasculated.

The other text, written by a woman, portrayed the countryside as a drunkards' paradise, where men come home to drink and lord it over women, only to leave them again, penniless and pregnant with another child. For her the city represented relative freedom, a place where she could find a job and enjoy the basic independence and degree of choice afforded by an income.

These two very different perspectives drew attention to contradictions which could form a framework for debate: questions of power and authority, patriarchy and dependency, constraints on the individual's freedom of choice, all operating in the context of the socio-political forces of apartheid. Again, however, I was unsure how much debate we should engage in and worried about the valuable time that should or could be spent on writing. I did not push the debate but let participants decide how far to go in their discussion. The result was another lost opportunity for my 'feminist agenda'.

Creating By this stage the threads had been spun and it was time to set up the loom and begin the weaving of stories. To facilitate the switch from an informative 'dry' text to a story, and to help participants add life, colour and sound to their thoughts and ideas, I asked them to go through a process of oral improvisations. Referring back to the drawings, participants identified individual people or groups of people who related directly to the theme of discrimination. Working in pairs or small groups, they assumed different roles and improvised a dialogue between those characters. Alternatively, participants identified a situation of dramatic conflict suggested by the drawing and enacted that conflict.

In either case, based on their experience and understanding, participants had to create the adopted roles for themselves. To guide them I restated a number of questions, such as: What power position is represented by your chosen character and what is this power based on? What kind of values and interests does the character represent? What is at stake for each of the roles? How does the character relate to others in terms of his/her class, race, gender and culture?

After lively improvisations, and without being given a chance to report back or divest themselves of the roles they had assumed, participants were asked to write the story or an aspect of the story they had just improvised. In this way, even participants who often suffered from 'writing block' had at least a starting-point from which to launch themselves and the often long stories generated at this point attested to the success of the process.

A feminist model?

What about this process could be labelled 'feminist' and on what basis could I claim that it is a model for feminist writing workshops? In order to offer some answers to these questions I will look at three aspects of the process. First, I will examine the role of the facilitator, specifically the power relations represented and played out in that role. Second, there is the issue of the format of the work: in what way is the choice of a creative writing workshop linked to feminist practice? Finally, I will examine the impulses generated by the process in terms of writing: what makes the texts feminist documents?

The role of facilitator From the outset, my position as teacher or facilitator was defined by the demands and expectations of the participants, on the one hand, and my own cultural and educational activism, on the other. Workers' willingness to participate was based on their trust that I could offer a skill which I had demonstrated, and that my actions both in and outside the workshops would not betray their cause. Included in the latter expectation was that I would refrain from imposing interpretations or topics. Further, in accord with the conditions for a creative educational interaction, initial agreements between myself and the participants about the process had to be constantly negotiated and renegotiated.

I responded to the call to act as facilitator in recognition of my privileged status as a white middle-class woman, moreover one who has reflected on her privilege sufficiently to know that the relative freedom my status affords me also demands that my actions be informed by a sense of responsibility and ethical consideration. My belief in the importance of a workers' cultural movement is a driving force in my role as woman, educator and cultural activist.

Thus, my planning was determined by participants' desire to express themselves and give voice to their narratives, not by my interests in creating pedagogy, formulating cultural policy or experimenting with feminist methodology. This seems to me a crucial point, as I made myself accountable to the learners' expressed intentions. Such a starting-point goes beyond a needs-driven curriculum or a learner-centred approach because it addresses the key area of power and control. Dismantling existing power relations, in this instance my membership of the dominant élite by virtue of being white and middle-class, is a prerequisite for a truly radical and truly feminist educational practice.

Power and empowerment In her detailed critical analysis of contending pedagogies, Jennifer Gore (1993: 120) maintains that neither feminist nor critical approaches have delivered a pedagogy that manages to go beyond its own contradictions:

> critical and feminist pedagogy discourses are grounded in conceptions of 'power-as-property' and 'power-as-dominance', while also maintaining a notion of 'power-as-productive', 'power-as-creative-energy'. Both pedagogies hold a notion of 'power as productive', allowing the reclamation of power for use by the critical or feminist teacher; power to be exercised with, rather than over the students and exercised for self and social empowerment.

Gore argues that 'power as productive' and 'power exercised with rather than over' are not exempt from repressive potential and warns of the dangers of domination inherent in the large degree of agency bestowed on the teacher or facilitator in relation to empowerment.

Ever since Freire set out to conscientize learners, the concept of empowerment has become central to progressive or popular education. However, unless it is used as a reflexive verb denoting self-empowerment, I find the term extremely problematic. Many so-called progressive educational endeavours operate with 'small group work' and 'sharing views' in a charade of power sharing. While they appear to hand over the 'talking stick' by 'allowing' a learner to 'take over' and facilitate, the process of this apparently emancipatory exercise can be every bit as regulated and controlling as 'non-progressive' education. No wonder then that Ellsworth (1992: 90), in her path-breaking article 'Working Through the Repressive Myths of Critical Pedagogy', asked: 'Why doesn't this feel empowering?'

The notion of empowerment implies both an agent and a desired state or condition, and this necessarily throws up considerations of the ethics of educators. In many educational endeavours the form the desired 'empowered' state might take remains unclear and one might ask whether there can ever be a general vision of 'empowered' learners. Unless power is defined in terms of being able to do something fairly specific as a result of learning, empowerment remains a popular slogan but not an achievable or, indeed, desirable aim of teaching. 'I taught them but they didn't learn' easily becomes 'I empowered them but they didn't get empowered'.

The suggestion from MacLaren and Da Silva (1993: 51) quoted below provides an example of the contradictory way in which pedagogues hold on to a position of power while professing to do the reverse. It seems to me that MacLaren and Da Silva are extraordinarily arrogant when they advise:

> So that critical pedagogy does not fall prey to forms of evangelising or enunciating its call for liberation as if it were the sole theoretical representative

of the oppressed, teachers should give the oppressed a preferential option for developing their own language of analysis as a means of interrogating the conditions of their own oppression.

Participants in the culture course described in this chapter possessed a well-developed sense of the conditions of their oppression. They did not wait for me as the teacher to 'allow' them to make choices. Rather they asserted clearly what they wished to discuss and how they wanted to proceed. Had I tried to impose subject matter or a process disagreeable to them, silence would have been a potent weapon: refusal to participate in a dialogue would have conveyed a clear message as to 'preferential option'. The nature of true dialogue and democratic interaction is that it is built on the confidence that I, as an educator, will not abuse the trust invested in me by violating learners' dignity. This is the foundation for ethical practice. All participants in a creative or educational encounter infuse a sense of self into the process. It is essential to understand and respect this if there is to be a shift in the relations of power and an educator's ethical practice. Although the participants in the writing workshops came to learn, they came with the clear understanding that they would be productive. They did not attend as passive recipients waiting to have learning bestowed on them, or to be 'empowered'. They came bearing their dignity as story-tellers and creative people, seeking to learn not as a result of any transfer of knowledge or skills, but through action and interaction with each other and with me as the educator.

They also had an astute sense of their own power in terms of their contribution to or withdrawal from production as a labour force. From the outset this precluded any notion of 'empowerment' as a handing over of power. Their demand was to learn more about writing and to improve their skills in the art of poetic composition. They expected to be en-abled, not as disabled or un-able people but rather as people who had managed to retain their valuable creative potential despite all the obstacles and destructive forces thrown in their way.

Power is not a commodity which can be traded. It is not something owned but rather something exercised in action. As an educator I am able to change relationships of power and control by changing my actions and modes of interaction. When the space and opportunities are created for learners to exercise their power as creative beings, as writers or thinkers or people who cope against incredible odds, they take charge and assume control of the process.

What, then, was my role as facilitator or educator? What decisions did I make in order to attempt to escape entrenched power relations?

I began with a thorough investigation of my own practice, assumptions and motives. I realized that I did not come to the process with an intention to conscientize, empower or emancipate. I reasserted my belief that participants are able to be in control but are in need of encouragement and a 'prod' to stretch their abilities beyond the first limitations. I decided that feminist/critical education practice involves an ethical choice to be accountable to participants in terms of subject matter, structure and mode of interaction.

However, the preceding description of the writing workshops suggests a fairly rigid succession of activities and the directive hand of an educator with a clear sense of purpose. How can I then claim to have escaped from the dominant power structures of teacher and learner? In the writing classes there were four main elements which helped to challenge orthodox power relations. These were the choice of subject matter; the mode of interaction, including considerations of language; the overall design of activities and exercises; and, finally, the negotiated process. All these must be considered in the context of the course as a whole. To begin with, the framework of the course was co-operative rather than competitive. In most cases participants had gone through exercises in listening and group participation in previous sessions.

In the design of the workshop, domination is averted through mixing varying co-operative and collective work with individual work. I took care to set up activities which established a common experience in the 'classroom'. For example, the drawing process ensures that no one is advantanged, since all go through the process together, accessing different experiences which are rooted in the common ground of their socio-economic condition. The subjective is mediated through contesting visions. Both individual experience and experience held in common find expression through collective action in images of a common condition.

In terms of power, this process favours women because socialization has made it easier for them than for men to speak about and share personal experiences and the emotions they generate. However, this is balanced by the sense of authority socialization confers on men when they speak, particularly if they have strong roots in rural areas where wives are expected to listen, not talk. Another important aspect of the workshop process is that when participants read their own written texts, and during discussion, any viewpoint presented is experienced as only one of many possible perspectives. There are many ways of looking at the world and constructing meaning, and each is valid for the particular speaker or writer. Alternative views are not dismissed or even attacked but given equal time and hearing. Having created a platform for open debate, all participants critique the offering, rather than the originator of the idea.

The strength of this openness is its encouragement of debate and the development of argument and debating skills. Its weakness is that tolerance of others' views can easily be perceived as an attitude of 'anything goes'. Viewpoints such as Khumalo's, quoted earlier, are not challenged enough and thus potential growth of understanding and even attitude changes are not realized. At times, also, openness can be experienced as a lack of direction and result in a sense of frustration arising from a perceived failure to improve. This tension in relation to openness is one that I have been unable to resolve successfully.

Far less problematic as an equalizing strategy, and also one that encourages shared leadership, is variation in type of activity. Different people favour different activities, depending on which learning style they feel most comfortable with. Variety creates a chance for different participants to move into the foreground. For example, the drawing exercise might favour a reticent speaker who finds it difficult to insert herself into a discussion. On the other hand, a 'high talker' confident in debates might step back and let others take the lead in the drawing process. In either case I, as the educator, can withdraw as other participants assume the leadership role and control.

Having set up the process, I was functional in my responses rather than instrumental to the discourse. I set up activities and kept track of the time, I steered participants through or around obstacles, I asked probing questions which led to deepened exploration of issues. However, unless specifically asked to, I did not offer viewpoints or opinions and for a lot of the time I remained on the outside of the process. This was made more obvious by repeated switches in language from English to Zulu, English being the medium of instruction but rarely the medium of discussion.

This stance was all the more crucial since white domination in South Africa has colonized the definition of what is mainstream art and literature, what is culture as opposed to 'indigenous craft'. If the margins are to be shifted and writing is to be a way of challenging the dominant culture, it is necessary that I, as a white middle-class educator, should step back and listen, rather than hold forth.

The discrimination workshops generated less writing around issues of gender than questions of race and class. Can this be taken as proof of my non-interference, evidence that participants were free to focus on their own concerns rather than being steered in a particular (gender) direction by my intervention?

bell hooks (1993: 150) claims that a lot of feminist books alienate black women who do not recognize themselves in the texts:

Since so many of the early feminist books really reflected a certain type of white bourgeois sensibility, this work did not touch many black women deeply, not because we did not recognize the common experiences shared but because those commonalities were mediated by profound differences in our realities created by the politics of race and class.

The texts created during the writing workshops support this position. In the initial texts, challenges to patriarchal practices as major problems in women's lives featured strongly, as demonstrated by the opening quote from Mahlaba. In the stories composed during the final phase of the process, other relations assumed greater prominence. For women participants, experiences of racial discrimination dominated; male writers reflected particularly incidents of class oppression.

A story written by Mahlaba describes a black woman going from house to house in search of a job as a domestic worker. She is attacked by a dog. The white owner of the dog watches and laughs: 'I thought that if my skin was white that woman would have helped me and saved me from the dog biting me ... Since that day I have not wanted to look for a job in a white woman's house.'

Similarly, Marjory Njeje's story describes a domestic worker being stripped of her dignity by her employer: 'The white woman shouted: "Stupid! Rubbish! Go home and take your clothes. Your job is finished and your salary is here on the floor. You dropped my basket!"'

In the story written by Ntombiyenkosi Shinga (1992), a pregnant black woman with a baby on her back and a heavy load on her head is walking with her employer.

> As they were walking they talked and I heard the pregnant woman calling the Indian woman 'Mrs'. I became very angry and kept on thinking about that incident in which a black woman called an Indian woman 'Mrs'. The other racial groups are living a good kind of life because they have everything they need for their daily lives, while we blacks are deprived of many things. We are very poor. Our houses are not in good condition and when it rains they fall down because they are built of mud. We do not have cars, we have to rely on buses and trains to commute to and from work. African women are most exploited.

These texts are examples of the treatment meted out to African women by women of other race groups. There is no common experience for women of different races as they define themselves in terms of their racial identity, not their gender. For both men and women writers in the workshop, the differences created by the politics of race and class appeared greater than those created between men and women by the politics of gender.

Feminist pedagogy Weiler (1988: 58) postulates three essential characteristics of feminist methodology, all of which reflect De Beauvoir's
(1972) insight that women's starting-point is their own position in society.

> First, feminist researchers begin their investigation of the social world from
> a grounded position in their own subjective oppression ... Secondly, feminist
> research is characterised by an emphasis on lived experience and the signi-
> ficance of everyday life ... Thirdly, feminist research is politically committed.
> In rejecting the possibility of value-free research, feminists instead assert
> their commitment to changing the position of women and therefore to
> changing society.

Participants in the writing workshops clearly fulfilled the first two
conditions. It remains to be asked whether any political commitment
was manifested in their participation in the workshops, in the act of
writing itself and in their stories. Finally, was there an expressed intention to change the world?

At their best, the texts which arose out of the workshops do offer
suggestions for a transformed society. For example, in Mahlaba's story
a gardener who witnesses the attack by the dog is described as wanting
to help but feeling unable to do so for fear of dismissal. The story ends
on a note of solidarity: a domestic worker helps the injured woman,
giving her a bandage and food, and her mother-in-law offers herbal
remedies for healing.

Acts of solidarity between women of the same race and class are a
common feature of Mahlaba's writing, illustrating her critique of a
feminist position defined outside the forces of class and race. She is also
critical of liberal white and Asian women who proclaim that 'we are all
the same' in our oppression as women. The enemy is not only the
system of patriarchy. The painful experiences described by Mahlaba
and other participants in the workshops strip away the different layers
of oppression and reveal how they support one another in their interrelationship. Their message is that male domination must be seen in the
context of capitalism, racist divisions and specific cultural traditions.

However, Mahlaba's stories go beyond critique to offer concrete
suggestions for both personal behaviour and strategic action. Her view
is that women and men should treat each other with compassion and
regard for each other's dignity, standing together in solidarity and working together for social change through such structures as trade unions.

The characters in her stories suggest through their actions that
helping each other, sharing available resources, and avoiding personal
gain that depends on detriment to others, are the kind of values which
should inform our behaviour. They also affirm the view that there should

not be a gap between belief and action, and that the values we hold should be realized in our practical daily lives.

Mahlaba's writing, as much as her characters, faces with courage Freire's challenge to the committed educator in relation to the poor and oppressed:

> Authentic help means that all who are involved help each other mutually, growing together in the common effort to understand the reality which they seek to transform. Only through such praxis – in which those who can help and those who are being helped help each other simultaneously – can the act of helping become free from the distortion in which the helper dominates the helped. (hooks, 1993: 51)

A feminist activity? Giroux (1992: 101) claims that critical pedagogy 'excavates, affirms and interrogates the histories, memories, and stories of the devalued others who have been marginalized from the official discourse. It attempts to recover and mediate those knowledge forms and social practices that have been displaced to the edge of the discourse of power.' In the writing workshops described in this chapter, the 'devalued others' take over the tools and do the excavating, affirming and interrogating of their own histories, the narratives which they, as the oppressed, know best. The marginalized reclaim the centre and speak up, choosing for themselves on what to focus. Writing, and seeing the writing published and read by others, is a way of placing oneself in the world, asserting the reality of one's experience. It is a way of lending weight to the challenge of existing narratives by counter-memory. At the same time, the process of talking about what hurts is often a way of healing.

The 'creaking of the Word' is thus an act of protest and challenge. As Eduardo Galeano (1988: 119) puts it:

> To awaken consciousness, to reveal reality – can literature claim a better function in these times and in these lands of ours? We are what we do, especially what we do to change what we are: our identity resides in action and in struggle. Therefore, the revelation of what we are implies the denunciation of those who stop us from being what we can become. In defining ourselves our point of departure is challenge, and struggle against obstacles.

The stories produced in the workshops reveal the writers' own lived experience as the foundation for their social vision, in relation to the past, the present and the future. Writing is more than a process of articulating a counter-memory or a viewpoint from the alternative perspective of a worker or a woman. It is an act of resistance and defiance, a refusal to be relegated to the margins, a process of claiming and occupying a space at the centre, which, in this instance, has been mainly and in the first place white and middle class, and then male. The 'creaking of the Word' is a combination of education and work. The Dogon's simultaneous spinning and story-telling finds its counterpart in the construction of narratives about working lives.

Workshops such as those described here carry the seed of feminist pedagogy because they allow learners to take control of their 'weaving of words' and to develop their skills and powers as story-tellers. As creative producers they assemble their experiences and spin them into tales, and this process of making meaning, of producing knowledge, is essentially political. Importantly, also, the process should lead to the imagining of alternatives, so that readers of the stories are able to catch the impulses that are challenges for social transformation.

The workshops provide the conditions in which participants can critically reflect on their experiences and beliefs, strip away the layers of different forms of oppression, understand their interrelationship in the wider context of social forces, and share that new-found meaning through the act of writing.

Like literacy itself, writing links hope to possibility. If, as I have argued, the workshop methodology stimulates a process through which participants interrogate, destabilize and disorganize dominant strategies of power, and suggest, through the act of writing and in their stories, an alternative form of social relations, then these workshops qualify as a feminist activity and I am justified in my assertion that they offer a feminist model.

Notes

1. The development of the Durban Workers' Cultural Local is recorded in detail by Von Kotze (1988) while the work of Orkin (1991) contains many references to the development of working-class culture.

2. The Sarmcol workers' collective was formed in response to a strike situation in which over 1,000 workers were dismissed. Members of the CWLP assisted an elected group from the collective with the making and production of a play called *The Long March*, which tells the story of their strike. The play toured all over South Africa and parts of Europe to raise funds for the strikers and lobby support for their struggle. Another play, *Bambatha's Children*, was workshopped in 1988 and deals with events in the community leading up to the strike, highlighting relevant lessons from the Bambatha Rebellion of 1906. *Comments* (1991) dealt with the return of political exiles to a volatile situation and *Mbube* (1992) focused on the migrant labour system and the hostels at the centre of much current political violence.

3. The overall course curriculum was developed by a team made up of union officials, workers and cultural activists. It ran on Saturdays, over two years, for workers from all over KwaZulu/Natal. The creative writing component of the course was developed and run by Nise Malange, Zaida Harneker and myself. It usually consisted of ten sessions. Although the course has been suspended as a result of a loss of funding, creative writing continues informally, with a number of former students/participants meeting occasionally to share and discuss their texts.

4. *Umkhumulansika: The Destruction of the Pillars of the Home*, published by Working Life Publications, Durban, in 1992, is a compilation of narratives, written, edited and reworked during the writing workshops. In some cases, stories and dialogues written by different people were combined into one narrative, offering a collective experience in both production of a story and the product itself. One such example is 'Women Coming from the Market', a story written by a collective of women workers and published in *Umkhumulansika*.

5. Some of the subheadings in this chapter have been taken from Lippard (1990). An inspired book on how to learn from multi-cultural perspectives, it illustrates how visual artists have attempted to insert themselves into the mainstream of American culture. Gerunds are chosen because they are the grammatical form of process. As such they are an appropriate way of labelling something that is constantly in a state of flux, of being made.

6. A notable account is a paper by Louise Hall (1991) presented to the 'Women and Gender in Southern Africa Conference' held in Durban in 1991. Hall conducts development workshops with rural people in the Pietermaritzburg region of KwaZulu/Natal.

7. Another interesting debate arose later when course participants had to select texts for publication as part of *Umkhumulansika*. Should a text like Khumalo's be published? Would it reinforce sexist attitudes? How did Khumalo himself feel about his (by then revised) views being made public? Should he falsify his text, pretend a great conversion had occurred, and thereby risk alienating (male) readers while presenting a positive role model?

Bibliography

De Beauvoir, S. (1972) *The Second Sex*, Penguin, London.

Ellsworth, E. (1992) 'Why Doesn't This Feel Empowering? Working Through the Repressive Myths of Critical Pedagogy', in Luke, C. and Gore, J. (eds), *Feminisms and Critical Pedagogy*, Routledge, New York.

Galeano, E. (1988) 'In Defence of the Word', in Simonson, R. and Walker, S. (eds), *The Graywolf Annual Five: Multi-Cultural Literacy*, Graywolf Press, Minnesota.

Giroux, H. (1992) *Border Crossings: Cultural Workers and the Politics of Education*, Routledge, New York.

Gore, J. (1993) *The Struggle for Pedagogies: Critical and Feminist Discourses as Regimes of Truth*, Routledge, New York.

Hall, L. (1991) 'The Use of Drawing in the Development of a Gender-sensitive Participatory Training Methodology in the Natal/KwaZulu Area', paper presented at the conference on 'Women and Gender in Southern Africa', Durban.

hooks, b. (1993) 'Speaking about Paulo Freire: The Man, His Work', in McLaren, P. and Leonard, P. (eds), op. cit.

Illich, I. and Sanders, B. (1989) *ABC: The Alphabetization of the Popular Mind*, Vintage Books, New York.

Lippard, L. (1990) *Mixed Blessings: New Art in Multi-cultural America*, Pantheon Books, New York,

MacLaren, P. and Da Silva, T. (1993) 'Decentering Pedagogy: Critical Literacy, Resistance and the Politics of Memory', in McLaren, P. and Leonard, P. (eds), *Paulo Freire: A Critical Encounter*, Routledge, New York.

Mahlaba, B. (1992) 'Women', 'Discrimination' and 'A Worried Woman', in *Umkhumulansika: The Destruction of the Pillars of the Home*, Culture and Working Life Publications, Durban.

Orkin, M. (1991) *Drama and the South African Stage*, Wits University Press, Johannesburg.

Shinga, N. (1992) 'African Women are Most Exploited', in *Umkhumulansika: The Destruction of the Pillars of the Home*, Working Life Publications, Durban.

Shor, I. (1980) *Critical Teaching and Everyday Life*, University of Chicago Press, Chicago.

Von Kotze, A. (1988) *Organise and Act: The Natal Workers' Theatre Movement*, Culture and Working Life Publications, Durban.

Walters, S. (1991) 'Her Words on His Lips: Gender and Popular Education in South Africa', paper presented to the conference on 'Women and Gender in Southern Africa', Durban.

Weiler, K. (1988) *Women Teaching for Change: Gender, Class and Power*, Bergin and Garvey, MA.

9

Women learning in Appalachian grassroots organizations

BETH BINGMAN

Popular education is not widely known or discussed in the United States. Paulo Freire's ideas are known in (some) academic circles and in a few groups working for social change but, by and large, they have had little impact. Much of the conversation about participatory learning takes place in business circles and it refers to a kind of surface participation rather than a real sharing of power.

However, many grassroots groups in communities, unions and environmental struggles are practising popular education, although they might not know the term. The learning processes which take place in these groups are not called popular education, nor are they necessarily thought of as education; they are simply a part of what the groups do and how they operate as they work to build democratic organizations and initiate change. But this work leads to learning for the people involved and, to my mind, this is popular education in action.

A woman who is an active member of a grassroots organization running a community centre puts it like this: 'I finished school and I've taken night classes and I've been here and there, but actually the best education I've had was when I came to this centre. Communication with these people is the best education there is.' A fellow activist describes her experience as being one of having knowledge in her head 'but no place to express it' until she 'started getting involved in the community and with women'. Another remarks: 'My life is a complete turn-around from what it was before. I learned things I never thought I would ever learn. It really made a difference in my life. It is a completely different world.'

All three speakers belong to grassroots organizations which operate community centres in Appalachia, a mountainous rural area in the south-eastern part of the United States. This chapter is based on work I have done with women in these organizations for over a decade as a researcher, an educator and a community member. It describes the ways in which the women involved in these organizations learn and change, coming together to meet their own and community needs and creating a rich learning site for themselves in the process.

Working to survive

The Appalachian coalfields, like many mineral-rich regions of the world, have been a source of tremendous wealth which has gone primarily to owners outside the region. Outside ownership was largely the result of developments in the last decades of the nineteenth century, which saw mineral rights sold off by local landowners who had no conception of their value. In consequence, many local families moved off their small mountain farms into mining villages owned by the coal companies, and the men and boys went to work in the mines. When the mines were mechanized in the 1950s, nearly a million people left Appalachia to seek work in the industrial cities of the northern United States. Many families returned in the 1970s when coal-mining boomed and the region enjoyed a period of relative prosperity. But a new wave of mechanization began towards the end of the 1980s, resulting in high unemployment (25 per cent in some areas) and families were again forced to leave in search of work. At the same time, Appalachia has been targeted as a site for toxic waste dumps and prisons.

But while the people of the coal counties have been economically impoverished, they have maintained a rich heritage. Despite the mining industry's ravaging of the environment, the region retains much of its natural beauty. The hills are forested; at least some of the major rivers remain relatively unpolluted; the mountains are experienced as a refuge rather than as a barrier. The region has a rich musical tradition and traditional crafts such as quilting, wood carving, gardening and food preserving are still part of many people's everyday lives. Appalachia is home, a place few want to leave.

This combination of poverty and rootedness is probably why people in communities across the region have come together to try to confront the problems they face. They oppose toxic waste dumps. They fight for clean water. In many communities they have established community development organizations whose members operate community centres and try through various projects to meet the needs of local people.

The community centres are run democratically with small part-time staffs. Most of the work is done by volunteers from the community, mostly women. Their projects include pre-schools, housing rehabilitation work undertaken by college and church volunteers, food distribution programmes, used clothing sales and Christmas programmes for children. The centres are the sites for adult education classes, dances, community meetings and private parties. Centre members are often active in attempts to bring about changes in their communities, for example, confronting local authorities about water quality or working to develop community businesses. Two of these centres are described below.

The Lee City Community Center is an old store building in the middle of town. The space has been painted and equipped with second-hand furniture, including tables and chairs for adult education and community college classes, some comfortable lounge chairs and shelves for books. A painted mural of mountains decorates one wall and there is a small kitchen at the back. A new family literacy programme recently added eight computers to the centre's facilities.

A room for selling used clothing donated by churches from beyond the mountains has been walled off from the main room. Proceeds from the clothing sales are used for the centre's operating expenses, which run to approximately 150 dollars a month for lights, water, telephone and janitors. An additional source of income is rent charged for some community functions: five dollars for private parties and fifteen for fund-raising events. An environmental group and groups of senior citizens are among those who use the centre for meetings and various other functions.

The staff who maintain the building and conduct clothing sales and other events are all volunteers. The part-time adult education teacher, who is an active member of the centre board, is paid by the county schools. She also serves as the town manager.

The Lee City Community Center is thus, in many ways, the hub of both social and community development activities in the town. It seems to be a point of entry for people needing assistance of various kinds: food, clothing, emergency help, education. People who come for help often stay to help.

A similar dynamic operates in the Two Sisters Community Center in Hamilton County, an extremely poor and isolated region of rugged terrain, ribbed by long ridges and narrow valleys. More than half of the land is owned by the outside coal corporations which dominate the economy. Official unemployment is over 15 per cent, reduced from the 1985 level of 20.2 per cent by the number of people who have left in search of work. There are only a few miles of four-lane highway in the county, which has a total population of 17,620 people. The county seat and largest town has a population of 1,542.

The Two Sisters Community Center is in a large one-storey building squeezed between the road and the river. There is enough room in front of it to park a row of cars; at the back a stretch of weeds leads down to the river bank. A glass front door opens into a large, light-filled room with a tile floor and walls covered with photographs documenting centre activities. The largest photographs are of the two women after whom the centre is named, a missionary who came to the area in 1915 and a woman miner who was active in the community before she was killed in a mine explosion. Handwritten signs encourage good behaviour and announce forthcoming events.

The Walker River Community Development Commission operates its programmes from the centre, which is the location for many other activities. Some are private functions such as parties for which the building is rented; some are special events sponsored by the centre, for example, a vigil held on the eve of the war in the Persian Gulf, or an initiative of many months which provided meals to striking miners.

However, most of the activities are part of the development commission's ongoing efforts to meet the needs of the people in the community and include a food programme, a pre-school, aerobics classes, Saturday dances and educational/volunteer activities for groups of college students. Two women work part-time as staff members, supported by many volunteers.

Community centre work

These are community organizations, not women's organizations, but most of the active members and volunteers are women and women are usually the leaders. Men help with particular projects and may be board members but are normally not very active in day-to-day activities. Traditionally, men and women have tended to work separately in Appalachia, and this pattern seems to continue in the grassroots organizations under discussion. At least to some extent, it may also be described in terms of what Gilligan (1982) calls women's ethic of care, with women extending a care-giving role into their communities.

The initial reasons for their involvement in community centre work vary. Many first approach community organizations in hopes of assistance with individual personal needs. For example, a woman I will call Elaine had just left an abusive husband and came to the centre looking for clothing for their children. She started sitting in on adult education classes, persisted and went on to become a tutor.

Others stayed on as volunteer workers at community centres after being assigned a stint as summer youth workers, or volunteered after their children left home to find work. Several became active members after doing support work at the centre for striking miners. One woman became involved after her father and brother were killed in the mines. Backed by other women at the centre, she then encouraged her daughter, who was in an abusive marriage, to volunteer for work at the centre.

Interestingly, none of these women spoke of working for change or even wanting to help the community when they talked about why they initially became involved in the community centres. However, while some particular individual need was often what initiated involvement, the women stayed on to work for the community. Some volunteer nearly every day. Others work only a few hours a week.

Much of the ongoing work involves maintenance of the community centres. The buildings, often old stores, are cleaned, painted, kept pleasant and welcoming. There is also organizational maintenance: serving on various committees and the board of directors, raising funds, distributing information through mailings or posters, keeping membership records up to date.

Then there are the programmes run by each centre. Some operate pre-school programmes for young children. Many sell used clothing. Most provide emergency assistance to families in need and run food programmes. The centres also offer a variety of recreational activities such as dances, music and children's programmes. All these projects are organized and carried out by volunteers, sometimes with a paid person responsible for pre-school or day-care programmes. Centres also have special projects, ranging from serving dinners for visitors to regular forums which explore issues of concern to the community.

A third kind of activity undertaken in the community centres is what I call support work, although the women do not refer to it as work and it is not an organized activity. They talk about 'being there for people'. The centres are often places where people with problems, particularly women, come for help. What they find is other women, often from situations similar to their own, who are willing to listen. The result is that communities of support are built and maintained, with listening often the key, as one volunteer observed:

> Now I'm running into people who have the same kind of problems I did. And sometimes there's no easy answers. I don't care who you are and what you've been through, there's no easy answers. Sometimes the only thing you can do is just listen. And so I've learned, I just sit and listen.

Another woman described this work of 'being there' in these terms:

> Working in the community centre, you get to talk to a lot of people. You get to find out what they're going through and how they feel. And it's a really big help. I mean, you know, like someone could come in, and it's just like when I was going through my divorce: there was a lady come in here and she had just been through a divorce and we got talking and it helped a lot. I mean, people around here are helpful, as far as that goes.

Learning from working

Many of the women I interviewed had taken part in some form of formal adult education, usually in a secondary certificate programme or a community college. Those who had taken courses offered at a community centre, instead of at a school or college, had usually had positive experiences and talked about learning more than mere course content.

Important to them was being in classes with other women like themselves and feeling their support. Moreover, classes were offered in a familiar setting and community centre people were available to act as advocates with formal institutions if this was necessary. In this kind of milieu, taking classes was experienced as empowering, as was getting out of their homes and being recognized as learners. However, women whose adult education experience had taken place in more traditional, structured settings tended to feel that they had not gained much beyond access to skills which they hoped would improve their employment prospects.

When the women talked about what they had learned from working in and being involved in the community centres, they all talked about learning and changing in a variety of ways. In essence, they reported learning new skills and gaining a new sense of themselves and what they might do in their lives.

The skills they learned were those needed to do the work of the centre. Among the specific skills women mentioned learning were: how to draft and send out fund-raising letters and proposals; how to set up an agenda; how to arrange clothing sales and set prices according to what people can pay; and how to keep financial records. These were skills they learned on the job. As one woman put it: 'We train ourselves, we train our self. We have to.'

Many also also spoke of particular 'people skills' they had acquired. They talked of learning how to listen and how to communicate from other people in the centre. Two women mentioned training as adult literacy tutors after becoming involved in community centre work. Another described learning from her participation in a prejudice workshop that was part of a regional conference she attended. She and several other women talked about learning how to work and to be with people very different from themselves, often people in relation to whom they had entertained prejudices or stereotyped ideas. One remarked:

> When I first started, I don't think I'd ever seen myself working with a Catholic sister. And it blew my mind, because I'd always thought 'you don't mess with them people and them weird ideas'. I guess it was a stereotype, too, because I think you'll run into that in certain areas.

Another spoke about learning to abandon her mistrust of urban sophisticates: 'These big city people will come in here. I don't pay no attention to it. I really don't pay no attention to it no more. But I used to think it was funny, you know.'

But, while all the women reported that working in community centres had enabled them to learn new skills, to find support and friendship and to increase their knowledge of other people, their fairly unanimous feeling was that the most important learning and change they had experienced was in relation to their sense of themselves and their own abilities. All spoke of feeling stronger and more confident. Some examples will illustrate the point:

> It took me the longest time to figure out that I was smart. I was volunteering and I was helping a lady. I was tutoring her in second-year college algebra. And I thought to myself, 'Hey! I'm smart! If I can do this, then I'm an intelligent lady.'

> When I worked it out and no one else could, I thought, 'I'm not stupid'. And it's helped me ever since then. It made me realize that I wasn't stupid, that I could be taught. I could learn. And from then on I've just been learning as much as I have been able to learn.

> I guess the community centre sort of gave me my confidence back. The ladies up here did. And they started getting me out more and involving me in more activities and, before I knew it, I was back to the way I used to be. So I got all my confidence back and it's helped. I do a lot more here than I've done in a long time.

> Working at the centre was something that really brought me out and made me know that I was an individual, that I could say what I felt like saying and that I could do things that I had never felt like I could do before. It made me realize that I didn't have to depend on anybody else, that I was my own person.

An aspect of this growth in confidence mentioned by many women was the recovery of their own voices. One woman described working at the community centre as the first time she had really moved out of herself and talked to others: 'I guess they're the ones got me started out not being so bashful talking to people. So it's helped a lot because I was always a real shy person.' Another formerly 'shy' woman put it like this: 'Oh, yeah, I talk more. Now I can get out and talk to everybody. I feel like I growed up a lot working up here. And I can communicate better with people. I can stand on my own.'

While none of the women mentioned a commitment to social change as a reason for getting involved in community centres, it is significant that the development of this kind of activist mind-set was mentioned by some as one of the lessons they had learned from the work, and also a reason for their continuing involvement. Again, a typical comment will make the point:

> Well, the thing is, you have to realize what I came out of. When I come over here first, everything was just focused on me and my needs. And that took, like two years, you know, before I focused a little bit beyond that. Then I decided what I wanted to do and how I would accomplish it. But all of us work together in it and we want to see the community centre, well, we'd like to see it financially successful, but we want more to see it people successful. We want to see people's lives changed, improvement in their lives. We want to see our people have better lives.

For some of the women, being active in community groups is important as a way to deal with gender issues in their lives. This is particularly true for women who have been or are in difficult marriages. They are supported by friends and colleagues at the centre as they question or leave their marriages. They also come to new conceptions of who they are and might be. As one woman put it:

> They all talked to me and they treated me like an adult, not a little kid, which was what my husband was treating me as. I didn't go out of the house and didn't need to read books, didn't need to learn, didn't need to get out and do anything. I was supposed to stay at home while he ran around. Well, the ladies up here showed me that was wrong.

Community work as popular education

Several factors contribute to making these Appalachian community centres rich learning environments for women, and they impact on both the ongoing informal learning that takes place as women do the work of the organizations, and the more formal classes held at the centres.

A critical factor is the quality of the organizational leadership. The women who are leaders are important for their work in keeping the centres running. But they are also respected for their personal qualities, their encouragement of others, their honesty and their commitment to the work of the organizations. A mentoring role also seems an important aspect of leadership, as this comment demonstrates:

> I've learned a lot from her. I've learned how to communicate from her. I've learned that, I guess there were times that I didn't think I could do anything and she'd say, 'You can do it girl! Go on for it!' And it just seems like, because she said it, I believed it, and was actually able to do it.

Another important element which contributes to the creation of a learning environment is the fact that the development of leadership is an organizational value. There is a commitment to developing leadership, and people are encouraged to take initiative. One of the women talked about this in terms of a heritage that is passed on from person to person:

> I try to put as much responsibility on them as they can take. Because I believe that to get into something, to be a leader in it, you have to be involved in it. You can't do it from afar off. And sometimes, when you are doing something for your community, your problems won't seem as big to you.

A third factor that facilitates learning experiences is that community centres function to connect local residents with people from outside. The centres are indigenous grassroots organizations which take their form from the culture and needs of the communities in which they are based. But the access to outside people and organizations which they facilitate serves to extend skills, provide stimulation and add new ideas and perspectives on both individual and community levels. As one woman noted of this connection with the wider world:

> It's very important because they teach us how to write proposals and stuff. I see it like, a few years back we would not have known how to do that. We would not have been able to get through it. But she had the know-how and stuff and they help out with it. And any other problem that might arise, they seem to be able to help us work through it.

Important also is a work style in the centres based on team-work. Most work is done by informal teams and, while some people may have assigned tasks, more often than not such assignments are given to learners rather than to 'experts'. As one woman noted:

> There's no fussing or fighting in it. You know, well, we'll fuss and fight about normal stuff but, like, to get this place worked up like it is, we worked together to do it. There wasn't no 'Well, you do this,' or 'I'm too good to do that,' or not wanting to do things.

Also useful to the whole question of learning environments is the fact that the centres have a process for dealing with conflict. While this tends to be informal, like so much else in these organizations, it is clear that members have taken time to plan and establish processes for handling problems between people, who, in addition, seem to be willing to lose on occasion and still continue to work with the organization.

Not unimportant, either, is the fact that families and children are involved and supported by the centres. They are not simply places of work but also social centres where friends meet and families are welcome. Christmas parties, Thanksgiving dinner and dances are events that people attend for fun as well as to work. Teenaged children are involved and advice and help with caring for children is part of what is on offer.

Perhaps the most important factor in making the centres environments of learning and change is the support and friendship that the women provide to each other. Everyone interviewed for this study talked about this support and how crucial it was for them to feel encouraged to be active, to speak out and to change. This was a typical comment:

> When I got in the community centre, I figured everybody was out for their own good, and what did they want from me? It took time to understand that they did want something from me, but it wasn't bad. They wanted me to be the best that I could be, and it took me a long time to figure that out. And so, with each person that I met in here, it was the same attitude, the same goal, like, from all the people. They wanted me to be the best that I could be. And, little by little, I think I'm being the best that I can be.

Finally, although it was not specifically identified by the women, I believe that the democratic structure of the organizations plays a vital role in creating an environment conducive to learning, growth and change. All the women involved in each centre have a voice in what happens and exercise some shared power. This experience has contributed to their sense of their own capacity to make a difference. As Belenky et al. (1986: 229) note in a different context, women will be assisted in regaining their own voices if educators

> emphasize connection over separation, understanding and acceptance over assessment, and collaboration over debate; if they accord respect to and allow time for the knowledge that emerges from firsthand experience; if, instead of imposing their own expectations and arbitrary requirements, they encourage students to evolve their own patterns of work based on the problems they are pursuing.

This kind of supportive, collaborative learning environment is found in Appalachian community centres. It is an environment that has much in common with consciousness-raising, which begins with personal experience, values collaborative discussion in small groups, and assumes political commitment (hooks, 1989; Hart, 1990; Weiler, 1991; Lather, 1991). It also has similarities to the feminist pedagogy described by Hayes (1989) and Caffarella (1992), which emphasizes democratic and collaborative classrooms and the importance of relationship in women's lives. Finally, the milieu of the community centres exhibits many of the characteristics of popular education, listed by Arnold and Burke (1983: 9) as follows:

— The starting-point is the concrete experience of the learner
— Everyone teaches; everyone learns
— [It] involves a high level of participation
— [It] leads to action for change
— [It] is a collective effort, focusing on group rather than individual solutions to problems
— [It] stresses the creation of new knowledge rather than the passing on of existing knowledge
— The process is ongoing – any time, place or age
— And it's fun!

The women in Appalachian community centres come together to try to bring about changes in their own lives, the lives of their families and the lives of their communities. As they take on these challenges, they become popular educators for each other. However, it is probably true that a more conscious and deliberate use of popular education methods would deepen and augment the processes of individual and community learning that are already under way in the community centres. At the same time it must be said that not all community centres in Appalachia function with the same degree of success in this regard. For instance, the leadership is quite centralized in some organizations where women who have achieved a measure of influence and power, perhaps for the first time in their lives, have found it difficult to share power. This tendency has been aggravated by certain academics and local media who have constructed particularly active or outspoken women as 'stars'.

Similarly, while there is a strong commitment to democratic process in most of the organizations, they are hampered by limited access to models and information on how to build and maintain democratic organizations. So, also, while classes held in community centres are conducted in a supportive atmosphere, they tend to conform to the traditional teacher-led model. The legacies of poverty and seriously constrained resources are other difficulties impacting on the work of both organizations and the individuals involved. Community centres are rarely able to support full-time staff and volunteers are continually beset by problems such as poor health, limited access to transport and family crises.

The ideas and methodologies of popular education clearly cannot overcome all these difficulties but one community centre has made a deliberate attempt to use participatory methods to analyse problems and develop solutions, with good results. Some centres have examined the effects of racism and sexism in their organizations, while others are working to change the way classes are conducted by experimenting with more learner-centred popular approaches, and building a curriculum around issues important to the community. Participatory research has been tried in some communities. However, these efforts have been fragmented and there is no overall strategy for change either within organizations or between and among them.

There is a definite need for co-operation within and between these organizations and progressive adult educators so that the strengths and processes developed by women in community centres can be documented and built on. The relevance of these processes to both formal education programmes for women and informal learning is clear. This kind of approach to education has immense potential not only for helping women to gain skills but also for enabling them to make significant changes to their own lives and the life of their communities.

Bibliography

Arnold, B. and Burke, B. (1983) *A Popular Education Handbook*, Ontario Institute for Studies in Education, Toronto.

Belenky, M. et al., (1986) *Women's Ways of Knowing: The Development of Self, Voice and Mind*, Basic Books, New York.

Caffarella, R. S. (1992) *Psychosocial Development of Women*, ERIC Clearing-house on Adult, Career and Vocational Education, Columbus.

Gilligan, C. (1982) *In a Different Voice: Psychological Theory and Women's Development*, Harvard University Press, Cambridge, MA.

Hart, M. (1990) 'Liberation Through Consciousness Raising', in Mezirow, J. et al. (eds), *Fostering Critical Reflection in Adulthood: A Guide to Transformative and Emancipatory Learning*, Jossey-Bass, San Francisco.

Hayes, E. (1989) 'Insights from Women's Experiences for Teaching and Learning', in Hayes, E. (ed.), *Effective Teaching Styles: New Directions for Adult and Continuing Education*, Jossey-Bass, San Francisco.

hooks, b. (1989) *Talking Back: Thinking Feminist, Thinking Black*, South End Press, Boston.

Lather, P. (1991) *Getting Smart: Feminist Research and Pedagogy with/in the Postmodern*, Routledge, New York.

Maggard, S. W. (1994) 'From the Farm to Coal Camp to Back Office to McDonalds: Living in the Midst of Appalachia's Latest Transformation', *Journal of the Appalachian Studies Association*, Vol. 6.

Weiler, K. (1991) 'Freire and a Feminist Pedagogy of Difference', *Harvard Educational Review*, Vol. 61, no. 4, November.

10

'Some good long talks': cross-cultural feminist practice

HELEN MYLES AND ISABEL TARRAGO

This is a story about many women, but two in particular, one black (an Aranda woman from Boulia) and one white (of Irish and Welsh ancestry) who live and work in Australia. It is the story of a journey of discovery, difference, learning, growth, bonding and feminism. It took place in tropical North Queensland and involved the participation of many Aboriginal women from various communities in the state.

By sharing our experience of working together for community development in health, we hope to contribute to the debate about feminist popular education on two levels: team-work between black and white women workers and cross-cultural feminist practice.

The project

A health project with exciting long-term prospects for Aboriginal women has commenced in Queensland. It is working towards change for Aboriginal women giving birth and is planned to progress in three phases. The first phase consisted of consultation with Aboriginal women in their communities about the way birth used to be, how it is now and the changes they would like to introduce. This was followed by preparation of a policy report, outlining programmes to be tested in various communities.

The second phase will cover the period during which several trial programmes relating to pre-natal and post-natal care will be carried out in selected communities, and the third phase will be the establishment of a full-scale birthing programme for Aboriginal women in Queensland, following evaluation of the trial programmes in phase two.

The first phase was undertaken by the authors and the work provides a framework in which to discuss issues of tradition, culture, colour, class, gender and feminism. We believe that these consultations around women's health, described as 'some good long talks' by one of the Aboriginal participants, demonstrate key principles not only in relation to feminist team-work between black and white women, but also in relation to work within a community development model, since we were outsiders working in Aboriginal communities and also in policy development processes for both government and non-governmental agencies.

The historical setting

In order to form an understanding of the issues discussed in this chapter, it is necessary to have some knowledge of the historical and cultural perspective of Queensland Aboriginal women. The history following European invasion and colonization of their country is significant not only when discussing racism and sexism, but also when discussing the relationship between black and white feminism (Huggins, 1994).

It is now well known that Queensland history, written by white male historians, has failed to give an accurate description of what some have called a time of 'undeclared war' (Malezer et al., 1979). In the period from 1840 to 1900, brave and proud Aboriginal people fought attempts to drive them from land which, prior to European settlement, had provided them with food, shelter and spiritual nourishment.

During this time Aboriginal people found that their former territories, hunting grounds, burial and sacred sites were suddenly called 'stations'. This name meant 'private property' which was a totally alien notion and, in addition, the land which had been the central focus of their culture was now given over to grazing cattle and sheep. When they attempted to resist this change, Aboriginal men, women and children were slaughtered in large numbers, by poisoning and by bullets, so that by the end of the nineteenth century destruction of Aboriginal tribes, life-style, religion and culture was almost complete.

Aboriginal people had two main choices at this point. They could try to maintain their traditional life-style in the bush, resisting white settlement and constantly at risk of being killed by government forces still searching for them, or they could accept European occupation and take up residence near a station homestead. Here they were given food, clothing and other gifts in return for performing casual chores around the station.

These homestead situations present early examples of the oppression of black women who were domestic servants, by their white female employers. This is an issue as yet not clearly defined or addressed by the women's movement in Australia (Huggins, 1994).

Very little recorded information exists today about tribes, their languages, law and social organization, because Aboriginal people passed on their stories in forms other than writing: this is another major issue to be considered in developing sound cross-cultural feminist practice. In addition, most settlers failed to appreciate the richness of the Aboriginal culture, noticing neither its religious and social obligations nor the variations in language. As a result of this lack of knowledge, white settlers continually violated laws sacred to Aboriginal people. This was particularly true of the law which prevented an Aboriginal person from entering another's land without a good reason and prior permission.

During the twentieth century a series of government policies have been brought to bear on Aboriginal people in an attempt to deal with 'the Aboriginal problem'. This view that there is a 'problem' continues to be held by many in the Australian population today.

'Civilization' Towards the end of the nineteenth century Christian missions, supported by the government, were established in Queensland by various religious groups. Their stated aim was to improve the conditions of Aboriginal people and to make them into 'useful and good humanity', in other words, to 'civilize' them.

Those who staffed both these missions and later government settlements received very little, if any, instruction about Aboriginal people and their culture. Whether they were paternalistic and kind, or rigid and cruel, none believed that Aborigines deserved to be treated as other Australians were, or that they should have any say about how and where they lived.

'Protection' Many Aboriginal people were unwilling to remain in mission settlements, so in 1897 the government introduced the Aboriginals Protection and Restriction of the Sale of Opium Act. This legislation represented a shift in policy in terms of which Aborigines were to enjoy 'protection' from the evils of white society. This was the first legislation targeted specifically at Aboriginal people and it gave the government power forcibly to move Aborigines on to reserves and keep them there.

For decades in the early twentieth century, survivors of all the different tribes were gathered together on reserves. Here they were supervised under a series of subsequent Acts and subjected to white education, economic practices and life-style. This government policy caused the loss of much traditional Aboriginal culture which can never again be reclaimed.

These early Acts placed Aboriginal people totally under the control of government-nominated protectors, superintendents, managers or directors. People were moved from anywhere in the state to reserves selected by these officials and moved again if they disobeyed regulations and orders. The legislation and subordinate regulations were a direct result of the ignorance and prejudice of European politicians. There was no Aboriginal involvement in discussing or planning the future.

Assimilation　In the 1930s the policy of the government changed to one of assimilation of Aboriginal people, especially those of mixed descent. The aim of this policy was to bring about the eventual absorption of Aborigines into white culture. They were separated and exposed to European-style education and values, with the intention that they would then gradually ease into the white community and be indistinguishable from other members of that society.

Part of this policy involved what later became known as 'the stolen generations': thousands of light-skinned Aboriginal children were forcibly taken from their darker parents and lodged in children's homes or fostered out to European families, sometimes even in other states. Black women activists in Australia today are beginning to draw attention to the role played by white women in this 'stealing of Aboriginal children'. They point out that this issue continues to be of great political concern to Aboriginal women, who are still struggling to have their voices heard within the white feminist movement (Huggins, 1994).

Other attempts to break down Aboriginal culture within the settlements and missions included the establishment of a dormitory system. This strategy disrupted families by housing children together in dormitories, apart from other members of their family.

Careful reading of the Queensland government's approach to assimilation reveals its intention to reduce Aboriginal identity, genetically merge Aboriginal people into the European race, break down the 'problem' population and, in the long term, create a 'readiness' for rights and equality. However, the restrictive nature of legislation from 1897 onwards so severely limited mobility, self-responsibility and self-management, that absorption into the European community was not a realistic outcome.

The effects of these policies can be seen even today in Aboriginal communities. Problems relating to family and identity issues often result in chronic cycles of alcoholism, frequent detentions in jail, anxiety and further family breakdown. The loss of old values and difficulty in accepting new ones in their place can lead to a lack of a sense of purpose and meaning in life.

Integration　The right to vote was eventually recognized for Aboriginal people by legislation passed in 1965. A national referendum in 1967 showed overwhelming support for including Aborigines in the census, a right denied them until that time. According to Jackie Huggins (1994), many Aboriginal women played vital political roles in the campaign before the referendum.

The mid-1970s saw a modified version of assimilation introduced – integration. In terms of this policy, Aboriginal people would receive special assistance to move from the reserves to towns and cities where they could 'live in the general community as an accepted and integral part of it, proud of their race and religion with their own cultural background yet in harmony with the broad society of the State' (Malezer et al., 1979: 17).

The government failed to recognize that this was intolerable for Aboriginal people whose religion and identity is inextricably linked to their traditional land.

Self-determination   During the 1960s an Aboriginal rights movement emerged in Australia and began to criticize the assimilationist policies of state governments. While the federal government declared in 1972 that Aboriginal people were to be encouraged to preserve their own culture, languages, traditions and arts, policies of assimilation and integration continued in the state of Queensland.

Some mission groups and Aboriginal communities in Queensland began to press for federal intervention with regard to land rights and self-determination, and in 1984 the Community Services Act converted the remaining Aboriginal reserves in Queensland into communities founded on deeds of grant in trust. Within the next few years local government responsibility was assumed by Aboriginal community councils.

A change of government in Queensland saw the Aboriginal Land Act passed in 1991 and this legislation, together with the more recent Commonwealth Native Title Act, is providing a basis for current struggles of Aboriginal people towards reclaiming their traditional lands.

The birthing project begins

Issues relating to birthing have long been of concern to Aboriginal women in Queensland. Robyrta Felton, an elder clanswoman from Mornington Island who describes herself as having 'a tongue of fire and wild breath in her lungs', put it like this: 'These things about birth have been in our hearts for many years.' Until fairly recently, however, 'these things about birth' have remained a concern held tightly within Aboriginal culture and mostly ignored by Europeans.

The black American feminist bell hooks (1989: 3) is among those who have urged black women to break this silence:

It has been a political struggle for me to hold to the belief that there is much which we – black people – must speak about, much that is private that must be openly shared, if we are to heal our wounds (hurts caused by domination and exploitation and oppression), if we are to recover and realize ourselves.

Similarly, Audre Lorde (1984: 40) has called for 'the transformation of silence into language and action', and this approach is gaining support among Aboriginal women. As they speak out, it becomes more difficult for the dominant white culture to maintain its disregard of their views. As recently as 1991, however, Marjorie Baldwin, a woman from the Kimberley area who was removed from her people as a child and raised in North Queensland, pointed out at a Remote Area Aboriginal and Torres Strait Islander women's meeting that 'no one has, as yet, asked black women how they could help to improve maternal and neo-natal mortality'.

In a nutshell, the issue is a desire to see Aboriginal babies born in their own communities and according to their own customs. In a paper on birthing issues presented in 1991 to the State Tripartite Forum, a body composed of Aboriginal community representatives and state and Commonwealth government health representatives, Felton stated that birthing should take place in home communities whenever possible; that a woman should have her close female relatives with her during the birth of her child, and that traditional Aboriginal values relating to birth should be respected.

Commonwealth government funding, made available through the National Alternative Birthing Services Programme, made it possible for the State Tripartite Forum to respond. The forum approached the Aboriginal and Torres Strait Islander Health Policy Unit and the Women's Health Policy Unit of the Queensland Health Department about developing a birthing project for Aboriginal and Torres Strait Islander women in remote areas of Queensland.

A joint proposal was developed by these two units and approved by the State Tripartite Forum, which then chose five communities within the state to participate in the project – Cherbourg, Doomadgee, Mornington Island, Palm Island and Yarrabah.

Principals of the project Both the design and implementation of the 'Birthing for Aboriginal Women in Remote Areas of Queensland' project reflect the view of the World Health Organization (1986, 1991) that primary health-care:

> pays special attention to high risk and vulnerable groups, as a precondition for equity in health outcomes and health care access ... is based on a social

view of health which takes into account social, emotional, cultural, economic and environmental factors which influence daily life; [and] structures community participation to provide significant and purposeful community involvement.

In addition, a community development approach underpins the project, one based on the idea that people leading an unsatisfying life are in the best position to address that lack of satisfaction, given the wherewithal to do so. Outside workers do have a role to play, but ideally this role should be limited to accord with what the community decides is appropriate.

A further important principle acknowledged by the project is that birthing, or 'borning' as it is called in Aboriginal culture, is traditionally women's business.

Borning: the cultural perspective

The cultural approach of Aboriginal women to anything which is 'women's business' is to keep it to themselves. However, borning has become an increasingly important issue with the recent introduction of land rights for indigenous people, since birthplace establishes ancestral connections and these are significant in claiming rights to land.

'Borning' describes much more than the process of labour and birth. It is about being conceived or 'found' in one's own country, about the rebirth of a 'spirit child' from the Dreamtime ancestors who belong to a particular area of country, which may be that of the baby's grandmother or grandfather. Thus, a child has strong traditional affiliations to the part of the country where she or he was 'found', and this affects rights and responsibilities in relation to law, land and people which that child will assume on reaching adulthood (Carter et al., 1987).

Traditionally, older women with familial connections, usually grandmothers and aunts, attend women giving birth. A women's camp is constructed some distance from the main camp and the women remain there together for a couple of weeks. In this warm and private atmosphere, the attendants provide massage and other support during the birth of the baby. There is no interference unless difficulties arise and the birthing woman has total control over the process (Carter et al., 1987).

After birth the cord is cut with stone, shell or scissors and warm sand or ash is applied to the baby's umbilicus. Similar warmth is used to relieve the mother's pain as she expels the placenta. The baby may be put to the breast straight away or after the mother has rested (Hamilton, 1981; Carter et al., 1987).

Procedures relating to the cord and the afterbirth differ from people to people. The cord may be tied around the baby's neck or portions of it given to certain relatives. In other nations the placenta or afterbirth is often buried. Later, both baby and mother are 'smoked', using special bushes, to strengthen them, relieve bruising and tears, prevent bleeding and ensure a good supply of breast milk (Hamilton, 1981; Carter et al., 1987).

In summary then, borning by the Grandmother's Law is 'a process guided by rites and skills, an oral tradition passed down through successive generations by experience. The Aboriginal women have control over their own lives, bodies and babies in this borning process' (Carter et al., 1987: 11).

The medical model

Western obstetrics, which currently governs birthing among women in Queensland Aboriginal communities, has been criticized world-wide by non-Western women for usurping their traditional control over their bodies and birth. Derived from the Latin *obstetrix*, meaning midwife, obstetrics is defined as the science dealing with the care of the pregnant woman during the ante-natal, parturient and post-natal phases. Throughout much of history and in many cultures, women controlled their own reproductive activities and functioned as midwives. Midwives were usually older women who had children of their own, and they acquired their skills through generational exchange of informal knowledge and experience (Oakley, 1976; Donnison, 1977).

From the thirteenth century onwards, male barber-surgeons began to form guilds and formally train their members in ways of dealing with birth complications. This form of organization and education was not available to female midwives and gradually men began to preside at births, especially as midwives were not permitted to use any instruments and had to call in a barber-surgeon whenever complications arose.

Obstetrics developed as a science following the appearance of the male midwife during the seventeenth century. The invention of forceps for delivering babies bolstered the position of men in the field and came to symbolize the science of obstetrics as opposed to the art of midwifery. At the same time, witch-hunts under the auspices of the church in England, Europe and America took the lives of millions of midwives. Thus the role of women as birth attendants was challenged by men in numerous ways (Daly, 1978) and, although midwives continued to assist women in birth for another couple of centuries, their access to education was limited and as a result their independent role gradually diminished.

Male practitioners, wielding increasing technology, stepped into the gap they had done much to create.

There were two other major effects of the increased participation of 'professional' men in childbirth: the establishment of lying-in hospitals and high maternal mortality rates from puerperal fever. Lying-in hospitals were established by the male medical fraternity in the eighteenth century. Here they not only practised their techniques on working-class women, but also set a precedent for the medical management of childbirth in hospital which persists today.

It took another century to overcome the puerperal fever which proliferated in the hospitals, as infection was passed from woman to woman by male doctors who did not wash their hands between deliveries. Women who continued to give birth outside hospitals, in the care of midwives, were much less likely to suffer from puerperal fever because midwives tended to deal with only one woman at a time.

In Australia many pioneer women delivered their babies without medical assistance, often relying on Aboriginal or neighbouring women to help them (Hagger, 1979). However, women in the developing cities experienced a high rate of medical attention because there were few midwives among the early European settlers and also as a result of superior obstetrical training which began in Melbourne in 1865 (Teale, 1978).

In 1912 a maternity allowance for non-Aboriginal women was introduced in Australia, removing for these women the financial barrier to obtaining medical assistance and, in consequence, halving the proportion of births attended by midwives. However, no corresponding decrease in infant or maternal mortality rates was evident (Willis, 1983). This trend away from reliance on midwifery was strengthened when obstetrics and gynaecology became separate medical specialities. By 1928 midwifery had also become a speciality in nursing training, thereby denying employment as midwives to those women who were not trained as nurses. By the 1930s most women in Australia were having their babies in hospital.

Following the demise of birth as a natural process under the informal control of women, and of midwifery as the accompanying natural practice, doctors practising according to the Western medical model have continued to convince women, indigenous and non-indigenous, of the need to intervene routinely in the birth process in the interests of safety, comfort and convenience.

Beginnings of change

After World War II, new ideas about childbirth began to challenge the medical dominance of the process and by the 1960s white women in Australia and elsewhere were questioning the scientific approach to birth which denied so many of them the experience they desired. As a result, changes in relation to birthing preparation, practice, venue and decision-making have been taking place in Australia and in other Western countries. Natural childbirth, home births, family and spouse participation and water-birthing are some of the better-known developments.

In response to continuing pressure from women, many Australian states conducted reviews of birthing procedures during the 1980s. Widespread dissatisfaction among women with existing birthing services was revealed. In particular women expressed their discontent with what they perceived to be the medicalization of birth: hospital delivery, frequent intervention in the birthing process and control of the event by health professionals.

For indigenous women the situation was even worse. Not only did they suffer the medicalization of birth, but also the European, male, medical approach to birthing was diametrically opposed to their cultural beliefs and practice. Indeed, the gulf between Western and indigenous medicine is 'culturally wide and historically deep' (Carter et al., 1987). Although there are points of similarity in the two approaches, for example both involve forms of pregnancy care, birth attendants and specific procedures, techniques and medicinal care during childbirth, the differences between them are far-reaching.

> The approach of one is mainly specialist, gender specific, mechanistic and scientific, and in it the emphasis on pathology is paramount. The other is holistic and embedded in the cultural traditions of the Law and Dreaming. The practice of Western obstetrics is specialised, involving the presence of an educated elite and its individual clients, and childbirth is technologically managed in hospitals. The practice of borning is generalised, collective and comprehensible in the domain of women's business and the Law. It is non-interventionist (Aboriginal women literally 'catch the baby') and grants women control and autonomy. (Carter et al., 1987: 13)

Some significant changes have occurred in birthing practice in white Australian society as a result of consumer pressure on the established health system. However, these changes have not extended to birthing among indigenous women in remote areas of Queensland.

Since the early 1970s pregnant women from Aboriginal communities in Queensland have been transported to the nearest obstetric service point for the major component of their maternity care: the birth of their babies. The cultural, familial, spiritual and emotional aspects of childbirth, and the effects on Aboriginal women of separation from home and kin, were not addressed in the development and implementation of this long-standing policy.

The oppression of black women, especially those in remote communities, has silenced their discontent for many years. Their fear of speaking out, linked with the unwillingness of the white, male-dominated, technology-based medical system to listen, has denied them their right to culturally appropriate 'borning' which has specific symbolic connections for them with the Dreamtime, kin and the land.

The transformation of silence

The opportunity to reoccupy their traditional land seems to be encouraging Aboriginal women in remote communities to be more assertive about their need for culturally sound birth practices. The importance of this issue to women is evident, given that sacred women's business is usually not discussed in public.

Congress Alukura   Women in central Australia were the first to speak up, during an extensive consultation process which was conducted over a number of years through the Central Australian Aboriginal Congress. In 1983 they began to describe their reasons for delaying ante-natal check-ups and their 'lonely', 'frightened' and 'shaming' experiences during childbirth in the Alice Springs Hospital. In 1984, the policy and planning division of the Commonwealth Department of Health provided funding for a 'borning' project (Carter et al., 1987).

This made it possible for Aboriginal women of all counties in central Australia, tribal and non-tribal, to talk together about 'the old-time way, the whitefellah way, Aboriginal resistance and their preferences in health practices'. These talks revealed that the interaction of the two systems of health-care, Western and Aboriginal, is currently associated with shame and degradation for Aboriginal women. The question women asked was: 'How can a point of contact be developed in which the Aboriginal way and the mothers and children become, and remain, happy and healthy?' (Carter et al., 1987: 5).

One woman said:

> But you must look after your babies, and children, and the young girls: teach them both ways, our own way and the white way. Two. We've got two lines now: whitefellah's line and black people's line. These days we must live two ways, like our people before us and also the white way. (Carter et al., 1987: 7)

These women demonstrated a sophisticated knowledge of factors contributing to high mortality rates and the need to incorporate obstetric
care alongside borning practices. They saw the need for this integration
as arising from changes in the Aboriginal way of life, the introduction
of diseases formerly unknown to their people, and the subsequent
undermining of their Law.

After many conferences, the option of *Alukura* (the Loritja word for
a separate women's camp), a place where women can deliver babies in
the Aboriginal way but with access to the advantages Western obstetrics
can offer, was endorsed. Congress Alukura is now a women's place in
Alice Springs, controlled by the Central Australian Aboriginal Congress,
where normal deliveries take place without disruption of traditional
practices. The following fundamental principles underlying Congress
Alukura were ratified in 1985:

— Aboriginal people are a distinct and viable cultural group with their
   own cultural beliefs and practices, Law and social needs.
— Every woman has the right to participate fully in her pregnancy and
   childbirth care, and determine the environment and nature of such
   care unless medical complications indicate otherwise.
— Every Aboriginal woman has the right in pregnancy and childbirth
   to maintain and use her own heritage, customs, language and institutions, or to choose other options as she wishes. (Carter et al.,
   1987: 26)

Consultation the Aboriginal way

Consultation with women in the five Queensland Aboriginal communities nominated for the study was undertaken in the second half of
1992. The methodology and detail relating to the women consulted and
their recommendations are contained in the report *Some Good Long
Talks* (Myles and Tarrago, 1992). Our purpose here in discussing some
aspects of these consultations is to demonstrate the use of cross-cultural
feminist practice, raise issues relating to the politics of difference within
the feminist movement, and show the reality (in the sense of 'get real')
of unity and team-work between black and white women.

Ownership   The keystone of the birthing project is ownership by Aboriginal women and their involvement in all stages of its development.
This means their participation in design, implementation, monitoring
and evaluation.

Previous reports on Aboriginal women's involvement in aspects of their communities have highlighted the significance of the role women play in both family and community affairs. 'They remain the nurturers and teachers of the young, both their own and those they foster. In particular it is the women who are responsible for teaching young children about their Aboriginal identity' (Daylight and Johnstone, 1986: 1). The same report remarked that the reason so many Aboriginal women are active in their communities is because they recognize that 'the future of their people is in their hands'. In addition, ethical guidelines relating to research involving women's business in Aboriginal communities clearly state that the women themselves should monitor any such activities.

One of the steps we took to ensure ownership of the project by the women themselves was to arrange a process for them to check the first draft of *Some Good Long Talks* for its accuracy in reflecting what they had said. The following quote introduces the final version: 'This report belongs to the women of Palm Island, Mornington Island, Doomadgee, Cherbourg and Yarrabah who recently participated in some good long talks about birth. It is a reminder of their stories and knowledge, of their advice and of our listening' (Myles and Tarrago, 1992: 1).

The report consists mostly of the voices of the women themselves, with a minimum of introductory interpretation from us, reflecting the advice of bell hooks (1989: 3): 'We make the revolutionary history, telling the past as we have learnt it mouth-to-mouth, telling the present as we see, know, and feel it in our hearts and with our words.'

Quality feminist practice dictates that community consultation is a two-way exchange of information. The women who participated in our community talks contributed valuable, and often confidential, personal and cultural information. As a way of giving something in return for this generosity, some general and community-specific aspects of historical information were compiled, primarily from black writers, and added to the end of the consultation report.

A reference group Establishment of a reference group was another important aspect of ensuring ownership of the project by the women concerned. We negotiated with the communities about the choice of a key woman from each to form a reference group for the project. Selection of the women was undertaken by the communities themselves, through their governing councils. The reference group met twice during the first phase of the project: once at the beginning to discuss its design and implementation, and once to review the draft of the consultation report.

Community involvement Reference group members wanted other women in their communities to have a chance to talk about birthing and they therefore invited the consultation team to visit their communities at appropriate times. Negotiating and receiving these invitations was important to the legitimacy of the project, as Aboriginal custom has it that even Aboriginal people do not traverse others' country without prior permission.

In each community it was agreed that discussions between the women and the consulting team would centre loosely around how birthing of Aboriginal babies used to be, what happened currently when a woman had a baby, and what changes, if any, were needed.

The consulting team   We two comprised the bi-cultural consulting team. Isabel was then the principal policy officer in the Aboriginal and Torres Strait Islander Health Policy Unit, located in the state government health department in Brisbane. As stated earlier, she is an Aranda woman, born in Boulia near the border of Queensland and the Northern Territory, and she was a prime mover in this project from its inception. Her role included funding allocation, design and presentation of the project for acceptance by the State Tripartite Forum and the reference group, negotiation with Aboriginal community councils and participants in the project, organization of visits to the communities, and assistance with analysis of information collected in both an academic and cultural sense.

Isabel also played a central role in the selection of a non-Aboriginal consultant to work with her throughout the consultation process. Selection criteria included knowledge and previous experience but also complementary skills and openness to culturally appropriate processes. As this non-indigenous team member, Helen was mainly responsible for assistance in design of the consultation process, listening, recording and analysing information and then writing the reports.

Time   Most of the communities in this project are hundreds of kilometres from regional towns and small aircraft were the only workable access option. However, we ensured that we spent more time in each community than the familiar 'fly in, fly out' visit practised so commonly by those developing policy or providing services for Aboriginal communities in Queensland. A four-day stay was not unusual and we visited one community twice, because two funerals were celebrated on two of the days scheduled for talking during the initial visit, making it impossible for the women to participate in any other activity. During our visits we sometimes slept in community guest houses (some of which were previously homes of missionaries now used to house visitors to the community) and sometimes in women's shelters.

This policy of spending a substantial amount of time with each community met the following needs:

— Residents of the community had time to note and discuss our presence and thereby understand and support the reason for our visit.
— Plenty of time was available for meeting with and talking to women, in recognition of the pace and format favoured by Aboriginal women at gatherings.
— We had sufficient opportunity to familiarize ourselves with aspects of the community that might not have been evident during a shorter visit.

Protocol   Dates for community visits were negotiated at great length between members of the reference group and Isabel and arrangements were made in accordance with protocol drawn up for visiting and researching in Aboriginal communities.

A powerful cultural imperative upon which we relied during these consultations was the acknowledgement of the communication processes which exist between older and younger Aboriginal women in their own communities. Appropriate cultural behaviour demands that elders speak for the community, although we often also spoke with younger women who were less confident than their elders.

In discussing the cohesion among Aboriginal women, Jackie Huggins (1994: 19) emphasizes the communal nature of relationships and the 'powerful network of female support' that exists between them. She explains that it is this 'connectedness' which 'determines who actually does what, who has responsibility for what, who takes responsibility for saying things to whom, who does the saying, who does the writing'.

Methods and places   A range of methods for meeting with women were used during the consultations. Community women were alerted by reference group members and sometimes by Aboriginal health workers as well, of the arrival of the consultation team. In three communities, a group of women gathered at an appointed place and remained together for lengthy discussion. On one of the islands, a number of small groups of women visited the consulting team at their base camp over a number of days. In an inland community, the consulting team walked through the red dirt streets of the community with the health workers and met with small groups of women where they were gathered as part of their daily routine: in parks, front yards, on verandas and outside community resource buildings.

Women's centres were utilized by the local women as a safe and comfortable venue for talks in three communities and a local hall was used in another. On a number of occasions, women attending the gatherings in the women's centres remarked that it was their first visit to the building, so these consultations also performed an awareness-raising and networking role in the community.

Recording　At each meeting permission was sought and given for the consulting team to take written notes and also tape-record the conversation. Helen always explained that capturing the spoken word would provide a back-up tool for her as the documenter, and the tapes certainly provided a rich picture of language, expression and ideas.

Language　In all the communities we visited, English was the commonly used language and thus no interpreters were used. However, in some communities, a small number of older women who attended the gatherings still spoke their traditional language in addition to English and often shared with us the traditional names for aspects of the birthing process.

Success　We rated our consultation processes successful or otherwise in terms of the following criteria: the numbers of women who contributed their points of view; their willingness to share personal and cultural information with an outsider, bi-cultural consulting team; and the range of views expressed.

What the women said

Over eighty women of varying ages participated in our particular women's business. In sharing their stories with us, the women made some very clear points.

First, they want to give birth close to where they live. Women are unhappy with the current policy of aerial evacuation, sometimes as early as thirty-two weeks into their pregnancy, which means that they must spend many weeks away from their husbands and other children, whose welfare they worry about. In addition, aerial evacuation is costly and the women are lonely, frightened and often shamed in unfamiliar towns and institutions.

Second, they want birth with safety for mother and baby. Women acknowledge the need to have medical assistance available in case of mishap during birth. They realize that women classed as 'high risk' will still have to be evacuated from home for the birth of their babies but seek an approach to safe birthing that combines the contemporary and the traditional.

Third, the women want familiar, female birth attendants who are culturally sensitive. They are very often uncomfortable with current health staff, many of whom are young, male doctors or transient nursing staff who often lack cultural awareness. They feel that trained, indigenous health workers would provide acceptable continuity of care during pregnancy, labour, delivery and early parenthood.

The women also want a specially designed space to enable aunts, grandmothers or other family members and friends to be present during labour. In addition it should function as a friendly, women's place in which attention can be given to women's business. They often do not feel comfortable attending local hospitals for ante-natal care.

Another need expressed by the women is to have a say in how their birthing services are conducted. They recognize that community development and ownership of services is a crucial step towards self-determination in Aboriginal communities. They understand the importance of health promotion and education in the context of birthing, acknowledge that changes to life-style are necessary to improve the health status of their people and believe that culturally appropriate educational activities are the way to achieve this.

Finally, the women appreciate the need for a process of graduated steps towards returning birthing to the community. They are keen for this to be accomplished but, aware of the social as well as medical factors influencing the health of Aboriginal women, want to work in a co-ordinated and co-operative fashion towards the goal of birth rights for Aboriginal women.

Outcomes for black and white women

During our time together on this project we learned many things which we are beginning to share with others in our country and elsewhere. Certainly in Queensland we believe this bi-cultural approach to community development has not previously been seen as a way forward by either black or white women. The reality in the past has been a feeling among many black women that feminism and women's studies were 'white cultural products' which continued to oppress them. As Huggins (1994: 16) put it: 'Western theory, language, academia – to name a few – are foreign constructs in which Aboriginal women do not fit. Therefore an oppressive society controls and manipulates Aboriginal women and in turn dictates how they should behave, think, learn, speak, write.'

The hope is that a recent landmark in Aboriginal affairs in this country, the historic support across political parties for legislation initiating a process of reconciliation between Aboriginal and Torres Strait Islander people and the wider community, will bring about change. Effective reconciliation will provide opportunities for black and white women to talk and listen to each other about the different circumstances they face, the different ways in which they wish to address issues and the ways in which they can pool their talents.

As an interracial team or bi-cultural team, we have spent many hours in places distant from our homes, discussing differences, oppression, colonial history and white feminism, as well as the links we two women shared. We both know that there is a richness to be gained from a partnership such as ours, and we are keen to encourage other women to try it.

In addition, we know that the women who participated in the project accepted our way of working together, because of the verbal and non-verbal responses (so significant in Aboriginal culture) of some of the senior clanswomen involved in the reference group, particularly their responses to 'the white one' in the team.

Why it worked　We believe that the interaction of a number of factors contributed to the culturally appropriate outcomes of this phase of the birthing project.

In the first place, it was essential that one of the members of the consulting team was an Aborigine, a fact that gave the project credibility in terms of a cultural approach. In addition, Isabel's personal status, arising both from being her mother's daughter, and thus culturally sound in upbringing, and from success in her own career, lent strength to the processes we used. Isabel's 'authenticity' was acknowledged from community to community. When she mentioned her mother, who had earlier fought for Aboriginal rights, she was recognized among older people and welcomed wherever we went. The cultural status accorded to this was a unique element of the project.

Another important factor was the reversal of the usual power relationship between black and white women in the composition of our cross-cultural team. It was Isabel who conjured up ideas for the project and controlled its funds. In selecting a white woman with complementary skills to work with her, she chose 'from the heart' in an Aboriginal way, looking for a partner whom she felt 'knew inside about her place'. This challenge to the common scenario of the politics of domination, in terms of which white academics or bureaucrats control events and invite blacks along to sanction their activities, set the scene for a different and culturally authentic approach.

A third important ingredient for a successful outcome was acknowledgement of protocol and cultural processes. 'It's the Law, you know,' Isabel said to Helen many times. Her knowledge of basic tenets relating to the way things are said and done indicated to the participating women that they could speak to us on their terms, but also ensured that we were invited to visit their communities. In addition we were careful to submit and receive documentation about our intended visits from the appropriate local council.

A related factor was an approach of respect for consultation in the Aboriginal way. This meant quite an adjustment on Helen's part. Schooled in the white bureaucratic approach of written agendas, focusing on one issue at a time, keeping an eye on the clock and so on, she had to trust in Isabel's confidence that such devices could be dispensed with and that information gathering would 'just happen' if we took our time. Part of the reason for spending numerous days talking with relatively small numbers of women was to be able to work at a pace with which the women felt comfortable.

The settings and informal style of meetings – indoors and outdoors, sitting on the floor, the grass or the veranda, standing at the gate, watching a card game, eating together – were all important in contributing to an atmosphere of comfort in which real consultation could take place.

'Knowing our place' was also important, an issue not only for Helen as the white worker, but also for Isabel, the black woman indeed but one operating at times in other black women's country. For Helen, knowing her place largely meant that she listened very hard and spoke very little. It sometimes meant that she did not roam the community on the day of arrival but waited until the word had spread about her presence and the purpose for it. Walking together through the community was undertaken only after our visit was well on its way.

Knowing our place also related to a sense of respect which gradually pervaded our 'good long talks'. This esteem existed in a cultural sense between older and younger women but was also extended to us as a trusted conduit for the women's stories and visions.

Finally, the success of this phase of the project owed much to its acknowledgement of verbal traditions. Consultations were conducted as free-ranging talks with an unstructured agenda, and inferences from both verbal and non-verbal behaviour were given credibility by the consulting team. The report on the consultation process was written with consideration for Aboriginal verbal traditions and consisted largely of the voices of the women themselves. This was well received by the reference group.

By way of a postscript in relation to the ingredients of a successful outcome, we would also like to mention an awareness of connections. We learnt a lot about working in Aboriginal communities, about the Law, about traditional birthing and about the connectedness of everything. Spiritual connections between black and white women, between women and the Law and between women and the land are not easy to describe, but the feelings are strong and we each knew when it was happening to us.

Cross-cultural feminist practice

When the issue arises of black and white women working together to support a stronger future for women in Australia, a most significant aspect of discussion is yet to be resolved: that of white feminism versus indigenous thought, the politics of difference. Black women activists in Australia continue to draw the attention of white feminists to the fact that Aboriginal women remain discriminated against on the basis of their race rather than their gender.

> For example, a cosmetically apparent Aboriginal woman is regularly stereotyped on the basis of being a boong, coon, nigger, gin or abo far in excess of being a 'woman'. The lack of recognition and real understanding of this political difference is a major issue still to be resolved by the white women's movement. (Huggins, 1994: 16)

The implications of ignoring the differences of race between women are described by Lorde (1984) as 'the most serious threat to the mobilization of women's joint power'. The lack of patterns for relating across our differences and the need for feminists to recognize difference as a pivotal strength are two matters of contention we have endeavoured to surmount in our cross-cultural, feminist approach to community development.

Bibliography

Carter, B. et al. (1987) 'Borning: Pmere Laltyeke Anwerne Ampe Mpwaretyeke', *Australian Aboriginal Studies*, no. 1.

Daly, M. (1978) *Gyn/Ecology: The Metaethics of Radical Feminism*, Beacon Press, Boston.

Daylight, P. and Johnstone, M. (1986) *Women's Business: Report of the Aboriginal Women's Task Force*, Australian Government Publishing Service, Canberra.

Donnison, J. (1977) *Midwives and Medical Men: A History of Interprofessional Rivalries and Women's Rights*, Schocken Books, New York.

Hagger, J. (1979) *Australian Colonial Medicine*, Rigby, Adelaide.

Hamilton, A. (1981) *Nature and Nurture: Aboriginal Child-rearing in North Central Arnhem Land*, Australian Institute of Aboriginal Studies, Canberra.

hooks, b. (1989) *Talking Back: Thinking Feminist, Thinking Black*, Sheba, London.

Huggins, J. (1994) 'A Contemporary View of Aboriginal Women's Relationship to the White Women's Movement', in Grieves, N. and Burns, A. (eds), *Australian Contemporary Feminist Thought*, Oxford University Press, Melbourne.

Lorde, A. (1984) *Sister Outsider*, Crossing Press, New York.

Malezer, L. et al. (1979) *Beyond the Act*, Foundation for Aboriginal and Islander Research Action, Brisbane.

Myles, H. and Tarrago, I. (1992) *Some Good Long Talks*, Women's Health Policy Unit, Queensland.

Oakley, A. (1976) 'Wisewoman and Medicine Man: Changes in the Management of Childbirth', in Mitchell, J. and Oakley, A. (eds), *The Rights and Wrongs of Women*, Penguin, London.

Teale, R. (ed.) (1978) *Colonial Eve: Sources on Women in Australia 1788-1914*, Oxford University Press, Melbourne.

Willis, E. (1983) *Medical Dominance*, George Allen and Unwin, Sydney.

World Health Organization (1986) *Ottawa Charter for Health Promotion*, International Conference on Health Promotion, Copenhagen.

World Health Organization (1991) *Community Involvement in Health Development: Challenging Health Services*, report of a WHO study group, Geneva.

Talking pain: educational work with factory women in Malaysia

CHAN LEAN HENG

This chapter records and analyses educational work undertaken with female factory workers in Malaysia as a participatory research project which attempted to commence from the standpoints of the women themselves: their subjectivities, lived experiences and experienced feelings. It explores how educational work can enable women to unpack and break through the numbness resulting from suffering continuous subordination.

The 'factory women' referred to here are global assembly-line operators. They perform menial, tedious, repetitive tasks as unskilled or semi-skilled shift workers. They are at the bottom of the economic hierarchy in labour-intensive, export-oriented industries. Mostly, as young rural migrants associated with free trade zones, they are people working in industrial jobs for the first time. In Malaysia and other developing nations, they are the dexterous, docile, nimble-fingered, responsible for their nation's integration into the industrialized world economy, yet the most deprecated socially and morally.

The chapter begins by charting the gap between existing educational programmes aimed at these women and their experienced realities. It then examines how the education process can incorporate such realities, explores the experiences of the factory workers who participated in the project, and analyses what takes place in the process of reflective talking that was a vital part of the education work undertaken.

Current educational work

The work of unions, social service groups, grassroots groups and my own work with women factory workers in Malaysia is briefly reviewed here in terms of objectives, content and methodology.

Most educational programmes of unions and social service groups are formulated from the perspective of sponsors or providers and in terms of a deficit model (Wynne, 1988). Assumed ignorance in relation to the women's roles as workers and home-makers, and assumed deficiency in terms of loose morals, underlie the practice of education as information, motivation and chastisement. The aims are to equip the women morally and functionally to behave in pre-defined ways, to impart awareness of their responsibilities and rights as workers, and to convey the benefits of unionization.

The women are treated as target beneficiaries and are seldom consulted about or involved in the design of programmes. Even where their participation is sought, organizational goals and priorities take precedence in structuring curricula. Thus, a disjuncture exists between the contents and objectives of educational programmes and participants' personally felt concerns.

In addition, organizational practices and programmes tend to deny participants the space and authority to talk about their experiences. Far from gaining a voice and being helped to take control over their lives, the women are often silenced or made to feel stupid, with both oppressive stereotypes and the reinforcement of the experience of subjugation.

Although many programmes emphasize the importance of participation, they ignore the practical obstacles and internalized intimations of inferiority (Bartky, 1990) that make participation impossible. Current pedagogical practices rarely take on board women's subjectivities, their physical exhaustion and the disabling effect of being eternally in subordinate positions. Many women agree that they should and would like to participate actively but feel helpless about the lack of confidence which prevents them from doing so (Chan, 1991). Most of the women working in Malaysian factories have no experience of relating and speaking out in groups.

In grassroots groups, which are more women-centred, there is more consciousness about the need to start from the issues and interests of the women themselves. However, focusing on interests to attract and sustain participation has tended to reinforce stereotypes of traditional femininity.

Education is practised in grassroots groups as awareness-raising about the exploitation and subordination of women. Information about rights and leadership formation dominates the curriculum. The pedagogical practice is integrated into organizing for daily survival to develop confidence, knowledge, consciousness and leadership through 'learning by doing and by being involved'. The primary objective is to get the women organized. The assumption is that it is only when they are organized that they will have any power, and that they will become politicized in the process of mobilization for action.

Although grassroots groups have a woman-centred approach, this takes the form of a women-only space for dealing with practical, mainly material needs. It rarely encompasses the subjectivities of the women, their individual personal experience and feelings, their differences and diversity. Women workers are treated as a homogeneous category. Personally felt subordination and its effects are not tackled. The psychological and practical constraints on women are noted but not addressed systematically in the pedagogy. Activities aimed at developing a consciousness of the politics of gender are rare.

As to my own work, it focused on the objective conditions of women workers until exposure to writings on popular education and feminism alerted me to the need to start with women's personal experience. Programmes I ran aimed to foster awareness about exploitation, rights and the need to be organized collectively. I concentrated on cognitive faculties: equipping the women with the orientation, confidence, analytical and action-oriented skills essential for committed involvement.

My mistake was to aim at conscientization for purposes of building a power or organizational base, without first considering the lack of personal power of the women themselves and the disempowering experiences that had disabled them. I did not take into account sufficiently their experienced subjectivities, in particular their lack of emotional well-being. Personal individual processes were subsumed in pursuit of collective goals. I overlooked the internalized stereotypes, myths, feelings and beliefs which numb the agency of individuals. The learning that could be generated from daily experiences was not invoked to aid in the necessary processes of self-validation and self-recovery.

I was aware of reluctance and passivity among the women, aware of the existence of a wealth of unspoken feelings, thoughts and experiences among them, but I did not know what to do about it. This was not an issue of concern among activist colleagues so I did not think it warranted special attention. In fact, I feared that dealing with personal dimensions might promote individualism and self-centredness, and feared also that I would be labelled 'unprogressive'. I assumed that the women would develop skills as a result of active involvement in organizing activities, and that in due course they would overcome their habits of passivity and silence.

However, my work is now informed by an understanding of the centrality of emotion, an understanding derived originally from the role of emotions in my own life and experience of the mobilizing power of redefining and naming feelings from one's own standpoint. This initial hunch about the transformative potential of emotions, derived from practical knowledge, was affirmed by exposure to discussion of women's emotional welfare as a concern in feminist social work (Dominelli and McLeod, 1989). My confidence grew as I encountered Jaggar's (1992) description of emotion as an epistemological foundation of women's knowledge, and became increasingly familiar with feminist therapeutic approaches, particularly the attention given to the 'negative' emotions. Of special interest was the role anger can play in problematizing the incongruity between lived experience and sanctioned interpretations of that experience. As a response to injustice, anger can energize oppressed people to work for social change (Lyman, 1981).

Emotions have constituted a very powerful resource for liberation in the women's movement. Feminist educators, particularly women in the early consciousness-raising groups, have explored feelings as a 'critical way of knowing', or 'inner knowing': the source of true knowledge of the world for women living in a society that denies the value of their perceptions (Weiler, 1991: 463). Lorde (1984) helped me to understand unexpressed or unrecognized feelings as a source of oppositional knowledge, the revolutionary core of feminist activism.

Thus fortified, I started to revision and reposition feelings in and as educational work. Specifically I explored how interactive, reflective talking can lead to an experience of release and of being able to make sense of emotional responses to the experience of subordination. I became increasingly convinced that it is necessary to include experienced emotional subjectivities in our educational agenda if we are serious about education for empowerment.

The next sections of this chapter explore an experiment designed to address personal experiences and feelings in and as educational work.

Story-telling as education

The experiment was undertaken as a participatory research collaboration with the union of a multi-national factory. It involved a series of all-women workshops using personal narrative, discussion in small groups and popular communication methods to evoke reflexivity: recollection, expression, reflection and synthesis. This popular education methodology (see, for example, Arnold et al., 1991) was informed by a feminist perspective which acknowledges the central importance of women's lived experiences and subjectivities.

My preparations for the workshops included talking to two women about their lives. This process of interactive story-telling and reflective talking brought to the surface hidden feelings and thoughts which would not have emerged in an ordinary interview. My position as an involved outsider gave me an informed perspective from which to direct interventions. Sharing my own personally experienced difficulties and short-comings encouraged undefensive self-disclosure from them. All of us found the experience educative and meaningful.

Also influential in shaping the experiment was my exposure to the knowledge accumulated by others in participatory training in social work practice (Butler and Wintram, 1991), the consciousness-raising groups of the women's movement, adult or popular education and feminist pedagogy. Of particular importance were insights relating to the use of story-telling and work in small groups.

The various uses and powers of story-telling have been well documented (Christ, 1979; Buker, 1987). Story-telling has been used as a tool for consciousness-raising and mobilization in the women's movement particularly, but also by organizations of indigenous people struggling against the effects of colonization and by other oppressed groups. Within feminist discourse, voice and speech are metaphors for women's self-definitions (Collins, 1990), countervailing the constructions of others.

In the experiment under discussion, we used story-telling in small groups to evoke repressed voices: the recollection and articulation of denied feelings, thoughts and experiences for the purpose of reconstituting the self-esteem and self-definition of participants. I particularly explored techniques for eliciting stories (unpacking silence) about anguish and pain which the women had been made to believe was illegitimate and had therefore suppressed.

Photo-language (a popular education technique which uses photographs to evoke memories and feelings in the form of story-telling) and recalling concrete incidents of feeling undermined were useful in surfacing these memories. Warm-ups and and other support activities aimed at fostering feelings of safety and relaxation were included early in the workshops, while exercises around group dynamics, role-playing and drama followed later. Story-telling took place in small groups not only to bolster participants' sense of a safe space, but also to maximize the opportunity for collective learning, with information, interpretation and analysis fused in shared conversation through which participants began to recognize and validate past experience and present circumstance.

My awareness of women's suppressed experiences and their hesitation to talk about them helped me to listen to what was not said. As one of the women put it in a private conversation with me: 'It is not that I do not want to tell you. I find it difficult to express. I do not know what to say. I feel bad talking about it.' Reading silence evolved as a methodology of listening to restrained voices.

I realized that the difficulty of getting the women to talk about their lives did not revolve around any desire of theirs to hold back, or issues of confidentiality or privacy, although such risks and hesitations should not be under-estimated. Rather, the difficulty was one of repression and diffusion of feelings and experiences socially constructed as illegitimate. The challenge was therefore to find ways to trigger and precipitate these forbidden and therefore unspeakable feelings and experiences. From this insight emerged the concept of 'eliciting talk'.

Story-telling in this sense is not individual narrative. It takes place in interaction with the listening, questioning and reflecting of others. Henley et al. (1984) describe this as collaborative story-telling, akin to consciousness-raising in women's groups (Jenkins et al., 1978). One story or comment sparks the memory or reflection for another. It is in this informal conversational mode that connections, meanings and under-standings emerge through listening, questioning and reflecting on each other's stories, and it is this process that contributes to the recovery of participants' authentic realities.

Indeed, moving from silence to voice is to reclaim what has been denied and dismissed. It is to assert opposition to established meaning. It is an act of profound personal and political significance, reinstating the suppressed or submerged knowledge of the marginalized (see, for example, Daly, 1978; Christ, 1979; Rich, 1975; Spender, 1980). I was amazed by the impact of this kind of story-telling on the perceptions and capacities of participants, and I became convinced during the course of my research that this is the basic educational work required first with women whose experience of subordination has been pervasive.

Cautionary notes have been sounded, however. Ellsworth (1989) warns that stories are not always empowering and that collaborative story-telling is a problematic strategy for empowerment, given the diversity and difference among the oppressed and the fact that varied meanings are constructed in multifarious ways by our multiple subjectivities. Razack (1993) points to the need to pay attention to the context in which we hear and tell stories, in particular the effects of the different subject positions of teller and listener. Similarly, Spivak (1990: 42) calls for 'unlearning privilege', meaning that middle-class activists need to become able not only to listen to 'that other constituency', but also to speak in such a way that they can be heard and taken seriously.

A number of other guidelines emerge from the literature in relation to what Razack (1993) calls 'ground clearing activity' and Fishman (1978) describes as 'interaction work'. Ellsworth (1989) advises facilitators to include opportunities for social interaction in their programmes in order to build trust and reduce risk and fear. She warns against the silencing of diversity and argues for the need to take the initiative in learning about others' realities, rather than simply relying on them to inform us. Trinh (1990: 372) notes the need to understand silence as 'a will not to say or a will to unsay and a language of its own'. Narayan (1988) elaborates ground rules for communication in working together across differences, critically examining what we share and do not share. Feminist pedagogy in general stresses that how we hear and speak (process) is as important as what we hear and tell (content).

The usefulness of small groups as vehicles for active, experiential learning is also well established (Pria, 1987). They can facilitate exploration of identity issues (Brodsky, 1973); provide a 'free space' (Allen, 1970) for uncovering the political, economic and social context of individual experience; and, above all, offer a safe place in which women can make links between their own and others' experiences, thus facilitating both the validation of individual perception and experience, and an understanding of how this is shaped by the broader social context.

Carlock and Martin (1977) and Hagan (1983) note that all-women groups are less competitive than groups comprised of men and women, and deal with issues of intimacy and relationship more quickly. Aries (1976) found that women prefer all-female groups, feeling more restricted in mixed groups, while others note the advantage of the role models provided by women in all-female groups. Flynn et al. (1986) and Davis (1988) comment on the characteristic mutuality and ongoing learning of all-women groups in community work. For my part, I have found that participation is maximized in all-women groups and that they help women gain courage to speak and confidence to do things.

These insights both provided a frame and informed the process of my collaborative research with factory workers. All-women participatory workshops, working with collaborative story-telling in small groups, were the means to 'elicit talk'. However, facilitation was necessary not only to evoke repressed thoughts and feelings, but also to help make sense of them.

A total of eighteen workshops were held over four months, including a follow-up workshop for group leaders and a one-day leadership training workshop. Except for the one-day training workshop which was conducted in an outside venue, all sessions were held within the factory compound. Sessions were held immediately after the morning shift, from three to seven p.m. On average, each lasted for three and a half hours, with between twelve and fifteen women taking part. For practical reasons, participants were grouped according to language and shift. Whenever possible, the union secretary co-facilitated with me. When she was not available, another female executive committee member assisted.

Without adhering rigidly to a standardized format, each workshop covered three main areas: an introduction; uncovering lived experiences and feelings through photo-language or the recollection of incidents of being undermined; and focused discussion.

The introduction established the purpose of the gathering, clarified my role and, through group profiling and energizing exercises, aimed at relaxing participants and creating a climate for self-disclosure. Stress reduction exercises were incorporated later, when exhaustion and anxiety surfaced in the stories women told. The second part of the workshop focused on participants' stories: either the perceptions, feelings and experiences evoked by a picture each woman chose, or an account of specific lived experiences. Participants were encouraged to talk about their own emotional and physical well-being. This was followed by a summary and reflection of the experiences and viewpoints raised.

The focused discussion at the end of each workshop examined various dimensions of the self, the women's sense of themselves and to what extent and how this had been constructed by others. My agenda was to help them validate their conceptions and recognize their feelings and experienced realities in contrast to the negative stereotypes they had internalized. In addition, the women's understanding of the union and its relationship to their lives as workers was discussed, with particular reference to desired educational programmes. Subjects for exploration in future sessions were identified from the themes of their narrations.

The heart of the workshops – the 'elicited talk' – is described in the next section of this chapter.

Restrained voices

Emotional subordination was the recurrent theme in the narratives of workshop participants. They spoke of social stigmas, hardships, oppressive relationships, discrimination in the family, husbands' demands and infidelity, work pressure, sexual abuse, the experience of belittlement from intimates and strangers alike. They told of their pain, shame, anger and helplessness. The extracts below, excerpted from detailed narrations, are representative samples: each voice resonates with many others. My intermittent observations and interpretations are intended to link and contextualize these voices.

Women factory workers in Malaysia are automatically targets for ridicule and sexual harassment. They are made to feel that they are promiscuous by virtue of their role as 'factory women' and deserving of disparagement. Attempts to disregard and repress such derogation often deepen their feelings of shame and inferiority while, simultaneously, reactions of defence and defiance underlie their silence.

> People look down on us. They see us with only one eye. Society looks disparagingly on us. They say factory girls are cheap, they fall for any man in the street ... All this talk makes us feel inferior. Even when they are not saying anything, I can feel their belittlement from the way they gawk at us.

> Even my own family feels embarrassed with my factory job. I avoid my neighbour so as not to be asked insinuating questions. One day she asked: 'You came back around midnight yesterday and left again so early this morning. What do you actually do?' All I could say was 'work'. I felt ashamed, defensive, actually disgusted ... I am not what she is maybe thinking.

> Young men whistle as we alight from the factory bus: 'Look, they go day and night like prostitutes!' How to retaliate? You know what kind of characters they are! All creeps! If we retaliate, they may bring their gang to tackle us. We have to use this road every day. We just pretend not to hear.

While self-righteously accusing factory girls of promiscuity, men are the very ones hounding and intimidating them at bus-stops and in back-streets. They even encroach into women's residential privacy in search of opportunities for seduction. The women's stories of sexual harassment show how they are made to feel responsible for and shamed by the harassment inflicted on them. Though pervasive, such incidents are endured in silence because of the shame and blame they bring.

> When I first worked here I was very appreciative of my landlord, whom we fondly called 'uncle'. I was naive not to have any suspicions when he started coming to my room for chats ... One night, when his wife was not around and other girls were on night shift, he came in as usual to chat but this time he sat very close. As I was cautioning myself, I felt his hand on my breast ... I shouted and ran out the backdoor ... I was too shaken, too ashamed, to tell anyone.

Humiliation is not inflicted only by outsiders. Women are also denied respect at home. 'It is very difficult to tell anyone about hurts from your own family. Outsiders cannot know how it hurts.'

> Five years ago, in my first annual leave, I had a quarrel with my brother. He hit my niece for playing in the sun. I tried to stop him but he only shouted at me, 'Who are you to control me? Is this what the factory has taught you?' My mother, instead of reconciling us, reproached me. Such is the fate of girls in Indian families. This brother is much younger than me. Yet I have to obey him and get his approval for everything since my father's death. Maybe if I were an office clerk I would have a better say.

Ridicule and abuse come even from their dearest ones, making it difficult either to retaliate or to disregard the hurt. The result is an obliteration of their sense of themselves, their capabilities and self-esteem. Unpacking and talking through some of these experiences and feelings in the workshops revealed that such mistreatment is often the cause of women's apparent apathy and lack of self-confidence.

> My husband derides me until I am not worth a cent. Not only does he prevent me from participating in neighbourhood activities, he tells others that I am a stupid useless woman, that anything I do will bring chaos … How not to feel mad? But if I retaliate, I am no longer a good wife! More ammunition for him to run me down! Better to ignore him than invite more attacks.

However, even while they are finding the courage to speak of such abuses, women defend their husbands almost in the same breath, blaming themselves and apologizing for 'washing dirty linen in public'. Many believe that a good wife should be tolerant and understanding, not complaining against her husband and doing nothing to provoke his anger.

Religion plays a major role in shoring up this socialized guilt, self-censorship, subservience and obedience. 'When we were picketing the police reproached us, saying that as good Muslims we should be at home caring for our husbands and children instead of loitering in the streets like prostitutes!' One woman's husband forbade her to carry on attending the workshops. 'As a Muslim I have to get approval from my husband for everything. Even though the seminars are useful, I cannot attend any more as my husband feels that I am wasting time and neglecting my duties.'

When the needs and desires of these women are contradictory to the expectations and desires of others, they are relinquished and dismissed. Over time they adjust by becoming unaware of wanting anything for themselves. Most of their hopes and wishes are defined in relation to family members. In particular, they learn not to expect anything from their husbands although they yearn for support and affection. As one woman put it, 'Without expectation, there is less disappointment and frustration. I try not to expect, to avoid more hurt.'

> I dare not say but of course I yearn to have some help from my husband. If only he could show a little attention. This would make me so happy … I would not mind how hard I had to work. Instead I have to pretend and say that he is such a great guy.

When the women felt support and empathy from group members, they were able to air their frustrations about their marriages, in particular about the irresponsibility, unreasonable demands and infidelity of their husbands. One woman remarked with bitterness, 'Marriage is like being in a congested, smelly mini-bus at peak time – don't get into it when others are trying to get out. Being married is like digging one's own grave.'

> Even at night I can't get a peaceful rest. My husband often comes back late and he still wants to have sex. It is all right for him. He gets up late. I start the day at five a.m. and don't get to lie down till midnight. Then he comes nudging me as I have just fallen asleep.

> If it were not for my two children I would have divorced long ago. Except for the first four months of our marriage, he has shown no concern or consideration for me. At the slightest thing he raises his voice. Very male ego. He has to exert control over me. There is no talk between us. He does not lift a finger in the house. Comes home late and is glued to the television. At this point I don't care any more if there is another woman. Makes no difference whether he is around or not.

> I feel very shy and wrong to say this. God forgive me. My husband is a sex maniac. He cannot leave me alone. He wants sex every day, even when I am on night shift. If I refuse he wallops me. When I cannot take it any more, I wear a pad. I can only blame myself. I should have heeded the rumours. Maybe this is my fate.

Despite these miseries, and although in one workshop session all seven married women said they would prefer to be single, many women said it was necessary to have a husband, even if he was shared. They feared the shame and blame they would attract if their husbands left them for other women, and they dreaded the treatment meted out to single women. As one participant observed, 'I have to stick it out and tolerate his nonsense. I take care of the children and all house-keeping expenses. What to do? As single divorced parents we are not accepted by our community and it's even worse for our children.' Another noted, 'As a widow I feel restricted. Other women are suspicious that I am out to tackle their husbands. I feel out of place, inferior in that I am not like them.'

In addition to such marital problems, women are physically strained and emotionally drained by the demands of daily domestic routine, which saps their creativity, patience and initiative. Although regarded as emotionally weak, they must carry the emotional burden of their families, caring for the young and dependent elders and sometimes carrying sole responsibility for disabled children. One woman spoke of her difficulties with her four-year-old Down's syndrome son:

> I sometimes forget and become so short-tempered with Rahim, especially when I have to work overtime. I am mad with myself for not being patient

with him. I try not to do overtime and spend the time with him instead but then I need the money. Taking him out incurs more expense for taxi fare as he cannot walk the distance.

As if this were not enough, the load and pressure of monotonous but physically tiring work at home and in the factory is enough to cause derangement. One woman described life as 'a continuous spin of endless chores'.

> If not work at home it's factory work. I work till I am dizzy. The men are lucky. I want to be a man in my next life! After the day's work, when they return home, they do not bother any more. The wife is there to prepare everything even though she is working.

> I am like an octopus with my hands, legs, eyes and ears, working all the time. I have to do everything. As I cook dinner I am supervising the children over their homework. Even now, although my body is in this room, my mind is thinking what to cook for dinner.

For many women, however, it is motherhood that provides meaning, giving them the courage and determination to face their trials and tribulations. When asked about empowering experiences, many referred to their children and mothering as affirmations which warmed them through their beaten-down numbness. As one woman said: 'Even though it has been a horrible day, the welcoming call of my daughter as she hears me opening the gate is enough to cheer me, despite all the shit I get the whole day.' Another observed, 'My children are the only ones who appreciate me. They are the only people who look up to me and make me feel I am somebody.'

Another major reality for these women is the sheer exhaustion caused by very long hours of work in the factory in addition to the domestic work they must handle alone. 'Sometimes we don't get to see daylight for days, even weeks. When I leave for work the sun has not risen yet. When I return after overtime the moon is out.' Beyond the long hours and the tedium, what makes the work almost intolerable is the rigid discipline, pressure, verbal abuse and intimidation the women must endure.

> We are petrified all the time. You can literally see some jerking when shouted at, stammering and shivering. You can imagine the kind of tension we work in. I do not know any more how to think, only anticipating when I will be shouted at.

> They call it possession of spirits. It is the pressures, exhaustion and fear, an overflow of all the bad vibes and sufferings absorbed. I saw what happened to Fatimah before she went hysterical. Everyday she was yelled at for not

achieving the target. She works very hard, even forgoes her break, is very quiet and timid, always apologizing for her slowness and begging for another chance. When we asked her what happened, she did not know, only remembering 'I felt my whole body exploding. My head was bursting. I screamed to let go the steaming turbulence.' She could not 'make don't know' any more.

For all their hard work, the women are seldom acknowledged or appreciated. Instead they are constantly told that they are not good enough, serving as scapegoats for others' frustration. 'Even the foremen take their frustration out on us,' one woman said. 'When the machine breaks down they shout at us 'Stupid!' They blame us for mishandling the machine. I am very nervous whenever there is a breakdown.'

> My husband always complains that my cooking is not good, that I am a lousy wife. For no reason he shouts at me. His shouting makes me very nervous and confused. No matter what I do, how hard I please him, it is never good enough. I feel so inadequate. Please tell me how to be a good wife.

> My superviser likes to shout at me, 'Stupid, why did your parents never teach you? Are you a descendant of the stupid? If you think you cannot cope, the gate is wide open for you.' I get scolded all the time, scolded until I do not know how to think. I dare not and do not answer – the only way for the scolding to stop. What to do? I need the money.

Given this all-pervading experience of exploitation and abuse, it is not surprising that the women describe themselves as feeling scared, insulted, reluctant, humiliated, looked down upon and ashamed. Under their 'no mood' perception of themselves as worthless, inferior or emotionally deranged, lie truly terrible hurts, worries, fears and insecurities, a perpetual state of 'troubled heart, troubled mind'. As one woman said, 'I am like a thing that does not exist but is being used, a tool that nobody takes notice of.'

Indeed, over time the minds of these exhausted and persecuted women seem to cloud over with blankness and numbness. 'I feel stupid and do not know how to think any more from all the scolding,' as one put it. Without words or tears, they cry in their hearts. 'The sorrow suffocates me, making me feel so numb and incapable.'

However, existing side by side with their deeply buried emotional suffering, is a seed of resistance. Their stories resonate with both vulnerability and strength, shuttling between distressed anxiety and resilience, submission and subtle defiance, incapacity and resourcefulness. Silence is their defence against multiple hurts, their strategy for avoiding further affliction.

> What can I do? I don't want to be shouted at further. This is more than I can

bear already. Better to avoid further attack. They bang you until you cannot stand any more. The more you speak your mind, the more shouting, retaliation and victimization you will get. So we learn to keep quiet.

It's almost a slogan: 'better to play mute and make don't know.' The women 'make don't know' to deflect and dissipate attacks and pressure. Most prefer to adopt a 'not bothered', or 'make don't know', or 'be stupid as they want us' attitude, so as to avoid 'unnecessary trouble' and being shouted at.

Indeed, they are silenced and learn to be silent. They adopt postures of ignorance, avoidance and passivity as survival strategies. Their silence, seeming lack of interest, apathy, indifference and fatalism are conscious, experienced responses, their lived wisdom.

We are so saturated with problems and pressure that we are concerned only with our own survival. We have no interest nor time to know what is happening in the world out there. Most important is to get by the day with the least hassle. The least we want to know about are things that bring trouble.

Making sense

From the outset of the workshops it was clear that, with the exception of a few articulate individuals, the women were reticent, unable or unwilling to talk spontaneously about their lives. Talk had to be evoked. It is clear from the preceding section that this did occur: when participants had warmed up and broken their defensive numbness, they participated passionately in the shared disclosure of experiences, thoughts and feelings.

The next stage in the workshops was a process of making sense of these experiences, not as a purely intellectual activity but rather as an affective–cognitive knowing, centred and pursued subjectively, but unfolding through interactive and reflective talking, listening, questioning and introspecting with others.

The overlapping stages in this process of making sense were punctuated by such exclamations as 'Now I see' and 'Only now am I aware it is like that' and 'I am getting to know now'. Each person was first encouraged to connect with herself, to recall, figure out and verbalize her self-perceptions, experiences and feelings. In doing so, she differentiated the core of 'I' from the self constructed by others.

A redefined 'I' and a sense of being part of a 'we' (relating, linking, comparing, noting similarities, differences and patterns) emerged for each woman as she interacted with others and their stories through listening, validation and supportive questioning. Individual experiences became collectivized as similar themes surfaced in the variety of stories. This movement from the personal to the collective and back to a reconstituted personal evolved in three phases which are discussed separately below: building bonds, breaking silence; talking stories, talking pain; and making sense.

Building bonds, breaking silence   Eliciting talk about their lived experience and helping the 'factory women' to make sense of it called for particular conditions, sensitivities, methods and skills. Initially most were hesitant to talk about their personal feelings and experiences in a group. Isolated and deprived of interaction, most viewed their problems in individual, personal terms and habitually censored and blamed themselves, withheld and withdrew at the slightest hint of a negative reaction.

The primary task in the facilitation of this phase was therefore the creation of a safe atmosphere of caring mutuality, trust and empathy in which the women could risk active participation and self-disclosure. While facilitation aimed at eliciting talk took place throughout the workshop, breaking the silence right at the start was essential. Likewise, a sense of shared purpose had to be cultivated to promote bonding and collaboration.

Accordingly, the first step was to introduce ourselves to each other and to introduce the workshop process itself. The latter involved clarifying context and objectives, levelling expectations and explaining how the sessions would be conducted. Participants were assured that there was no right or wrong way of participating; that each person's experience, however different from others', was important and valid; and that feeling afraid or uneasy was very normal.

We introduced ourselves to each other by taking it in turns to describe ourselves briefly. Though many were shy and some found it nerve-racking, the experience of speaking out to a group fostered a sense of their own value. Among the comments made during subsequent evaluation were: 'I was heard instead of being reprimanded'; 'something positive was charged in me'; and 'I was nervous but the attention made me feel you all were really interested and this encouraged me'. The exercise gave voice and attention to each. Being listened to has the effect of prompting feelings of self-worth, confidence in one's judgement and a sense of the legitimacy of one's experiences and feelings. A surer, clearer sense of the self emerges.

Next were two structured exercises: a group profiling activity and a human knot, which reduced tension levels at the same time as drawing out information on the backgrounds of participants and the characteristics of the group as a whole. The activities helped to break down inhibitions and generated much laughter and fun. Bonds began to be forged as the women giggled away their awkwardness and moved towards a sense of being comfortable in the group and in a mutually created emotionally safe space.

Talking stories, talking pain The first phase of this 'talking stage' of the workshops was to facilitate an inward focus for each individual, using three evocative techniques: visualization, photo-language and the recollection of specific incidents of personally experienced subordination. Focused questions aimed at drawing out the multiple aspects and contexts of recalled incidents, identifying different reactions to them, and validating subjugated voices through challenges to the dominant response.

Visualization helped the women to recall and re-experience repressed subjectivities. The photo-language exercise was very effective in precipitating memories of relationships and surfacing strongly felt but unarticulated experiences. Recalling and narrating incidents of subordination aroused in participants both 'forbidden, unspeakable' feelings and negative thoughts about themselves.

Subsequent self-disclosure and naming were encouraged by attentive listening, empathy, gentleness, validation/affirmation and the interaction extended by group members and the facilitator. Most of all it was facilitated by a sense of awareness and responsiveness to the subjectivity of each person. With some coaxing and assurance, most embraced the opportunity to break silence, to say the unspeakable. Once participants felt that they were 'allowed' to do this, and to cry, be upset, feel ashamed or express anger, most took the risk of disclosing their vulnerabilities, sharing what they really felt, how they really reacted. They were encouraged by the self-disclosure of others and by the affirming responses of the group.

Listening is crucial to processes of disclosure. The kind of listening encouraged is 'listening with the heart', an attentiveness that includes emotional responsiveness. Elsewhere (Chan, 1991) I have written about emotions as a resource in women and how singing together from the heart generates bonding affections. The same thing happens through talking and listening with attentive compassion, a bonding Janeway (1980) describes as a power of the weak which can be reclaimed through small-group work. We attempted and experienced this in our workshops.

While listeners did not necessarily understand everything they were told, they communicated acceptance, interest and concern. Acceptance was conveyed by not criticizing, ridiculing, advising or interjecting their own viewpoints too quickly, and by affirming the normality and legitimacy of the story-teller's feelings. Interest was expressed by the giving of undistracted attention, especially by means of sustained eye contact and thoughtful questions. Concern was communicated by appropriate facial expressions and, when necessary, by touching or holding a hand, staying emotionally present with the speaker. Appropriate questions helped the speaker to focus her recollection and to explore her feelings and thoughts more deeply.

As the women told their painful stories, many for the first time in their lives, they experienced a sense of release and relief. 'I am so relieved to be able to talk about my problem which I tried to bury for the past forty years,' was a typical comment. Many expressed their hurts openly with tears. This evoked tears in other women as they identified with and personally felt the pains and sorrow. Though expression may not in itself solve a problem, simply being allowed to verbalize, particularly in an atmosphere of empathy and support, was therapeutic for participants.

The narrative form enabled the naming of suppressed reactions without fear of the criticism usually attendant on the assertion of a different or controversial point of view. The process of reminiscence and 'permitted articulation' helped the women to discharge their hurt and to begin to reclaim a sense of both their own agency and the validity of their own feelings and standpoints.

Making sense   The third stage of the workshop process involved making connections, reflective talking and reconstituting subjectivity and self-identity in opposition to the negative constructions of others. At the interpersonal or collective level, reflective talking built bonds of empathy and fostered understanding, commonality and solidarity. Reactions such as 'I would have been more sympathetic to you if I had know about your situation. I extend my apologies,' were common.

Hearing each other's divergent views and reactions, in an atmosphere devoid of criticism, defensiveness or debate about who was right or better, facilitated acceptance of difference and thawed conditioned attitudes of unwillingness to explore alternatives. The process nudged the women into considering new ways of looking at their experiences, integrating the insights of fellow participants in the collaborative development of new perspectives on themselves and the world.

As the women recognized their own situations in others' descriptions, they realized that their painful, seemingly personal problems were shared by many of their workmates. Together they explored the issues behind their experiences: why they behaved and felt the way they did. They teased out the who, what, why and how of their encounters and emotions, particularly feelings and perceptions about themselves, to arrive at an understanding of internalized stereotypes and social construction of the self. Exploring the ways, however small, in which they had contested and defied these constructions, enabled them to recognize the fact of their own agency and a sense that they were not utterly powerless after all.

In other words, the processes of articulation and collective reflection, unfolding both sequentially and together, enable a degree of liberation from socially imposed constructions and the emergence of a reclaimed self. Heard and interpreted together, the women's narratives uncover their experiential knowing (Rowbotham, 1972; Reinharz, 1983; Donnelly, 1986), or what I term their lived wisdom. The consciousness which unfolds from this realization of their own capacity, singly and together, to make sense of lived experience, becomes the basis for both self-recovery and social agency. The retrieval and reconstruction of sub-jugated knowledge enables participants in the process 'to create effective and meaningful resistance, to make revolutionary transformations' (hooks, 1989: 26).

Differences and commonalities

The need to address the question of difference has been raised by women of colour (hooks, 1989; Collins, 1990; Aziz, 1992), post-modernist theorists (Lather, 1991; Usher, 1992), Third World feminists (Sen and Grown, 1987) and in feminist pedagogy (Weiler, 1991). Put differently, there is growing awareness of the fact of partial perspectives, 'situated knowledges' (Haraway, 1991) and the 'insurrection of sub-jugated knowledge' (Sawicki, 1991: 224). However, these differences need not be a source of division or weakness among women (Lorde, 1984) and, properly approached, may serve as a 'scientific and political resource' (Jaggar, 1992: 386).

Differences in ethnicity (and language), age and marital status are common sources of animosity and division among Malaysian women factory workers. Real or suspected racial discrimination and distrust arising from ethnic differences deter co-operation and interaction on the shopfloor. Cultural norms privilege older, and especially married, women so that younger women will talk only when asked, often deferring to and agreeing with their elders so as to avoid giving offence or seeming disrespectful.

Equally, there can be ill feeling between married and unmarried women, the latter struggling with feelings of envy and defensiveness imposed by their socially constructed lower status. This surfaced in one workshop when a middle-aged unmarried woman talked about hurts that discussion revealed as shared by other unmarried peers. She described her dejection and her sense of being sneered at by those who told her she had missed out in life by not marrying. She felt defensive, uneasy and apologetic.

Different feelings and standpoints were heard and misunderstandings clarified. The married women apologized for insensitivity, explaining that it was not their intention to 'rub salt into wounds'. This process mended misconceptions and negative feelings, facilitating a more relaxed and candid discussion. It became clear that when differences are examined with care, antagonisms resulting from them can be dispelled, even when contradictions and conflicts remain unresolved. Approached with sensitivity and compassion, difference itself can generate bonds of empathy, affection and caring support.

The need for sensitivity cannot be over-emphasized, if dealing with difference is to generate bonds. This particular session brought out unconventional views about marriage, family life, women's strength and self-reliance. Different reasons for singlehood were articulated. While some yearned for marriage, some chose to be single. While some fretted over being unmarried, others were enjoying themselves in ways not possible to those with children and husbands. A story about adoption inspired listeners and sparked insights about unspoken alternatives. The case of a single parent with a disabled child evoked compassion and admiration. The narration of her pains transformed the way others perceived her, from one who always looked down-trodden and scared to one with courage, love, strength and determination. The practice of lesbianism was acknowledged, although reactions were controversial. In general, aspects of women's lives which are invisible, rendered insignificant or denigrated were acknowledged and reinterpreted, along with their hidden and diverse capacities.

Notwithstanding the importance of difference, the notion of a commonality underlying the diversity of women's experience (Eisenstein, 1984: 38) remains crucial. It was on the basis of this concept that I came to understand the experience of emotional subordination as the thread linking the individual sufferings of the factory workers. Examining women's experience from a women-centred perspective has also unfolded common gynocentric concerns and values: women's responsiveness and concern for others' welfare, their interpersonal caretaking (Wine, 1989). Women's relational needs, capacities and ways of being, defined and devalued as weakness in terms of the dominant patriarchal discourse, have been recognized as desirable values, pro-social skills and sensitivities that enhance human functioning (Gilligan, 1982; Belenky et al., 1986; Miller, 1986; Jordan et al., 1991).

Existing educational work with factory women has included a focus on commonality in terms of structural oppression; that is, class exploitation and gender subordination. However, the more subjective commonalities of thought and feeling tend to be overlooked, as are the gynocentric practices and values which not only enrich social interactions and relationships in general but also contribute to effective pedagogy.

In the workshops I facilitated, a subjective commonality among the factory women was clear. It was characterized by silence, apathy, anxiety, worry, repressed anger and feelings of inferiority; in short, the low self-esteem and lack of confidence one might expect to result from a continual experience of emotional subordination. Because the women are routinely blamed and made to feel guilty or immoral, they rarely show directly what they genuinely feel. Most of the time, authentic feelings of anger, hurt or disgust, particularly in relation to husbands, are repressed or brushed aside as illegitimate or immoral, and grouchiness, disinterest, listlessness and indifference are projected instead. This syndrome then becomes labelled the 'problematic emotionality of women'.

The pertinent question for educational work in this context is: how do we help women to uncover, comprehend and take charge of their authentic feelings?

When first gathered together, women often appear quiet, restless, anxious, withdrawn, distracted and void of opinion. They are described and describe themselves as not interested. Indeed, this was the starting scenario in most of the sessions described above.

Most of the women began by being apprehensive and withdrawn, even openly reluctant and negative. Some showed displeasure at having to stay on at the factory after eight hours of tiring work. However, over the three hours interest grew. Everyone talked with some facilitation. Many even enjoyed it. Some added that they had never shared so much before. They appreciated the listening and caring extended to them. All groups wanted follow-up sessions. Some even identified topics for future sessions.

Subsequent collective evaluation of the workshops revealed that it was the supportiveness and emotional responsiveness of fellow participants, coupled with effective facilitation, that elicited talk and enabled reflection. These gynocentric values of empathy, emotional responsiveness, interpersonal sensitivity and connectedness are among women's resources that should be tapped in educational work with them. Such an approach affirms women's strength and capacities while also contributing to the effectiveness of the work.

It became clear during the sessions that what came across initially as lack of interest was actually anxiety and lack of confidence about having to do something they did not know, since this was an 'education session' which they all associated with the demonstration of one's brain and ability to articulate. Anxiety about waiting family demands was a further distraction, impacting negatively on their interest, mood and level of energy for participation. As one woman put it: 'Even though my body is here, my mind is thinking the different things I have to do as soon as I reach home.'

In addition to such daily domestic anxieties as 'my children may be loitering in the streets', or 'my husband will be angry when he returns and I am not in the house', or 'I have to wash and feed my bed-ridden mother before cooking dinner for my family', women's worries included having 'to convince the landlord to let us stay on' and 'where to borrow enough money to pay the doctor'. The ongoing experience of ridicule and contempt was a major source of anxiety, which, above all, related to their ability to participate and perform correctly. 'I don't want to be laughed at. I am always conscious that I will make a fool of myself,' was a typical comment.

They are anxious about being called upon to speak when unprepared. They fear saying the wrong things, fear mixing with people they do not know and operating in unfamiliar situations. They worry about being caught unexpectedly and not knowing what to do. They are anxious about being embarrassed. Non-participation and silence become the way to cope. Such deconstructions, emerging during reflective talking, enabled the women to recognize that they were in a continual state of anxiety.

Suppression and denial of feelings of anger and disgust were other commonalities identified during the workshops. Initially, women neither acknowledged nor recognized these feelings. Instead, they blamed themselves for 'moodiness', lack of perseverance or self-discipline, and 'outbursts' of anger or impatience. In the process of story-telling, some discovered their anger and also that it was justified.

As incidents and comments quoted earlier make plain, their stories mostly described emotional suffering: put-downs, blame, experiences of being shouted at, sneered at, coerced, humiliated, ridiculed and demeaned. The women's accounts illustrated how daily experiences of emotional subordination, at the hands of close kin and strangers alike, generate feelings of shame, guilt, inadequacy, self-doubt, low self-esteem and inferiority. Such devaluation affects not only how they feel, but also their self-image and sense of their capacities – their entire subjectivity. It negates the women's confidence and sense of themselves, inhibiting the development of their potential, immobilizing their very capacity to act. They cope with a mask of silence, indifference and passivity, repressing their anguish and appearing submissive and inert.

The debilitating effects of internalized oppression, commonly depicted as powerlessness and learned helplessness, have been a core concern of the women's movement (Steinem, 1992). Consciousness-raising groups have been a means for overcoming some of these psychological obstacles (Butler and Wintram, 1991), exploring feelings as a 'critical way of knowing' or 'inner knowing', the source of true knowledge of the world for women living in a society that denies the value of their perceptions (Weiler, 1991: 463).

A growing body of feminist literature and practice emphasizes the need to address the emotional welfare of women, whether in feminist therapy (Krzowski and Land, 1988), in organizing work aimed at asserting individual and collective rights (Dominelli and McLeod, 1989), in feminist popular education (Perg, 1992) or practical programmes for women's empowerment (Gutierrez, 1990). The workshops with factory women confirmed the validity of this approach. Education work concerned with empowerment cannot fail to address the pervasiveness of debilitating emotional subjectivities among women. Indeed, that is where it must begin.

Sharing their stories in small groups enabled the factory women to experience the commonality of their emotional suffering. 'Talking pain' in an interactive small group context enabled the reclamation of suppressed feelings and the reconstruction of lived experience. Group validation of forbidden emotions was powerful in changing perceptions that were guilt-ridden and paralysing. Naming both their own feelings and the ways in which they had been victimized was liberating, demonstrating that the movement from silence to voice does indeed change 'discourse politics' (Best and Kellner, 1991: 57) and that the 'politics of naming' (Scheman, 1980) is a powerful strategy for the recovery and reinterpretation of submerged feelings and ways of being.

Thus, in very real ways, the process of reflective talking in small groups enabled the women to reconstruct their subjectivities in relation to the experiences and views of their peers. Their tales of struggle and survival uncovered their strength and capacity to act. Their shared image of themselves as passive, powerless victims was transformed into an image of strong, active survivors. The hegemony of the audible social voice, and the fact that their silence could perpetuate the illegitimacy of their own unheard voices, became evident.

As feelings of self-blame and inadequacy diminished, so interest, enthusiasm, energy and feelings of 'wanting to' were recovered. These recovered psychological resources helped to develop a sense of personal power, the power to define and determine oneself and to act in ways congruent with that definition (Miller, 1986). This is a concept similar to yet more potent than Freire's (1972) notion of becoming a subject rather than remaining a powerless object. This process of interactive self-realization which enables women to reclaim their self-worth and self-integrity is fundamental to feminist education (Ferguson, 1992) and critical for the process of women's empowerment.

Conclusion

Though the research discussed here yielded substantial insights, it was only a small window into the large issue of how to surface and address women's experienced subordination in ways that are empowering. The emphasis in the workshops was largely on getting the women to talk and express their feelings, and consciousness-raising must go beyond this to engage analysis and formulation of a vision and strategy for change. I had neither sufficient time nor adequate know-how during the field-work to facilitate this. Nevertheless, a number of important conclusions can be drawn from the work.

First, although emotional suffering is only one dimension of women's subordination (Eichenbaum and Orbach, 1984; Ernst and Goodison, 1981), it is an essential area to address in educational work concerned with empowerment. Second, collaborative story-telling can facilitate the constructive unfolding of differences and commonalities while also fostering an emotionally safe space in which women can rebuild self-esteem and confidence and discover solidarity. Indeed, story-telling in combination with reflective talking is the educational method *par excellence* that commences with lived experiences and experienced feelings to reconstitute women's subjectivities.

Third, it is vital to address, acknowledge and validate both differences and commonalities among those participating in educational work. The transformative potential of problematic differences and unearthed commonalities must be recognized and constituted as educational concerns. In other words, they must be consciously anticipated and planned for in education programmes.

Finally, it is essential that the facilitation skills and methods learned and deployed by educators go beyond the means to forge participation and active learning. Facilitators need to have an understanding of the dynamic between subjectivity and experience, and of the particularities which impact on it in the specific context in which educational work is undertaken. They also need to be able to recognize and use the resources women themselves bring to the educational process in terms of gynocentric attributes and ways of being.

Bibliography

Allen, P. (1970) *Free Space: A Perspective on the Small Group in Women's Liberation*, Times Change Press, New York.

Aries, E. (1976) 'Interaction Patterns and Theories of Male, Female and Mixed Groups', *Small Group Behaviour*, no. 7.

Arnold, R. et al. (1991) *Educating for a Change*, Between the Lines and Doris Marshall Institute for Education and Action, Toronto.

Aziz, R. (1992) 'Feminism and the Challenge of Racism: Deviance or Difference', in Crowley, H. and Himmelweit, S. (eds), *Knowing Women: Feminism and Knowledge*, Polity Press, Cambridge.

Bartky, S. L. (1990) *Femininity and Domination: Studies in the Phenomenology of Oppression*, Routledge and Kegan Paul, New York.

Belenky, M. et al. (1986) *Women's Ways of Knowing: The Development of Self, Voice and Mind*, Basic Books, New York.

Best, S. and Kellner, D. (1991) *Postmodern Theory: Critical Interrogations*, Guilford Press, New York.

Brodsky, A. (1973) 'The Consciousness-raising Group as a Model for Therapy with Women', *Psychotherapy: Theory, Reasearch and Practice*, Vol. 10, no. 1, Spring.

Buker, E. (1987) 'Storytelling Power: Personal Narratives and Political Analysis', *Women and Politics*, Vol. 7, no. 3.

Butler, S. and Wintram, C. (1991) *Feminist Groupwork*, Sage, London.

Carlock, C. J. and Martin, P. Y. (1977) 'Sex Composition and the Intensive Group Experience', *Social Work*, no. 22.

Chan, L. H. (1991) 'Reflections of an Organizer', in *Many Paths, One Goal: Organising Women Workers in Asia*, Committee for Women in Asia, Hong Kong.

Chan, L. H. (1992) *Weaving Connections*, World Council of Churches, Geneva.

Christ, C. (1979) 'Spiritual Quest and Women's Experience', in Christ, C. and Plasskow, J. (eds) *Womanspirit Rising: A Feminist Reader in Religion*, Harper and Row, San Francisco.

Collins, P. H. (1990) *Black Feminist Thought: Knowledge, Consciousness and the Politics of Empowerment*, Unwin Hyman, New York and London.

Crowley, H. and Himmelweit, S. (1992) *Knowing Women: Feminism and Knowledge*, Polity Press, Cambridge.

Daly, M. (1978) *Gyn/Ecology: The Metaethics of Radical Feminism*, Beacon Press, Boston.

Davis, R. (1988) 'Learning From Working-Class Women', *Community Development Journal*, Vol. 23, no. 2.

Dominelli, L. and McLeod, E. (1989) *Feminist Social Work*, Macmillan, London.

Donnelly, A. (1986) 'Feminist Social Work with a Women's Group', Monograph 41, University of East Anglia, Norwich.

Eichenbaum, L. and Orbach, S. (1984) *What Do Women Want?*, Fontana, London.

Eisenstein, H. (1984) *Contemporary Feminist Thought*, Unwin, London.

Ellsworth, E. (1989) 'Why Doesn't This Feel Empowering? Working Through the Repressive Myths of Critical Pedagogy', *Harvard Educational Review*, Vol. 59, no. 3, August.

Ernst, S. and Goodison, L. (1981) *In Our Own Hands: A Book of Self-Help Therapy*, Women's Press, London.

Ferguson, A. (1992) 'A Feminist Aspect Theory of the Self', in Garry, A. and Pearsall, M. (eds), *Women, Knowledge and Reality: Explorations in Feminist Philosophy*, Routledge, New York.

Fishman, P. (1978) 'Interaction: The Work Women Do', *Social Problems*, no. 25.

Flynn, P. et al. (1986) *You're Learning All the Time: Women, Education and Community Work*, Atlantic Highlands, Nottingham.

Freire, P. (1972) *The Pedagogy of the Oppressed*, Penguin, London.

Gardner, H. (1983) *Frames of Mind: The Theory of Multiple Intelligences*, Heinemann, London.

Gilligan, C. (1982) *In a Different Voice: Psychological Theory and Women's Development*, Harvard University Press, Cambridge, MA.

Gutierrez, L. (1990) 'Working with Women of Color: An Empowerment Perspective', *Social Work*, March.

Hagan, B. H. (1983) 'Managing Conflict in All-women Groups, *Social Work with Groups*, Vol. 6, nos 3 and 4.

Haraway, D. (1991) 'Situated Knowledges: The Science Question in Feminism and the Privilege of Partial Perspective', in Haraway, D. (ed.), *Simians, Cyborgs and Women: The Reinvention of Nature*, Free Association Books, London.

Henley, N. et al. (1984) 'Imagining a Different World of Talk', in Hoffman, E. et al. (eds), *Women in Search of Utopias*, Schoken, New York.

Hinton, W. (1966) *Fanshen*, Vintage Books, New York.

hooks, b. (1989) *Talking Back: Thinking Feminist, Thinking Black*, Sheba, London.

Hope, A. and Timmel, S. (1986) *Training for Transformation*, Mambo Press, Harare.

Jaggar, A. (1992) 'Love and Knowledge: Emotion in Feminist Epistemology', in Garry, A. and Pearsall, M. (eds), *Women, Knowledge and Reality*, Routledge and Chapman Hall, New York.

Janeway, E. (1980) 'Women and the Uses of Power', in Eisenstein, H. and Jardine, A. (eds), *The Future of Difference*, Rutgers University Press, New Brunswick.

Jenkins, L. et al. (1978) 'Small Group Process: Learning from Women', *Women's Studies International Quarterly*, no. 1.

Jordan, J. et al. (eds) (1991) *Women's Growth in Connection: Writings from the Stone Center*, Guilford Press, New York.

Krzowski, S. and Land, P. (eds) (1988) *In Our Experience: Workshops at the Women's Therapy Centre*, Women's Press, London.

Lather, P. (1991) *Getting Smart: Feminist Research and Pedagogy with/in the Postmodern*, Routledge, New York.

Lorde, A. (1984) *Sister Outsider*, Crossing Press, New York.

Lyman, P. (1981) 'The Politics of Anger: On Silence, Resentment and Political Speech', *Socialist Review*, no. 57.

Miller, J. (1986) *Toward a New Psychology of Women*, Beacon Press, Boston.

Miller, J. (1991a) 'The Development of Women's Sense of Self', in Jordan, J. et al. (eds), op. cit.

— (1991b) 'The Construction of Anger in Women and Men', in Jordan, J. et al. (eds), op. cit.

Narayan, U. (1988) 'Working Across Differences', *Hypatia*, Vol. 3, no. 2.

Perg (1992) *Women Educating to End Violence Against Women*, Popular Education Research Group, Toronto.

Pria (1987) *Training of Trainers: A Manual for Participatory Training Methodology in Development*, Society for Participatory Research in Asia (Pria), New Delhi.

Razack, S. (1993) 'Storytelling for Social Change', *Gender and Education*, Vol. 5, no. 1.

Reinharz, S. (1983) 'Experiential Analysis: A Contribution to Feminist Research', in Bowles, G. et al. (eds) *Theories of Women's Studies*, Routledge and Kegan Paul, London.

Rich, A. (1975) 'For a Sister', in *Poems: Selected and New, 1950-1974*, W. W. Norton, New York.

Rowbotham, S. (1972) 'Women's Liberation and the New Politics', in Wandor, M. (ed.) *The Body Politic*, Stage 1, London.

Sawicki, J. (1991) 'Foucault and Feminism: Toward a Politics of Difference', in Shanley, M. L. and Pateman, C. (eds), *Feminist Interpretations and Political Theory*, Polity Press, Cambridge.

Scheman, N. (1980) 'Anger and the Politics of Naming', in McConell-Ginet, S. et al. (eds), *Women and Language in Literature and Society*, Praeger, New York.

Sen, G. and Grown, C. (1987), *Development Crises and Alternative Visions: Third World Women's Perspectives*, Monthly Review Press, New York.

Shrivastava, O. (1987) 'Participatory Training: Some Philosophical and Methodological Dimensions', paper presented at workshop on 'Building a Movement of Grassroots Educators', Icheon, Korea, July.

Spender, D. (1980) *Man Made Language*, Routledge and Kegan Paul, Boston.

Spivak, G. (1990) 'Interviews, Strategies, Dialogues', in Harasym, S. (ed.), *The Post-Colonial Critic*, Routledge, London.

Steinem, G. (1992) *Revolution From Within: A Book of Self-Esteem*, Little, Brown, London.

Surrey, J. (1991) 'The "Self-in-Relation": A Theory of Women's Development', in Jordan, J. et al. (eds), op. cit.

Trinh, M. T. (1990) 'Not You/Like You: Post-Colonial Women and the Interlocking Questions of Identity and Difference', in Anzaldua, G. (ed.), *Making Face, Making Soul*, Aunt Lute Foundation Books, San Francisco.

Usher, R. (1992) 'Experience in Adult Education: A Postmodern Critique', *Journal of Philosophy of Education*, Vol. 26, no. 2.

Wagner, P. (1991) 'Semangat in the Zone', *Pepe en Pilar*, Vol. 2, no. 1, Institute of Popular Education, Manila.

Weiler, K. (1991) 'Freire and a Feminist Pedagogy of Difference', *Harvard Educational Review*, Vol. 61, no. 4, November.

Weitz, R. (1982) 'Feminist Consciousness-raising, Self-concept and Depression', *Sex Roles*, Vol. 8, no. 3.

Wine, J. D. (1989) 'Gynocentric Values and Feminist Psychology', in Miles, A. and Finn, G. (eds), *Feminism: From Pressure to Politics*, Black Rose Books, Montreal.

Wynne, B. (1988) 'Knowledge, Interests and Utility', paper presented at a Science Policy Support Group workshop, Lancaster University.

Contributors

BETH BINGHAM works as Associate Director of the Center for Literacy Studies at the University of Tennessee, Knoxville. Her work includes research, staff development, writing and editing, curriculum development and programme evaluation. She has wide experience as an educator in a variety of settings including rural community development organizations. She is particularly interested in working with women. She lives with her family on a farm in mountains in Dungannon, Virginia.

CHAN LEAN HENG earns her living as a lecturer in feminist social work and is completing her PhD on 'Educational Work with Factory Women in Malaysia'. However, she prefers the identity of a feminist popular educator. She is a founder member of the Workers' Education Centre, the first women workers' centre in Malaysia. She is currently involved in participatory training for empowerment and in women's and worker education. She enjoys recycling discarded items into valuable usables and is an earnest scavenging walker.

COLLEEN CRAWFORD COUSINS has lived in Europe, Swaziland and Zimbabwe since going into exile in 1972. She has written and illustrated books for children, adolescents and the co-operative sector, including *Lwaano Lwanika*, *Tonga Book of the Earth* (with Pamela Reynolds), published by Panos, London, in 1993. She has been involved in rural development and participatory learning activities for the past 15 years. She has worked with non-governmental organizations to design materials and methodology for rural and urban development in a wide range of contexts, including health-care, water and sanitation, educare, organization development, in-service teacher training, land reform and gender rights. She returned to South Africa in 1991 and lives in Cape Town.

MICHELLE FRIEDMAN is programme officer for the Africa Gender Institute based at the University of Cape Town. She has worked as national gender co-ordinator for the National Land Committee and as a researcher for the Institute of Natural Resources attached to the University of Natal, Pietermaritzburg. Voluntary work for Durban Rape Crisis introduced her to practical feminist politics and participatory methods of learning. She is a member of the collective which publishes the feminist journal *Agenda*, a member of the advisory board for the environment and development journal *New Ground* and serves on the steering committee of the Gender and Education Trainers' Network. Her most passionate personal interest currently is an exploration of process at various levels, including how to develop a balanced life-style.

LINZI MANICOM left South Africa as a political exile in 1976. She lived and worked as a researcher and community worker in Tanzania and Mozambique before moving to Toronto, Canada, in 1984. She has worked for several years on the staff and as a consultant to the Women's Programme of the International Council for Adult Education. She is currently teaching a Women and Development course part-time at York University in Toronto, and working as a freelance writer and editor in the field of women's organizing and gender issues in global economic restructuring. She is a PhD candidate at the Ontario Institute for Studies in Education, working on a dissertation on gendered state formation in South Africa.

CAROLYN MEDEL-ANONUEVO taught sociology at the University of the Philippines for almost twelve years. She worked for nine years with the Centre for Women's Resources, for six years as executive director. She is currently working as a research specialist on women's education at the Unesco Institute of Education in Hamburg, Germany. She was involved in research on the situation of women while lecturing in sociology, and has participated as resource person, designer, facilitator and trainer in many women's seminars and workshops and, lately, in gender and development workshops. The nature of her work has meant that she has not been 'involved', in the traditional sense, as a wife and mother of four children and she is now grappling with this part of her identity. She is interested in the way women work and organize themselves and 'constantly amazed by their strength'. She loves nature and being at peace with herself.

HELEN MYLES has worked in the areas of health, welfare and adult education over the last 35 years. Workplaces have ranged from community organizations to government departments in the United States, Britain and three Australian states. She has been a nurse, midwife, Family Planning Association educator, equal opportunity officer for the Council of Adult Education in Melbourne and a member of the first Queensland Women's Consultative Council. She is now based in a rural area of Australia which verges on remote, and works as a consultant, teaching social welfare studies, community work skills in small rural towns, the politics of women's health and self-awareness for women. An important component of her life is acting as mentor to younger women 'whose lives often begin to blossom after contact with feminist popular education'.

DENISE NADEAU is a Canadian popular educator who has recently reclaimed her identity as a dancer. She has worked for 20 years as a mother and as an educator and organizer within the women's movement. Since the mid-1980s she has worked with labour and Christian social justice groups around the challenges of global economic restructuring. She has a master's degree in divinity and is now also exploring how to bring spirituality into grassroots organising in a secular culture. She has taught at the University of British Columbia School of Social Work and the Vancouver School of Theology. She lives in British Columbia.

SHEELA PATEL is a founder member of the Society for Promotion of Area Resource Centres (Sparc) and currently works as a Sparc activist and educator based in Bombay. She holds a master's degree in social work from Bombay University. Working with women in welfare situations sowed the seeds of dissatisfaction with an orthodox social work role and led to the change in attitudes and values which became the basis of Sparc activism in India and abroad.

KATE PRITCHARD HUGHES has worked for many years in community education, particularly in the areas of literacy and women's programmes. She became interested in the work of Paulo Freire while studying for a diploma in adult education at the University of Nottingham, England. Since migrating to Australia she has worked in the Community Education Unit at the Victoria University of Technology in Melbourne and more recently in the Department of Social and Cultural Studies where she teaches women's studies. She is interested in the relationship between power and knowledge and tries to use education as a vehicle for empowerment in both a personal and collective sense. When not agonising about applying the work of Freire and various feminist theorists to classroom practice, she reads feminist detective fiction in between the demands of her daughter and twin sons.

RIEKY STUART is an adult educator who has worked in international development for many years. Between 1985 and 1994 she taught at Coady International Institute, St Francis Xavier University, in the diploma programme in social development and consulted with a variety of development organizations on their gender policies and practice. She is currently programme director at the Canadian Council for International Co-operation, an umbrella group for Canadian non-governmental organizations active in international development.

ISABEL TARRAGO has been concerned with Aboriginal affairs for 25 years, working with both federal and state governments and with Aboriginal and Torres Strait Islander community organizations. She has worked with the Department of Social Security, the Department of Employment Education and Training, the Department of Health and, currently, the Department of Family Services and Aboriginal and Islander Affairs. She has represented Aboriginal women at international, national, state and local levels, working to put women's issues on the agenda. She has been chairperson of the Westend School ASSPA committee for five years.

ASTRID VON KOTZE is senior lecturer in the Department of Adult and Community Education at the University of Natal, Durban, and coordinator of the Community Adult Educator Training Programme. Holder of a doctorate in literature, she developed an interest in popular education through participation in an experimental theatre company and cultural projects within the trade union movement. She is interested in helping people to confront and explore difference and otherness in interacting with each other and the world. She loves reading about women's experiences of cultural and linguistic 'border crossings', which help her to understand better what she is trying to do when she encourages others to enjoy learning, particularly about different ways of interpreting and making sense of the world.

SHIRLEY WALTERS is a cyclist, activist, educator and academic who lives on the slopes of Table Mountain in Cape Town and enjoys the beautiful environment in which she lives. She has been active in a wide range of cultural, educational and women's organizations over the last 20 years. She is founding director of the Centre for Adult and Continuing Education and Professor of Adult and Continuing Education at the University of the Western Cape. She has worked as a schoolteacher, industrial trainer, community educator, researcher and academic. She is currently deeply involved in the reconstruction of a democratic adult education system in South Africa.

Index

as birth attendants, 188; as
category, 17; as community
managers, 94; as story-tellers, 153;
bear brunt of spending cuts, 9;
black, 30, 149, 182, 197, 200
(oppression of, 182, 191); category
of, 30; exploitation of, 149, 163;
health of, 46; left out of
development projects, 127; middle-
class, 16, 103; not homogeneous
category, 15; poor, 97; relations
with men, 137, 139; rural, 63;
silencing of, 20; socialization of,
161; Western, 13; white, 5, 158,
182, 197, 200; workload of, 46, 127
Women and Work organization, 48
Women in Development (WID), 35,
126, 128
Women to Women Global Strategies,
54
Women's Charter, 24
women's collectives, 96, 98
women's movement, 8, 10, 16, 29, 88,
89, 104, 119, 182, 206

Women's Programme of International
Council for Adult Education, 1, 4
women's studies, 108–12
women-only spaces, 204, 208
workplace organization, 47
workshops, 32, 53, 54, 76, 215, 221,
223; analysis of dynamics, 78–81;
CACE, 31, 33; control of, 81;
creative-writing, 150, 151, 158,
161, 164, 165; design of, 69;
disturbers of, 78, 82; for training
educators, 24–7, 52; in body
education, 49; methodology of,
141, 153, 166; on participatory
method, 61, 62, 64, 66, 68, 69;
organization of, 208, 209, 216;
process of, 69–78, 152; rules of, 82;
using narrative, 205–9; utopia, 152
World Bank, 9, 55, 129, 131, 132
World Health Organization (WHO),
186

Yanz, Lynda, 1
youth, 67; organizations, 25